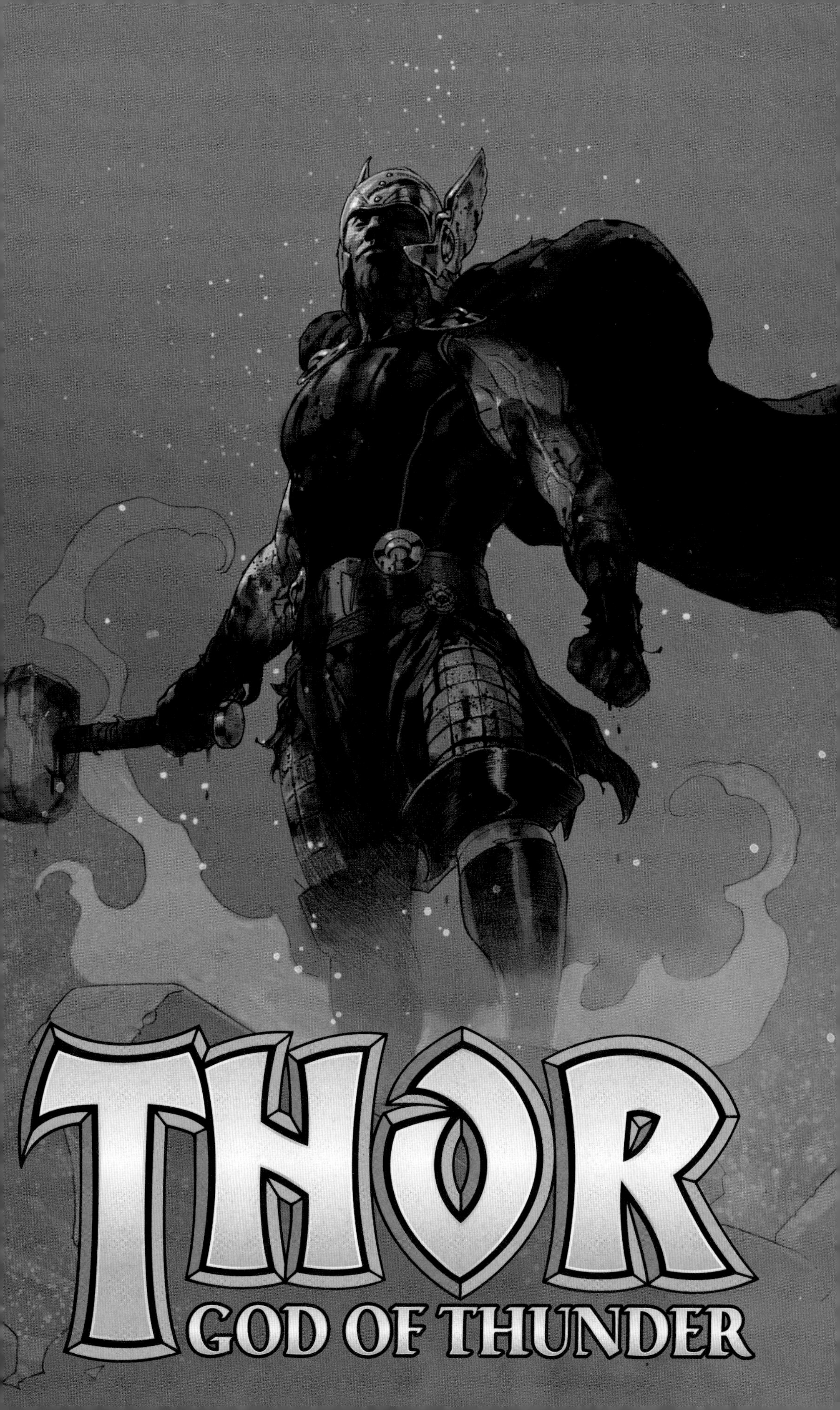
THOR
GOD OF THUNDER

Collection Editor: **Jennifer Grünwald**

Assistant Editors: **Alex Starbuck & Nelson Ribeiro**

Editor, Special Projects: **Mark D. Beazley**

Senior Editor, Special Projects: **Jeff Youngquist**

SVP of Print & Digital Publishing Sales: **David Gabriel**

Book Design: **Jeff Powell**

Editor in Chief: **Axel Alonso**

Chief Creative Officer: **Joe Quesada**

Publisher: **Dan Buckley**

Executive Producer: **Alan Fine**

THOR: GOD OF THUNDER VOL. 1 — THE GOD BUTCHER. Contains material originally published in magazine form as THOR: GOD OF THUNDER #1-5. First printing 2013. ISBN# 978-0-7851-6842-3. Published by MARVEL WORLDWIDE, INC., a subsidiary of MARVEL ENTERTAINMENT, LLC. OFFICE OF PUBLICATION: 135 West 50th Street, New York, NY 10020. Copyright © 2012 and 2013 Marvel Characters, Inc. All rights reserved. All characters featured in this issue and the distinctive names and likenesses thereof, and all related indicia are trademarks of Marvel Characters, Inc. No similarity between any of the names, characters, persons, and/or institutions in this magazine with those of any living or dead person or institution is intended, and any such similarity which may exist is purely coincidental. **Printed in the U.S.A.** ALAN FINE, EVP - Office of the President, Marvel Worldwide, Inc. and EVP & CMO Marvel Characters B.V.; DAN BUCKLEY, Publisher & President - Print, Animation & Digital Divisions; JOE QUESADA, Chief Creative Officer; TOM BREVOORT, SVP of Publishing; DAVID BOGART, SVP of Operations & Procurement, Publishing; C.B. CEBULSKI, SVP of Creator & Content Development; DAVID GABRIEL, SVP of Print & Digital Publishing Sales; JIM O'KEEFE, VP of Operations & Logistics; DAN CARR, Executive Director of Publishing Technology; SUSAN CRESPI, Editorial Operations Manager; ALEX MORALES, Publishing Operations Manager; STAN LEE, Chairman Emeritus. For information regarding advertising in Marvel Comics or on Marvel.com, please contact Niza Disla, Director of Marvel Partnerships, at ndisla@marvel.com. For Marvel subscription inquiries, please call 800-217-9158. **Manufactured between 4/1/2013 and 5/13/2013 by R.R. DONNELLEY, INC., SALEM, VA, USA.**

10 9 8 7 6 5 4 3 2 1

THOR
GOD OF THUNDER

the god butcher

WRITER
JASON AARON

ARTIST
ESAD RIBIC

COLOR ARTISTS
DEAN WHITE (#1) & IVE SVORCINA (#2-5)

LETTERER
VC'S JOE SABINO

COVER ART
ESAD RIBIC

ASSISTANT EDITOR
JAKE THOMAS

EDITOR
LAUREN SANKOVITCH

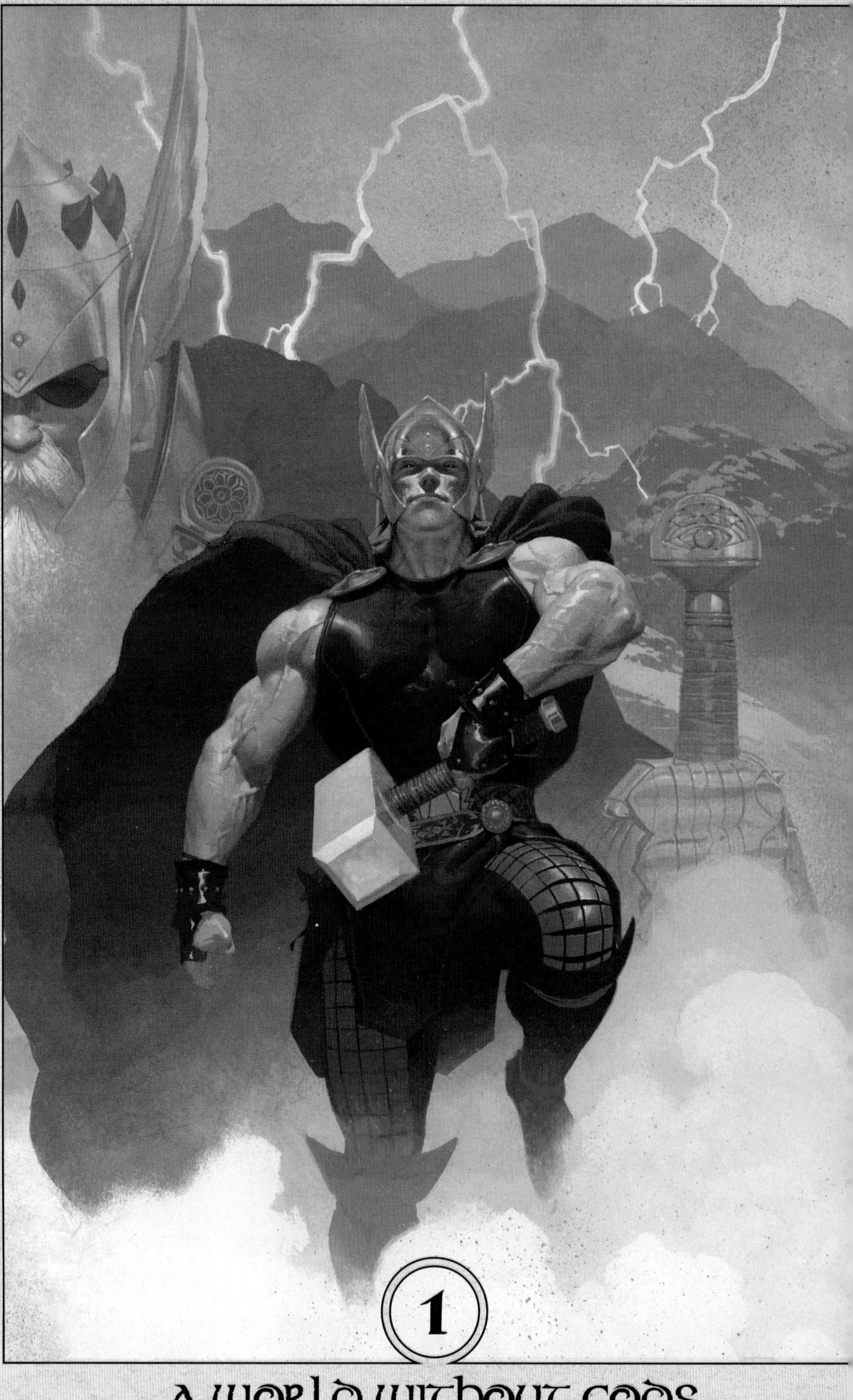

1

A WORLD WITHOUT GODS

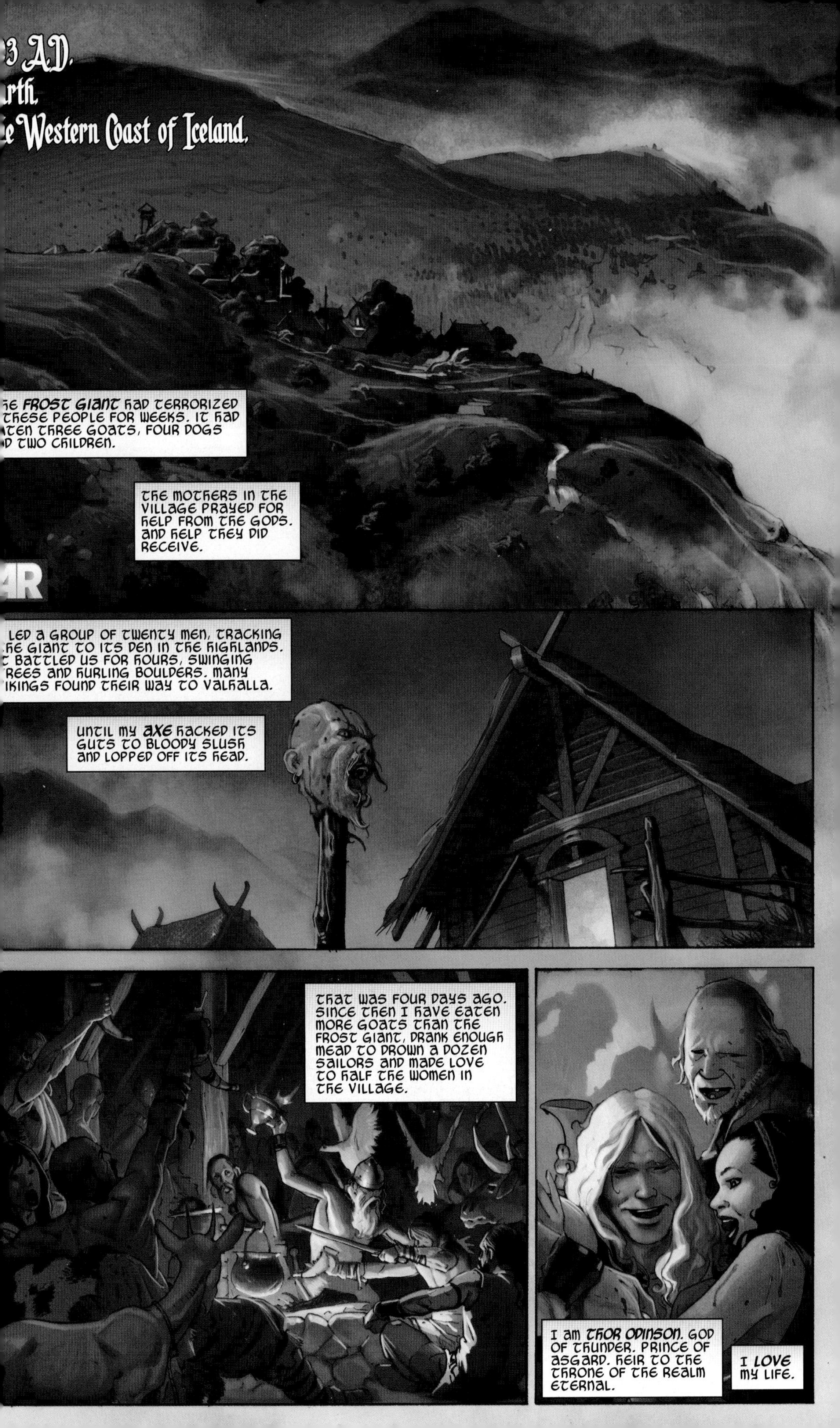

3 A.D.
rth.
e Western Coast of Iceland.
E FROST GIANT HAD TERRORIZED THESE PEOPLE FOR WEEKS. IT HAD TEN THREE GOATS, FOUR DOGS D TWO CHILDREN.
THE MOTHERS IN THE VILLAGE PRAYED FOR HELP FROM THE GODS. AND HELP THEY DID RECEIVE.
AR
LED A GROUP OF TWENTY MEN, TRACKING HE GIANT TO ITS DEN IN THE HIGHLANDS. BATTLED US FOR HOURS, SWINGING REES AND HURLING BOULDERS. MANY IKINGS FOUND THEIR WAY TO VALHALLA.
UNTIL MY AXE HACKED ITS GUTS TO BLOODY SLUSH AND LOPPED OFF ITS HEAD.
THAT WAS FOUR DAYS AGO. SINCE THEN I HAVE EATEN MORE GOATS THAN THE FROST GIANT, DRANK ENOUGH MEAD TO DROWN A DOZEN SAILORS AND MADE LOVE TO HALF THE WOMEN IN THE VILLAGE.
I AM THOR ODINSON. GOD OF THUNDER. PRINCE OF ASGARD. HEIR TO THE THRONE OF THE REALM ETERNAL.
I LOVE MY LIFE.

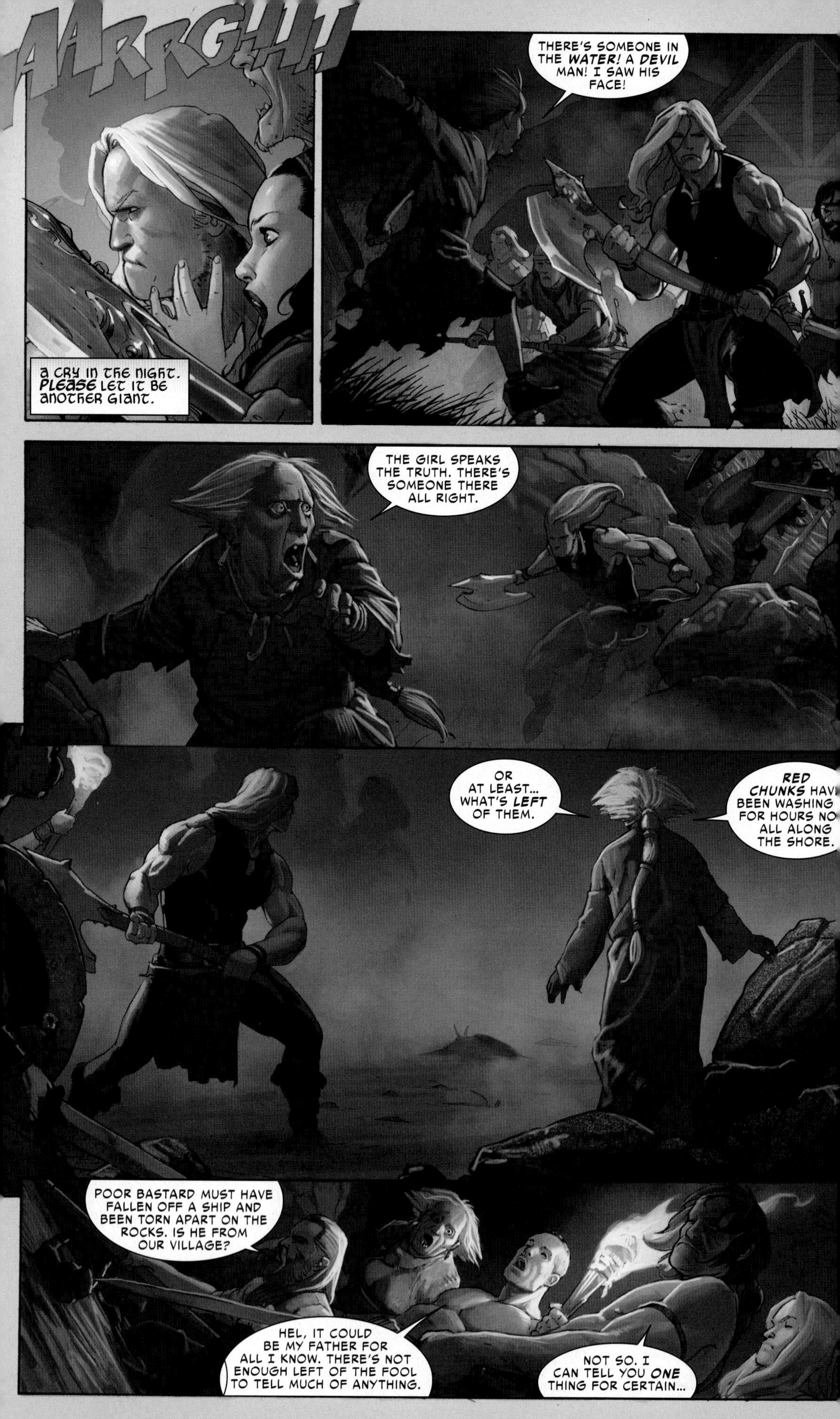
AARRGHH
A CRY IN THE NIGHT. PLEASE LET IT BE ANOTHER GIANT.
THERE'S SOMEONE IN THE WATER! A DEVIL MAN! I SAW HIS FACE!
THE GIRL SPEAKS THE TRUTH. THERE'S SOMEONE THERE ALL RIGHT.
OR AT LEAST... WHAT'S LEFT OF THEM.
RED CHUNKS HAV BEEN WASHING FOR HOURS NO ALL ALONG THE SHORE.
POOR BASTARD MUST HAVE FALLEN OFF A SHIP AND BEEN TORN APART ON THE ROCKS. IS HE FROM OUR VILLAGE?
HEL, IT COULD BE MY FATHER FOR ALL I KNOW. THERE'S NOT ENOUGH LEFT OF THE FOOL TO TELL MUCH OF ANYTHING.
NOT SO. I CAN TELL YOU ONE THING FOR CERTAIN...

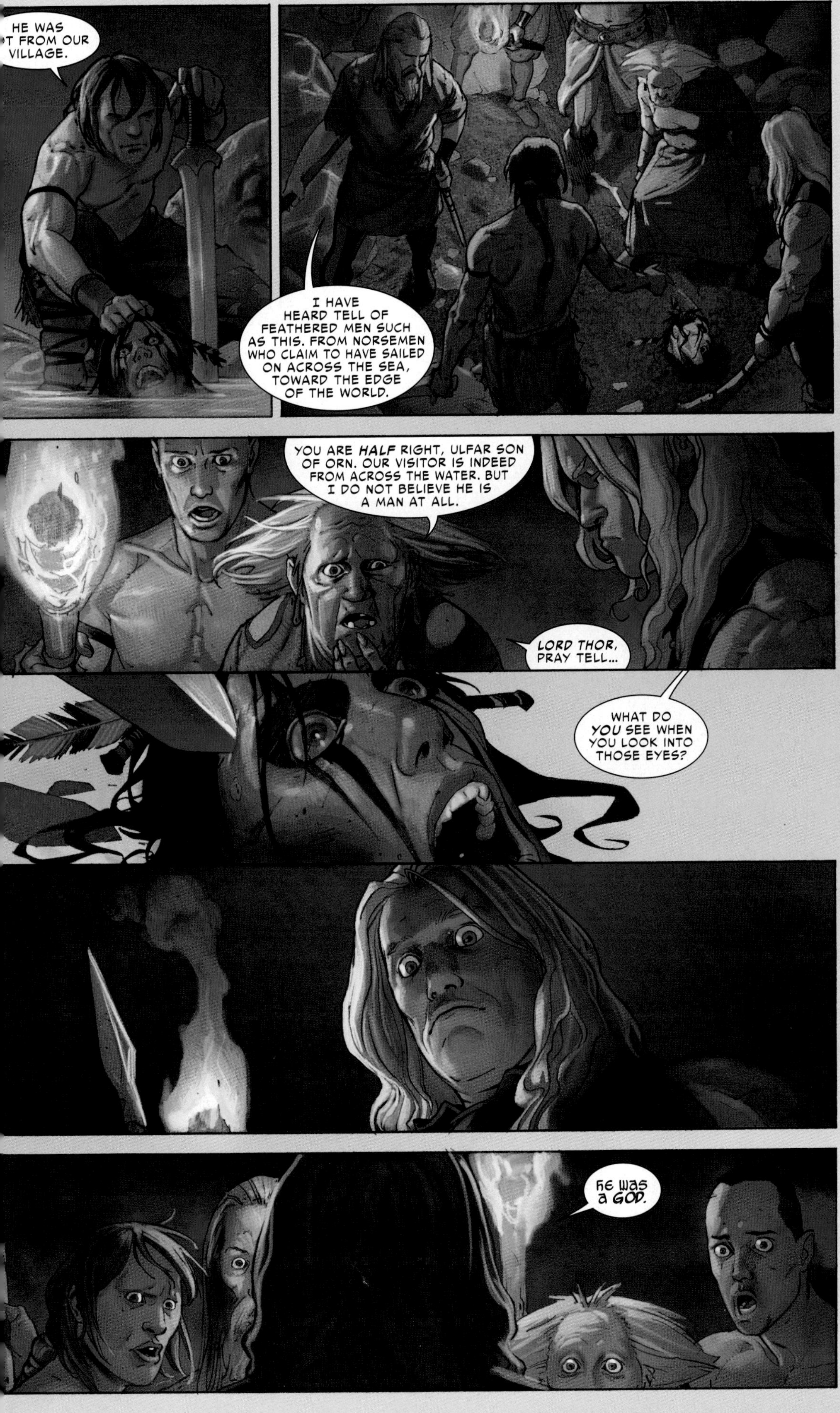
HE WAS
T FROM OUR
VILLAGE.
I HAVE HEARD TELL OF FEATHERED MEN SUCH AS THIS. FROM NORSEMEN WHO CLAIM TO HAVE SAILED ON ACROSS THE SEA, TOWARD THE EDGE OF THE WORLD.
YOU ARE HALF RIGHT, ULFAR SON OF ORN. OUR VISITOR IS INDEED FROM ACROSS THE WATER. BUT I DO NOT BELIEVE HE IS A MAN AT ALL.
LORD THOR, PRAY TELL...
WHAT DO YOU SEE WHEN YOU LOOK INTO THOSE EYES?
HE WAS A GOD.

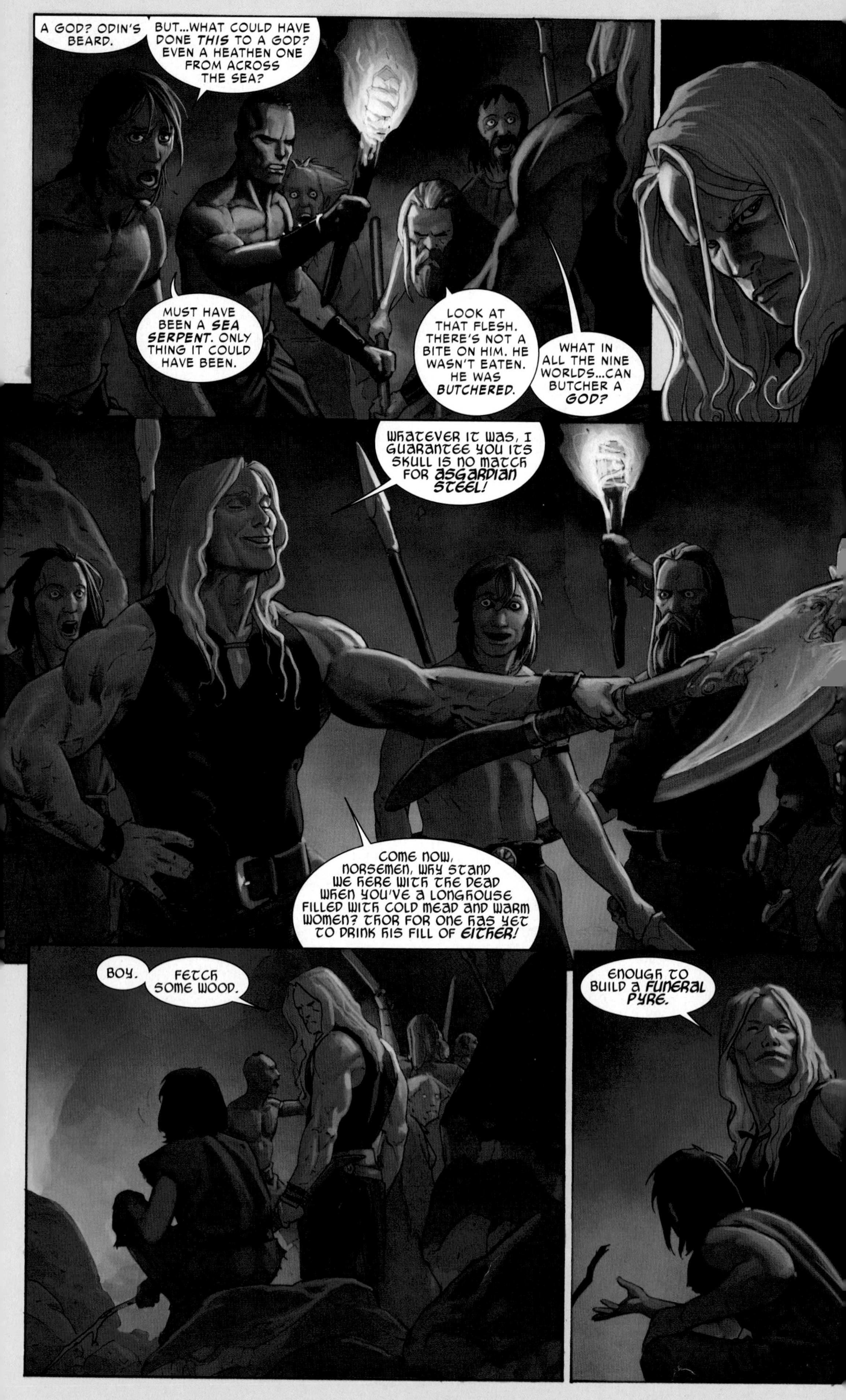
A GOD? ODIN'S BEARD.
BUT...WHAT COULD HAVE DONE THIS TO A GOD? EVEN A HEATHEN ONE FROM ACROSS THE SEA?
MUST HAVE BEEN A SEA SERPENT. ONLY THING IT COULD HAVE BEEN.
LOOK AT THAT FLESH. THERE'S NOT A BITE ON HIM. HE WASN'T EATEN. HE WAS BUTCHERED.
WHAT IN ALL THE NINE WORLDS...CAN BUTCHER A GOD?
WHATEVER IT WAS, I GUARANTEE YOU ITS SKULL IS NO MATCH FOR ASGARDIAN STEEL!
COME NOW, NORSEMEN, WHY STAND WE HERE WITH THE DEAD WHEN YOU'VE A LONGHOUSE FILLED WITH COLD MEAD AND WARM WOMEN? THOR FOR ONE HAS YET TO DRINK HIS FILL OF EITHER!
BOY.
FETCH SOME WOOD.
ENOUGH TO BUILD A FUNERAL PYRE.

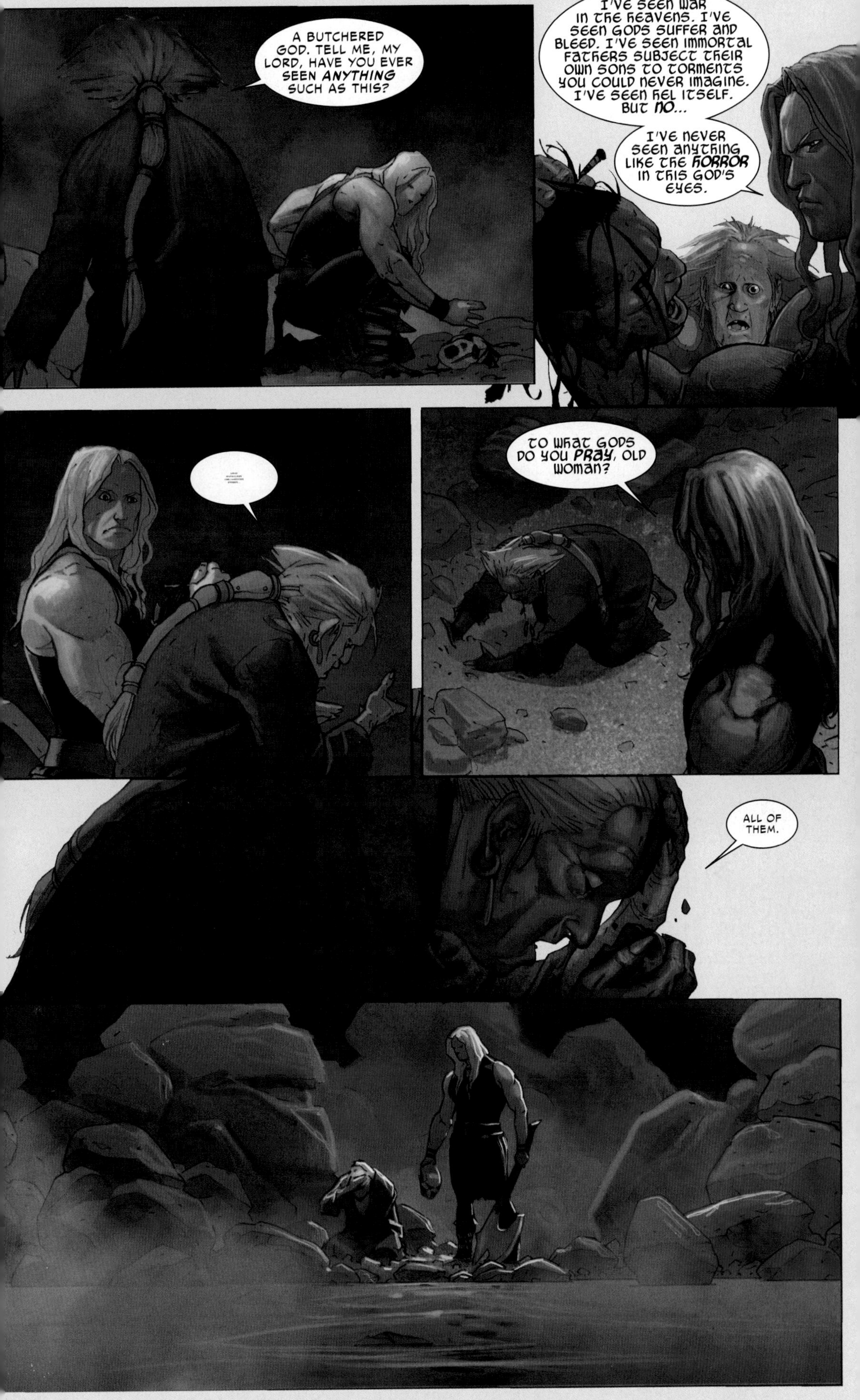

A BUTCHERED GOD. TELL ME, MY LORD, HAVE YOU EVER SEEN *ANYTHING* SUCH AS THIS?
I'VE SEEN WAR IN THE HEAVENS. I'VE SEEN GODS SUFFER AND BLEED. I'VE SEEN IMMORTAL FATHERS SUBJECT THEIR OWN SONS TO TORMENTS YOU COULD NEVER IMAGINE. I'VE SEEN HEL ITSELF. BUT *NO*...
I'VE NEVER SEEN ANYTHING LIKE THE *HORROR* IN THIS GOD'S EYES.
TO WHAT GODS DO YOU *PRAY*, OLD WOMAN?
ALL OF THEM.

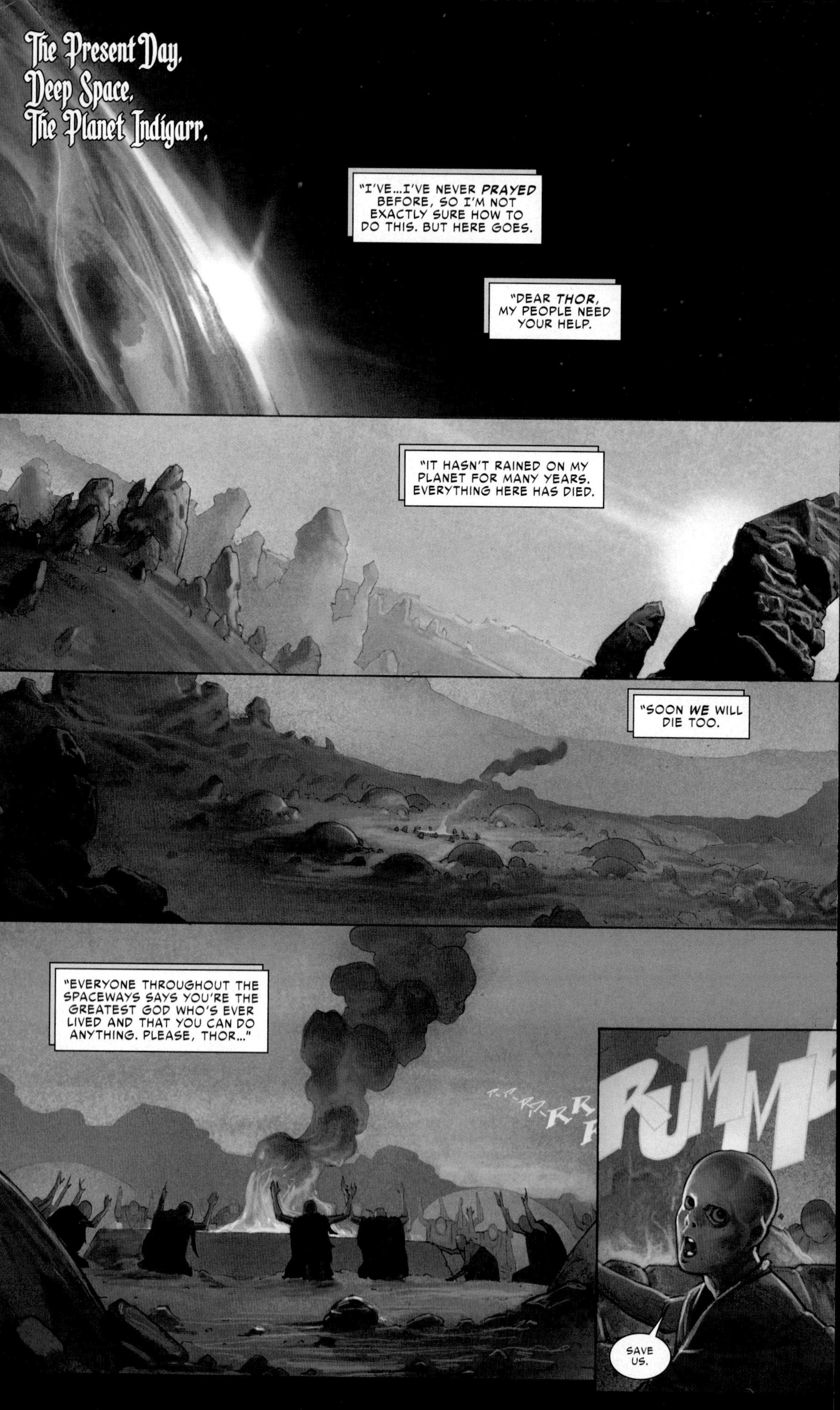
The Present Day.
Deep Space.
The Planet Indigarr.
"I'VE...I'VE NEVER PRAYED BEFORE, SO I'M NOT EXACTLY SURE HOW TO DO THIS. BUT HERE GOES.
"DEAR THOR, MY PEOPLE NEED YOUR HELP.
"IT HASN'T RAINED ON MY PLANET FOR MANY YEARS. EVERYTHING HERE HAS DIED.
"SOON WE WILL DIE TOO.
"EVERYONE THROUGHOUT THE SPACEWAYS SAYS YOU'RE THE GREATEST GOD WHO'S EVER LIVED AND THAT YOU CAN DO ANYTHING. PLEASE, THOR..."
SAVE US.

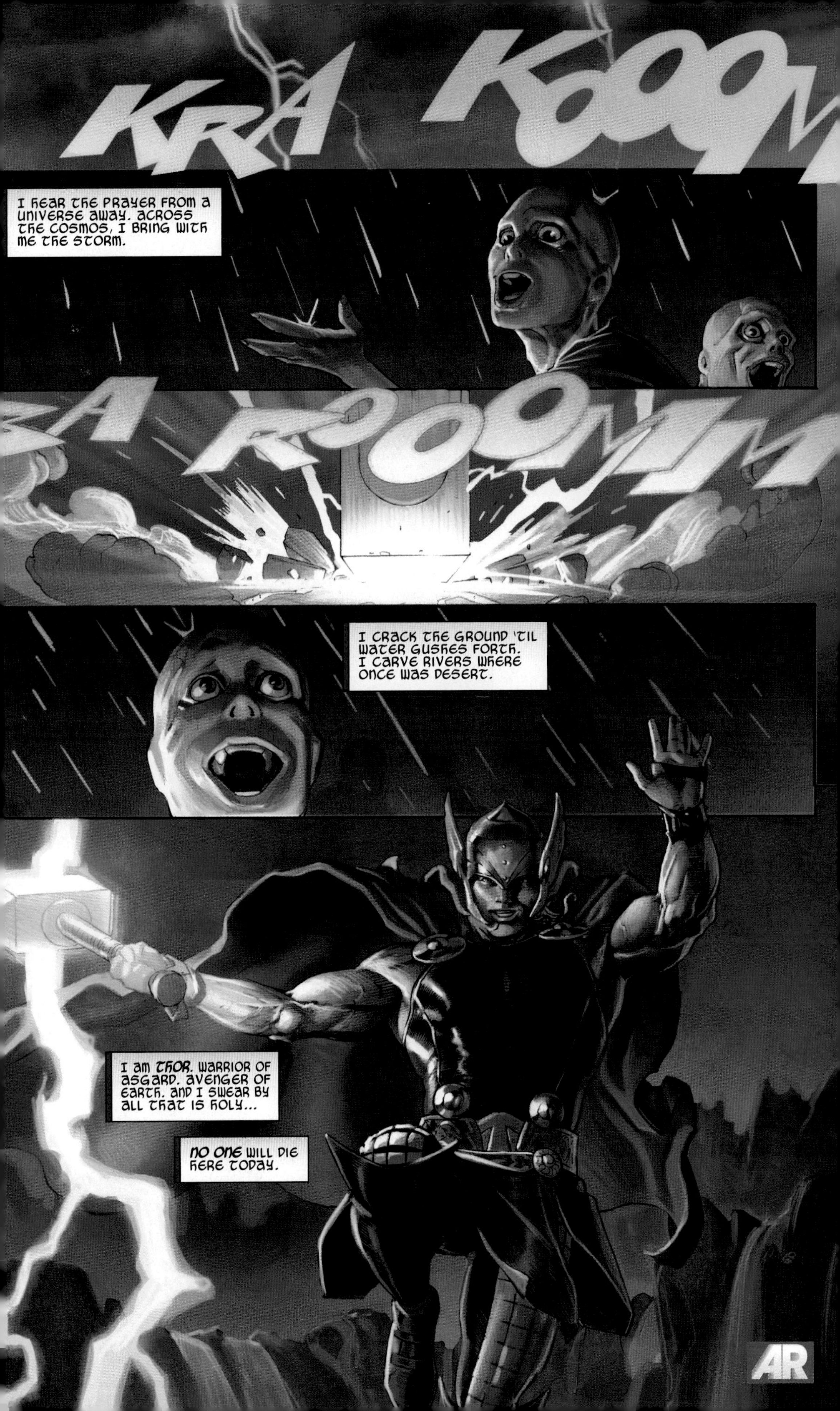
KRA KOOOM
I HEAR THE PRAYER FROM A UNIVERSE AWAY. ACROSS THE COSMOS, I BRING WITH ME THE STORM.
RA KROOOM
I CRACK THE GROUND 'TIL WATER GUSHES FORTH. I CARVE RIVERS WHERE ONCE WAS DESERT.
I AM *THOR*. WARRIOR OF ASGARD. AVENGER OF EARTH. AND I SWEAR BY ALL THAT IS HOLY...
NO ONE WILL DIE HERE TODAY.

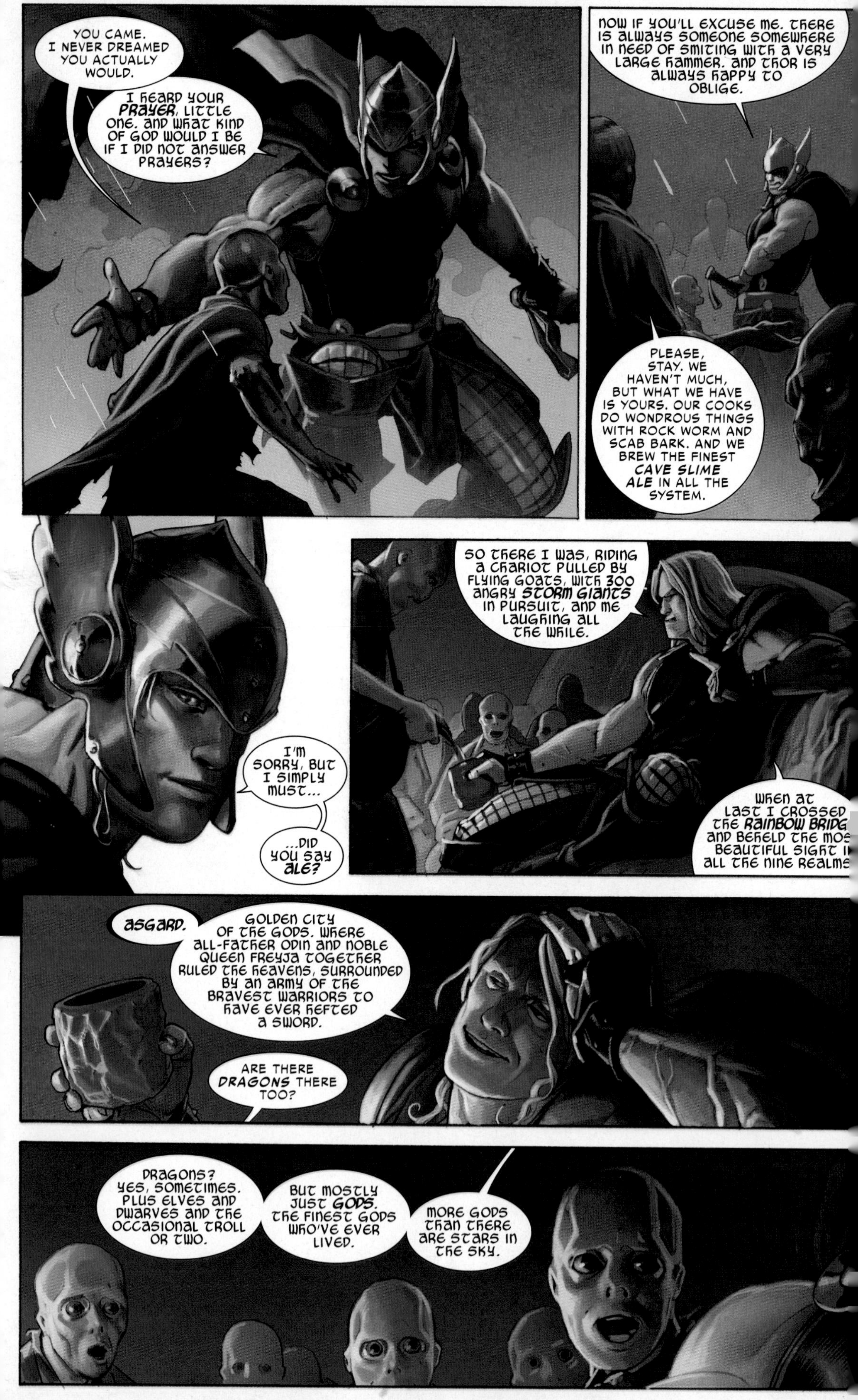
YOU CAME. I NEVER DREAMED YOU ACTUALLY WOULD.
I HEARD YOUR PRAYER, LITTLE ONE. AND WHAT KIND OF GOD WOULD I BE IF I DID NOT ANSWER PRAYERS?
NOW IF YOU'LL EXCUSE ME. THERE IS ALWAYS SOMEONE SOMEWHERE IN NEED OF SMITING WITH A VERY LARGE HAMMER. AND THOR IS ALWAYS HAPPY TO OBLIGE.
PLEASE, STAY. WE HAVEN'T MUCH, BUT WHAT WE HAVE IS YOURS. OUR COOKS DO WONDROUS THINGS WITH ROCK WORM AND SCAB BARK. AND WE BREW THE FINEST CAVE SLIME ALE IN ALL THE SYSTEM.
I'M SORRY, BUT I SIMPLY MUST...
...DID YOU SAY ALE?
SO THERE I WAS, RIDING A CHARIOT PULLED BY FLYING GOATS, WITH 300 ANGRY STORM GIANTS IN PURSUIT, AND ME LAUGHING ALL THE WHILE.
WHEN AT LAST I CROSSED THE RAINBOW BRIDG AND BEHELD THE MOS BEAUTIFUL SIGHT I ALL THE NINE REALMS
ASGARD.
GOLDEN CITY OF THE GODS. WHERE ALL-FATHER ODIN AND NOBLE QUEEN FREYJA TOGETHER RULED THE HEAVENS, SURROUNDED BY AN ARMY OF THE BRAVEST WARRIORS TO HAVE EVER HEFTED A SWORD.
ARE THERE DRAGONS THERE TOO?
DRAGONS? YES, SOMETIMES. PLUS ELVES AND DWARVES AND THE OCCASIONAL TROLL OR TWO.
BUT MOSTLY JUST GODS. THE FINEST GODS WHO'VE EVER LIVED.
MORE GODS THAN THERE ARE STARS IN THE SKY.

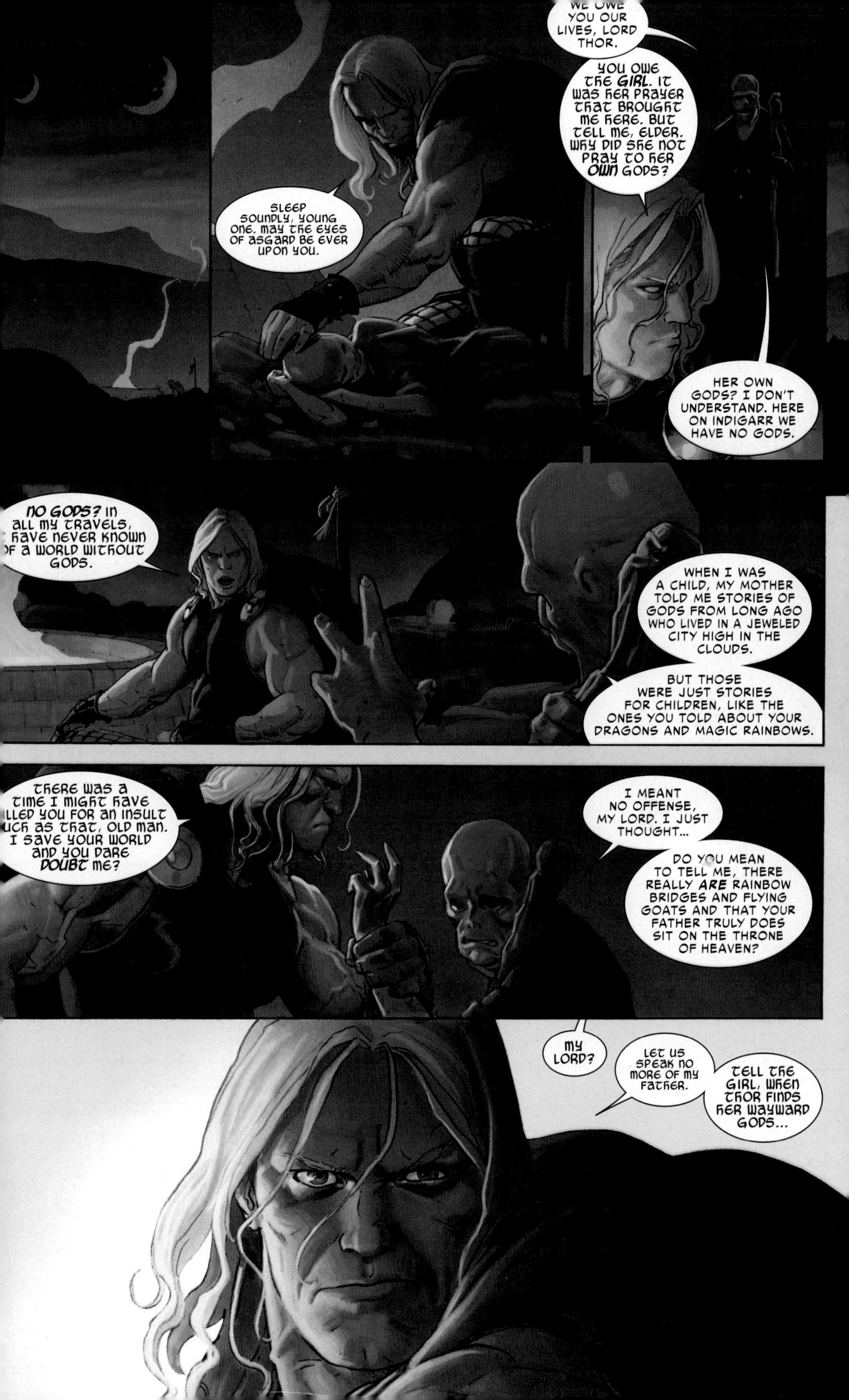

SLEEP SOUNDLY, YOUNG ONE. MAY THE EYES OF ASGARD BE EVER UPON YOU.
WE OWE YOU OUR LIVES, LORD THOR.
YOU OWE THE GIRL. IT WAS HER PRAYER THAT BROUGHT ME HERE. BUT TELL ME, ELDER. WHY DID SHE NOT PRAY TO HER OWN GODS?
HER OWN GODS? I DON'T UNDERSTAND. HERE ON INDIGARR WE HAVE NO GODS.
NO GODS? IN ALL MY TRAVELS, I HAVE NEVER KNOWN OF A WORLD WITHOUT GODS.
WHEN I WAS A CHILD, MY MOTHER TOLD ME STORIES OF GODS FROM LONG AGO WHO LIVED IN A JEWELED CITY HIGH IN THE CLOUDS.
BUT THOSE WERE JUST STORIES FOR CHILDREN, LIKE THE ONES YOU TOLD ABOUT YOUR DRAGONS AND MAGIC RAINBOWS.
THERE WAS A TIME I MIGHT HAVE KILLED YOU FOR AN INSULT SUCH AS THAT, OLD MAN. I SAVE YOUR WORLD AND YOU DARE DOUBT ME?
I MEANT NO OFFENSE, MY LORD. I JUST THOUGHT...
DO YOU MEAN TO TELL ME, THERE REALLY ARE RAINBOW BRIDGES AND FLYING GOATS AND THAT YOUR FATHER TRULY DOES SIT ON THE THRONE OF HEAVEN?
MY LORD?
LET US SPEAK NO MORE OF MY FATHER.
TELL THE GIRL, WHEN THOR FINDS HER WAYWARD GODS...

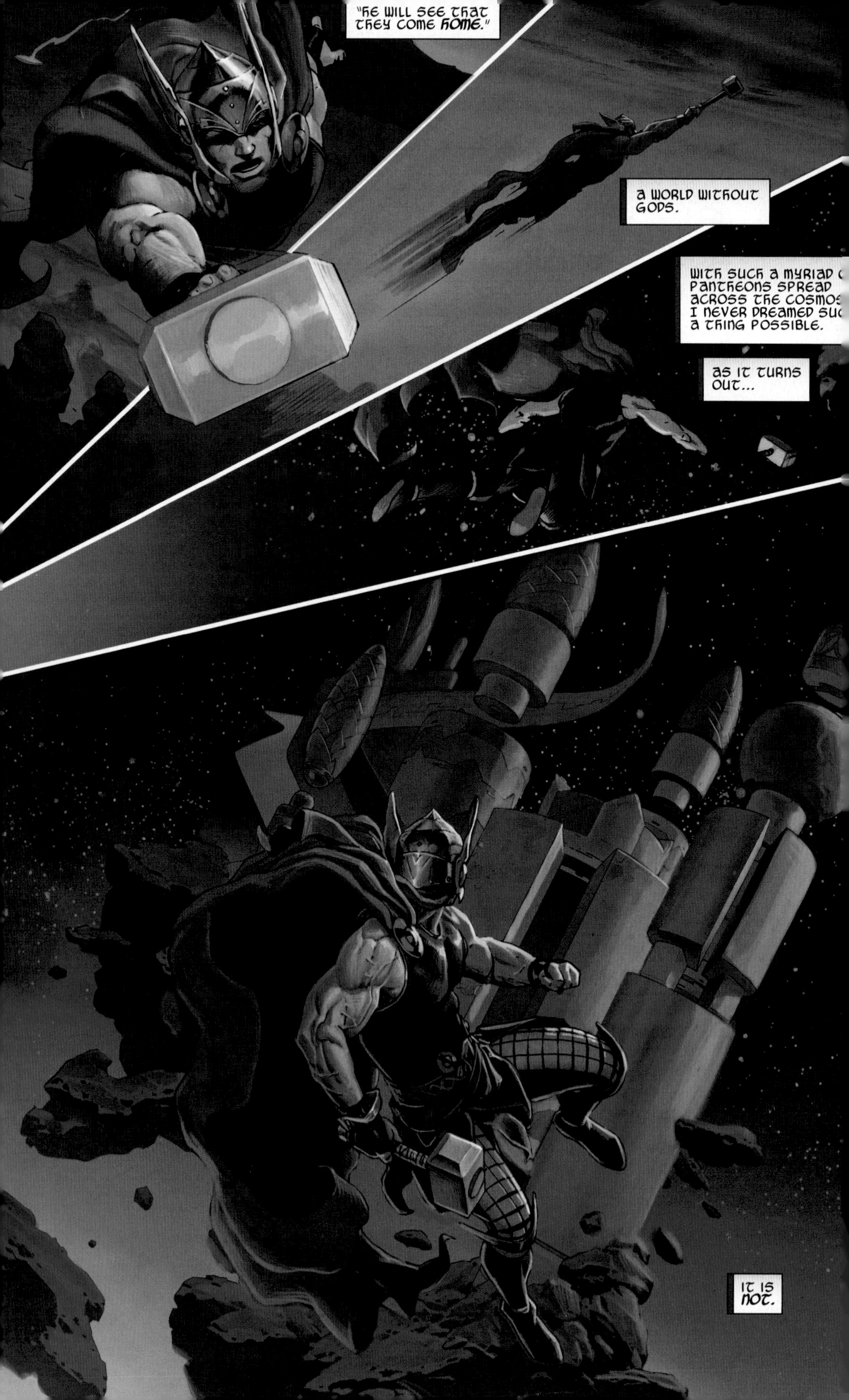
"HE WILL SEE THAT THEY COME HOME."
A WORLD WITHOUT GODS.
WITH SUCH A MYRIAD PANTHEONS SPREAD ACROSS THE COSMOS I NEVER DREAMED SUC A THING POSSIBLE.
AS IT TURNS OUT...
IT IS NOT.

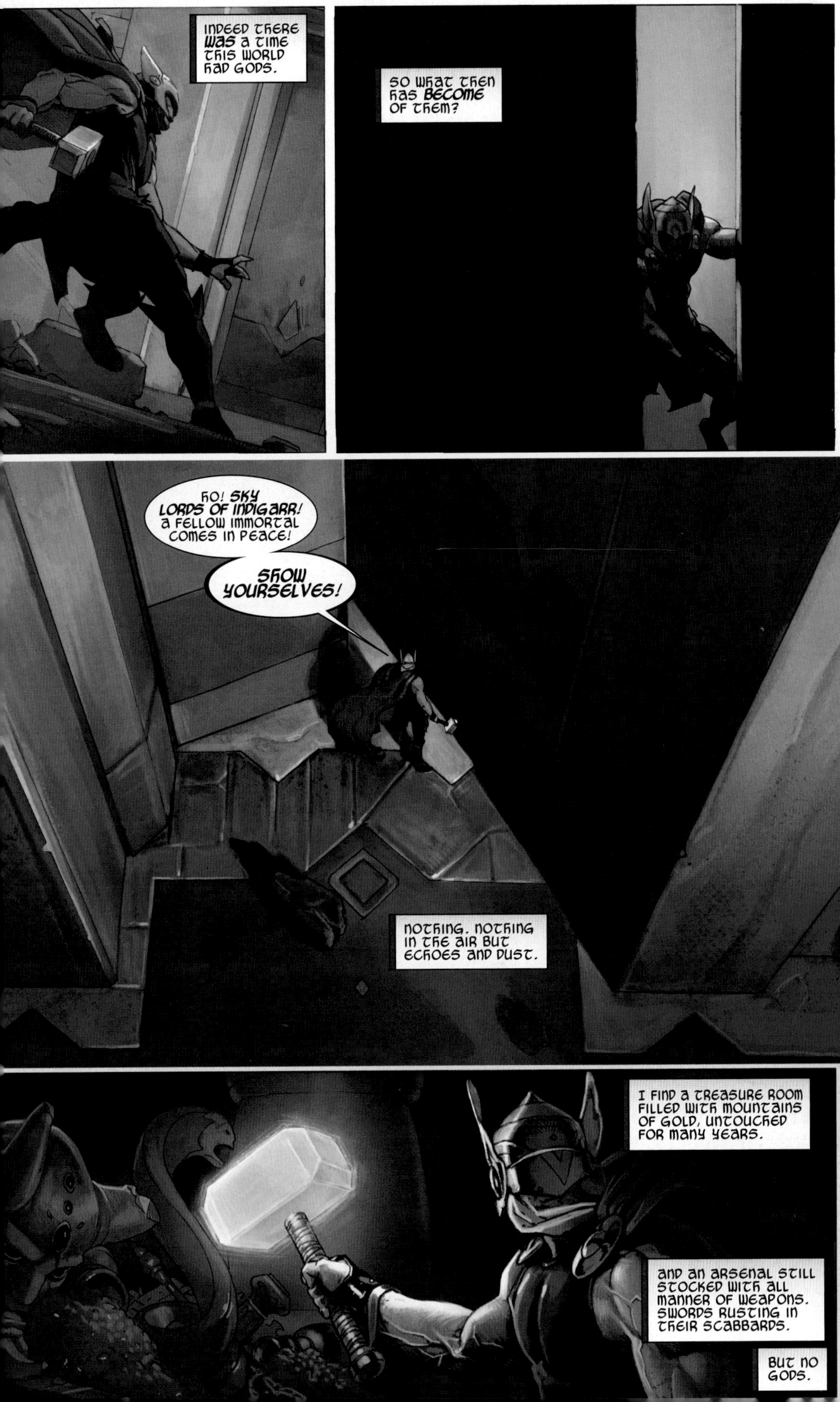
INDEED THERE WAS A TIME THIS WORLD HAD GODS.
SO WHAT THEN HAS BECOME OF THEM?
HO! SKY LORDS OF INDIGARR! A FELLOW IMMORTAL COMES IN PEACE!
SHOW YOURSELVES!
NOTHING. NOTHING IN THE AIR BUT ECHOES AND DUST.
I FIND A TREASURE ROOM FILLED WITH MOUNTAINS OF GOLD, UNTOUCHED FOR MANY YEARS.
AND AN ARSENAL STILL STOCKED WITH ALL MANNER OF WEAPONS. SWORDS RUSTING IN THEIR SCABBARDS.
BUT NO GODS.

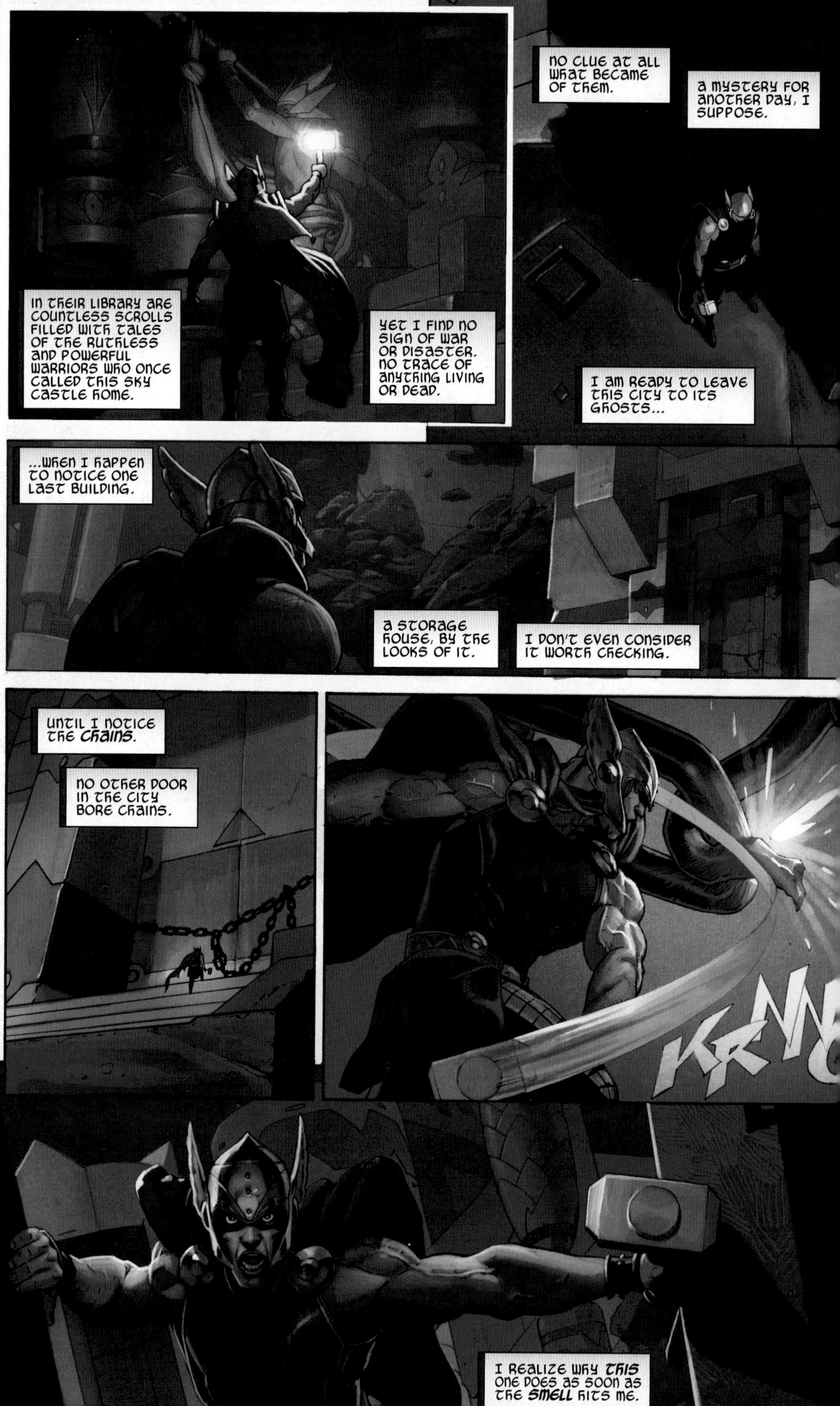
IN THEIR LIBRARY ARE COUNTLESS SCROLLS FILLED WITH TALES OF THE RUTHLESS AND POWERFUL WARRIORS WHO ONCE CALLED THIS SKY CASTLE HOME.
YET I FIND NO SIGN OF WAR OR DISASTER. NO TRACE OF ANYTHING LIVING OR DEAD.
NO CLUE AT ALL WHAT BECAME OF THEM.
A MYSTERY FOR ANOTHER DAY, I SUPPOSE.
I AM READY TO LEAVE THIS CITY TO ITS GHOSTS...
...WHEN I HAPPEN TO NOTICE ONE LAST BUILDING.
A STORAGE HOUSE, BY THE LOOKS OF IT.
I DON'T EVEN CONSIDER IT WORTH CHECKING.
UNTIL I NOTICE THE *CHAINS*.
NO OTHER DOOR IN THE CITY BORE CHAINS.
KRNN
I REALIZE WHY *THIS* ONE DOES AS SOON AS THE *SMELL* HITS ME.

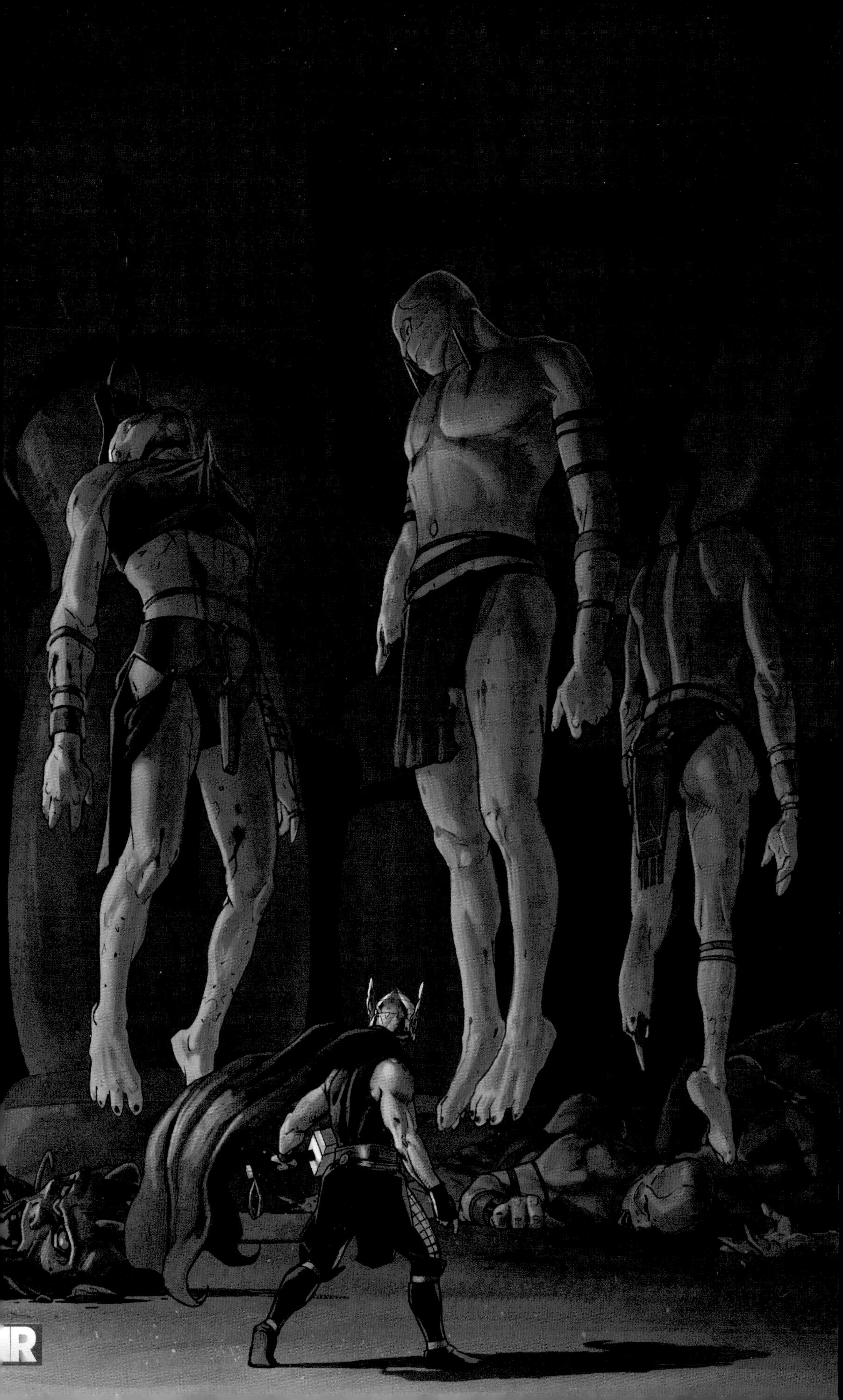

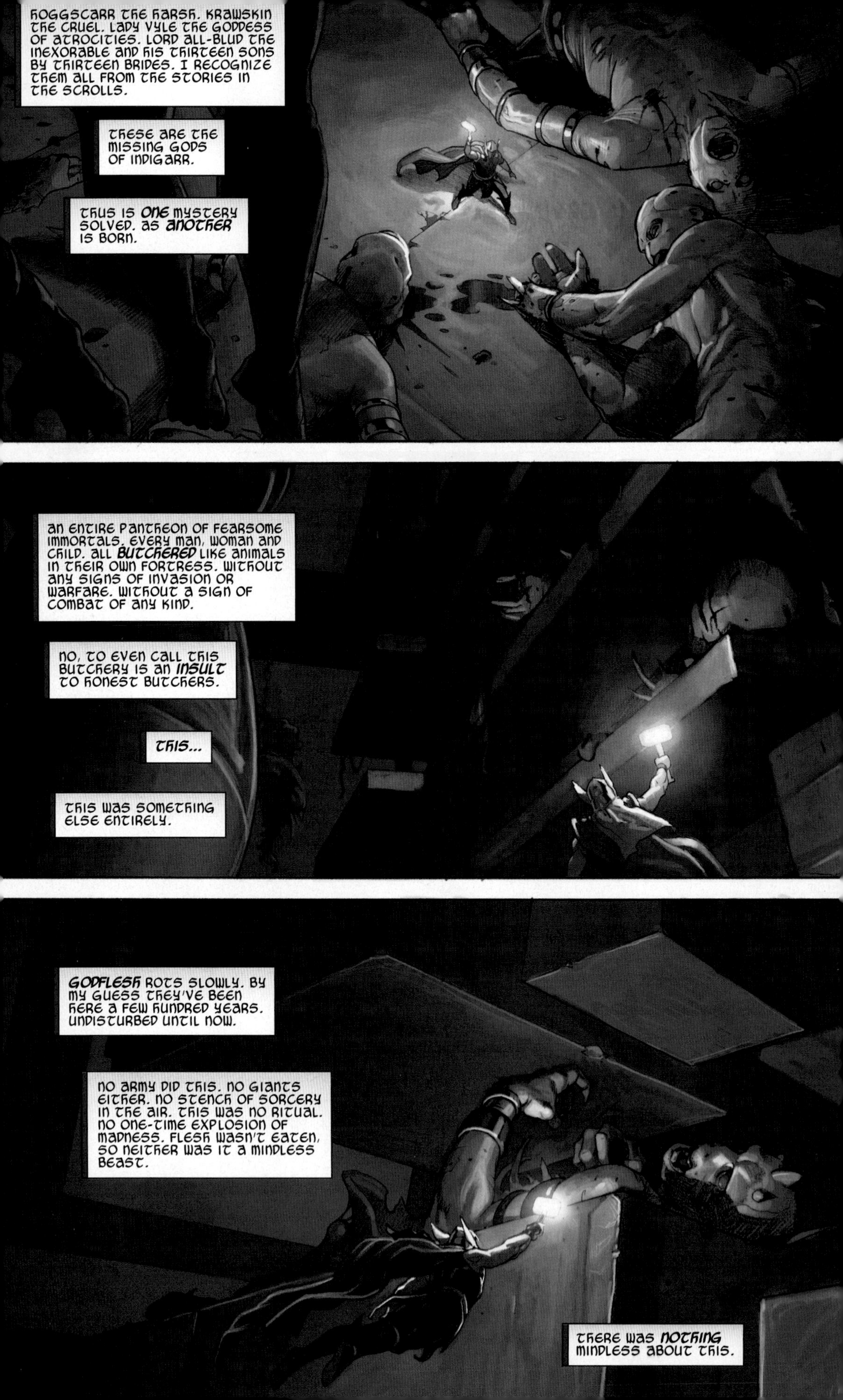
HOGGSCARR THE HARSH. KRAWSKIN THE CRUEL. LADY VYLE THE GODDESS OF ATROCITIES. LORD ALL-BLUD THE INEXORABLE AND HIS THIRTEEN SONS BY THIRTEEN BRIDES. I RECOGNIZE THEM ALL FROM THE STORIES IN THE SCROLLS.
THESE ARE THE MISSING GODS OF INDIGARR.
THUS IS ONE MYSTERY SOLVED. AS ANOTHER IS BORN.
AN ENTIRE PANTHEON OF FEARSOME IMMORTALS. EVERY MAN, WOMAN AND CHILD. ALL BUTCHERED LIKE ANIMALS IN THEIR OWN FORTRESS. WITHOUT ANY SIGNS OF INVASION OR WARFARE. WITHOUT A SIGN OF COMBAT OF ANY KIND.
NO, TO EVEN CALL THIS BUTCHERY IS AN INSULT TO HONEST BUTCHERS.
THIS...
THIS WAS SOMETHING ELSE ENTIRELY.
GODFLESH ROTS SLOWLY. BY MY GUESS THEY'VE BEEN HERE A FEW HUNDRED YEARS. UNDISTURBED UNTIL NOW.
NO ARMY DID THIS. NO GIANTS EITHER. NO STENCH OF SORCERY IN THE AIR. THIS WAS NO RITUAL. NO ONE-TIME EXPLOSION OF MADNESS. FLESH WASN'T EATEN, SO NEITHER WAS IT A MINDLESS BEAST.
THERE WAS NOTHING MINDLESS ABOUT THIS.

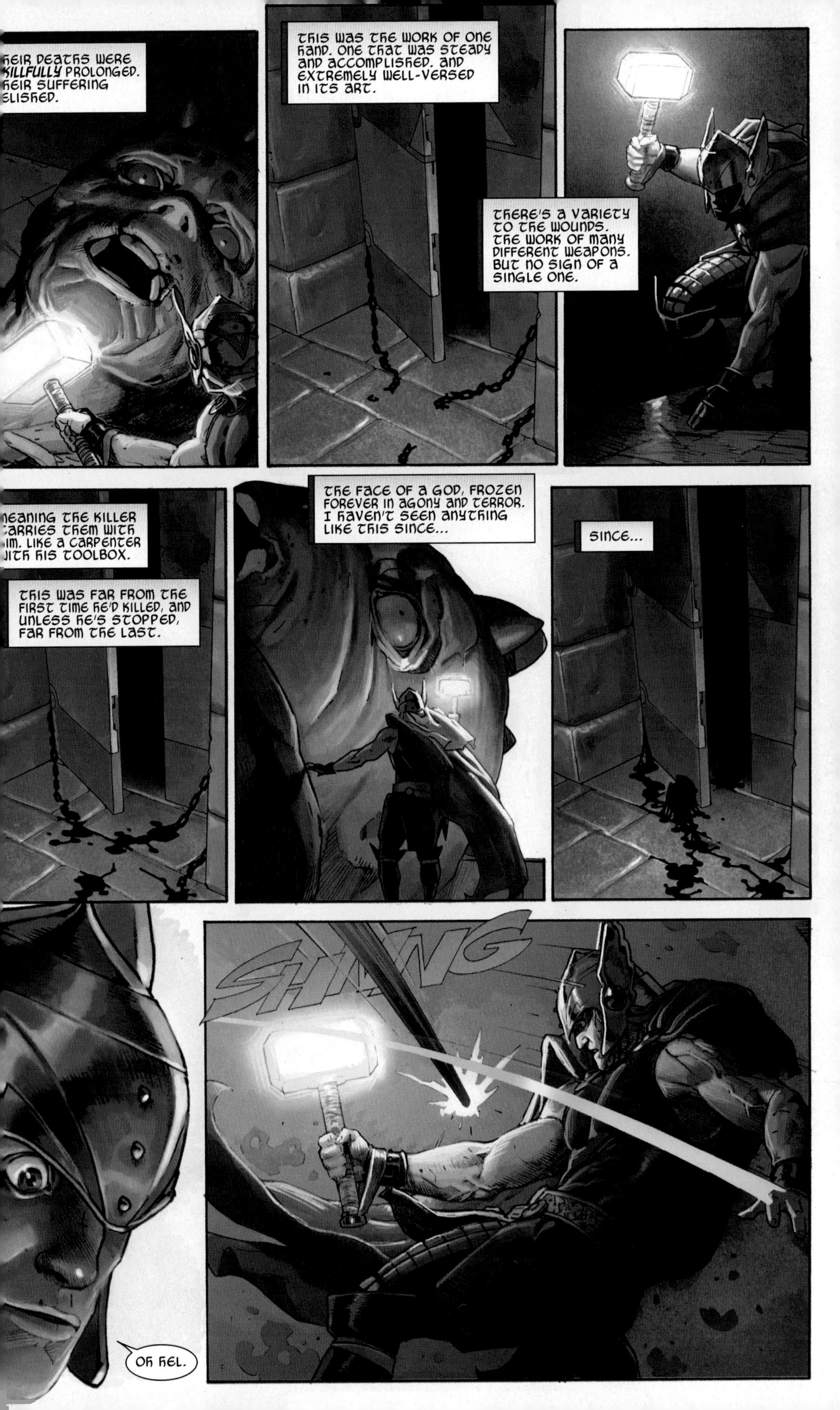
HEIR DEATHS WERE SKILLFULLY PROLONGED. HEIR SUFFERING ELISHED.
THIS WAS THE WORK OF ONE HAND. ONE THAT WAS STEADY AND ACCOMPLISHED. AND EXTREMELY WELL-VERSED IN ITS ART.
THERE'S A VARIETY TO THE WOUNDS. THE WORK OF MANY DIFFERENT WEAPONS. BUT NO SIGN OF A SINGLE ONE.
MEANING THE KILLER CARRIES THEM WITH IM. LIKE A CARPENTER WITH HIS TOOLBOX.
THIS WAS FAR FROM THE FIRST TIME HE'D KILLED, AND UNLESS HE'S STOPPED, FAR FROM THE LAST.
THE FACE OF A GOD, FROZEN FOREVER IN AGONY AND TERROR. I HAVEN'T SEEN ANYTHING LIKE THIS SINCE...
SINCE...
OH HEL.
SHHHNG

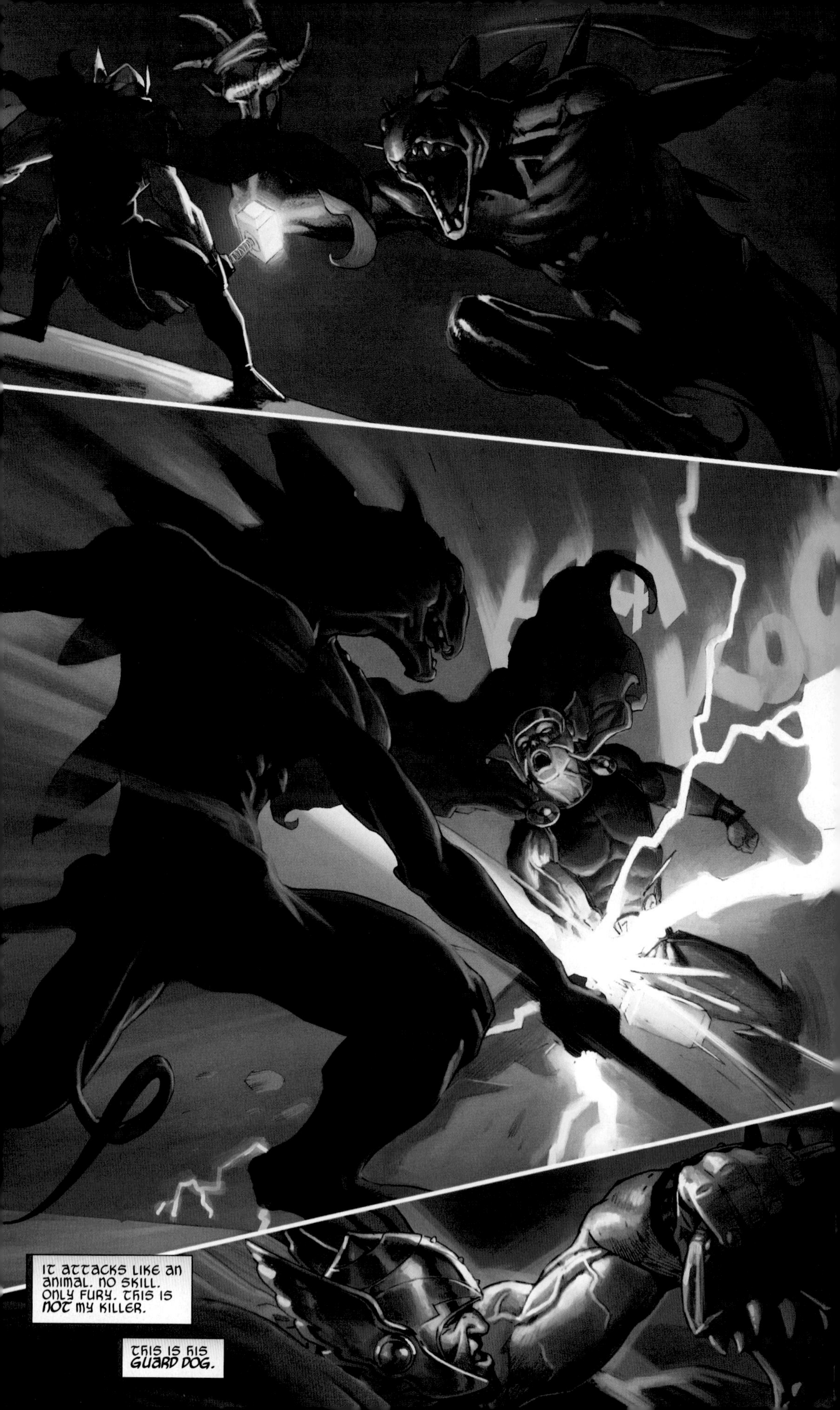
IT ATTACKS LIKE AN ANIMAL. NO SKILL. ONLY FURY. THIS IS NOT MY KILLER.
THIS IS HIS GUARD DOG.

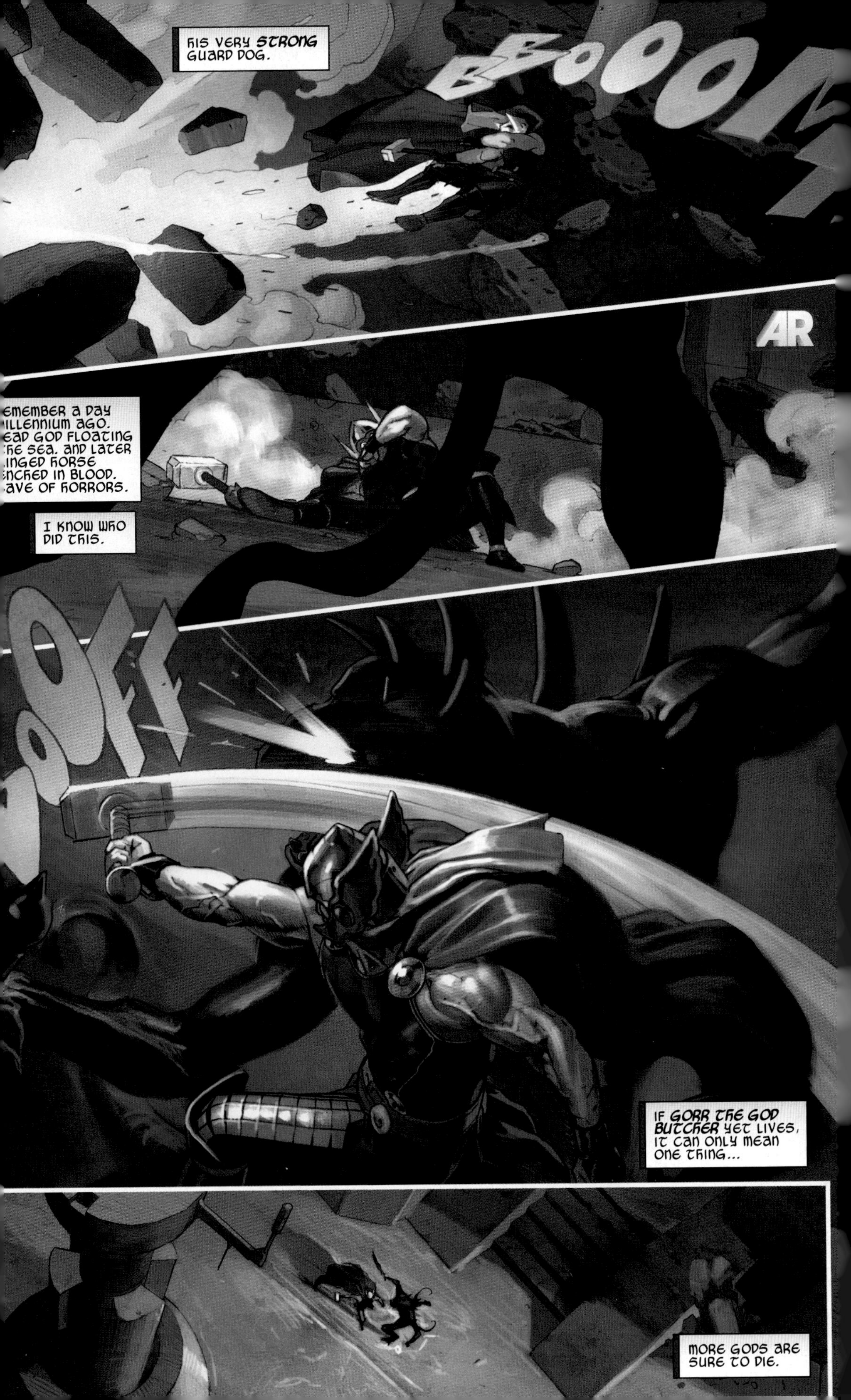
HIS VERY STRONG GUARD DOG.
BBOOOOM
AR
EMEMBER A DAY
ILLENNIUM AGO.
EAD GOD FLOATING
HE SEA. AND LATER
INGED HORSE
ENCHED IN BLOOD.
AVE OF HORRORS.
I KNOW WHO DID THIS.
OOFF
IF GORR THE GOD BUTCHER YET LIVES, IT CAN ONLY MEAN ONE THING...
MORE GODS ARE SURE TO DIE.

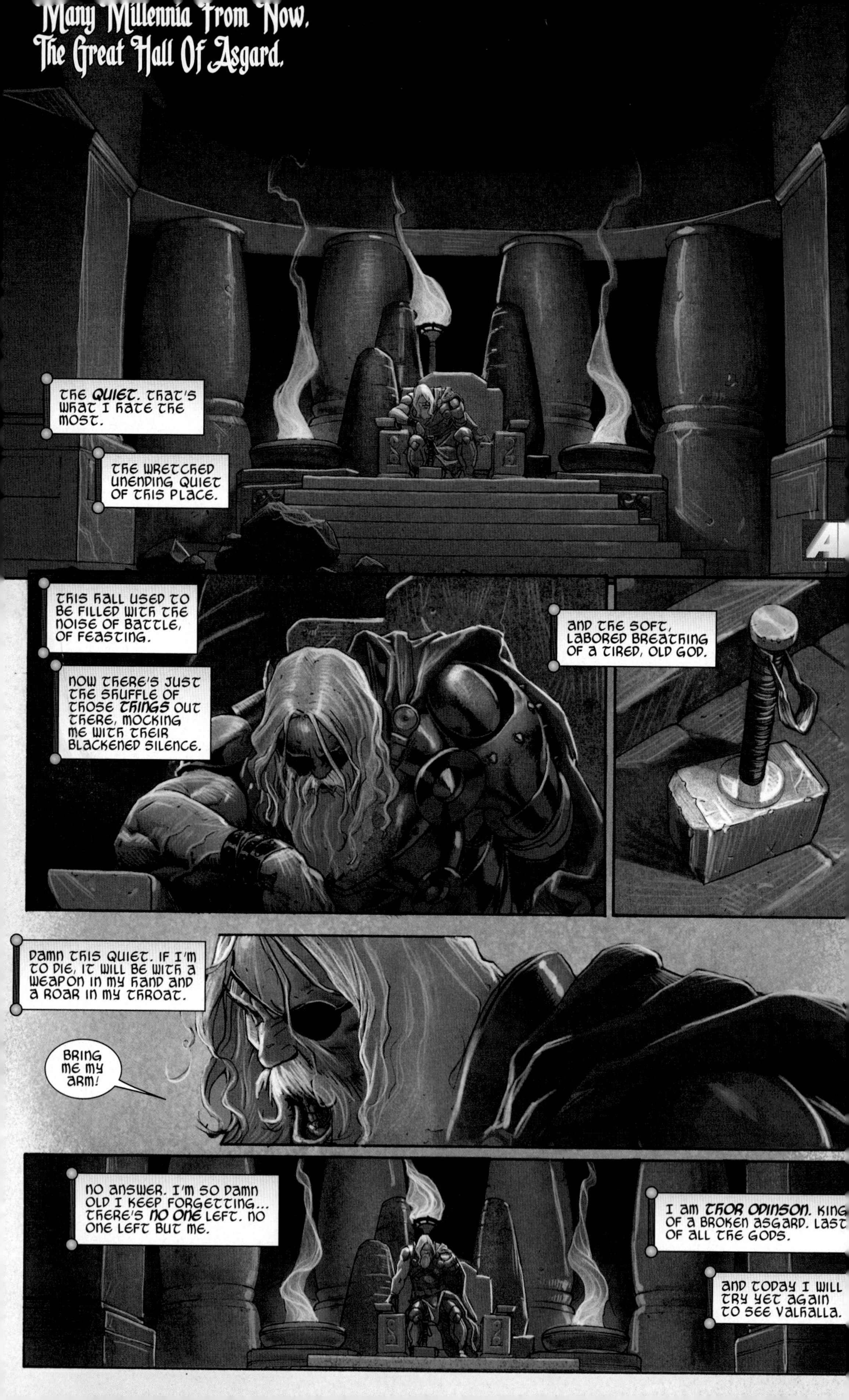
Many Millennia From Now,
The Great Hall Of Asgard.
THE QUIET. THAT'S WHAT I HATE THE MOST.
THE WRETCHED UNENDING QUIET OF THIS PLACE.
THIS HALL USED TO BE FILLED WITH THE NOISE OF BATTLE, OF FEASTING.
NOW THERE'S JUST THE SHUFFLE OF THOSE THINGS OUT THERE, MOCKING ME WITH THEIR BLACKENED SILENCE.
AND THE SOFT, LABORED BREATHING OF A TIRED, OLD GOD.
DAMN THIS QUIET. IF I'M TO DIE, IT WILL BE WITH A WEAPON IN MY HAND AND A ROAR IN MY THROAT.
BRING ME MY ARM!
NO ANSWER. I'M SO DAMN OLD I KEEP FORGETTING... THERE'S NO ONE LEFT. NO ONE LEFT BUT ME.
I AM THOR ODINSON. KING OF A BROKEN ASGARD. LAST OF ALL THE GODS.
AND TODAY I WILL TRY YET AGAIN TO SEE VALHALLA.

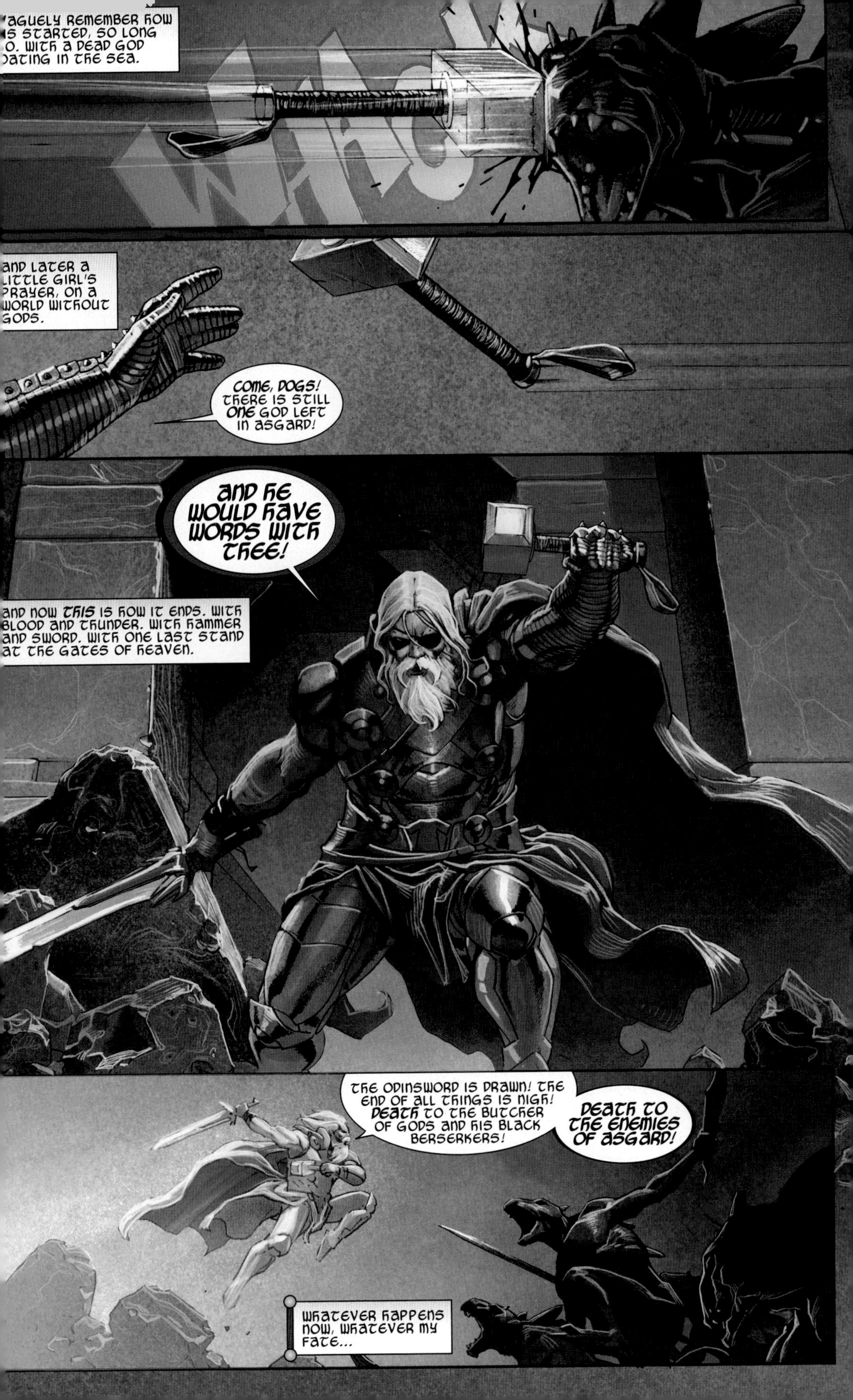
AGUELY REMEMBER HOW
S STARTED, SO LONG
O. WITH A DEAD GOD
DATING IN THE SEA.
AND LATER A LITTLE GIRL'S PRAYER, ON A WORLD WITHOUT GODS.
COME, DOGS! THERE IS STILL ONE GOD LEFT IN ASGARD!
AND HE WOULD HAVE WORDS WITH THEE!
AND NOW THIS IS HOW IT ENDS. WITH BLOOD AND THUNDER. WITH HAMMER AND SWORD. WITH ONE LAST STAND AT THE GATES OF HEAVEN.
THE ODINSWORD IS DRAWN! THE END OF ALL THINGS IS NIGH! DEATH TO THE BUTCHER OF GODS AND HIS BLACK BERSERKERS!
DEATH TO THE ENEMIES OF ASGARD!
WHATEVER HAPPENS NOW, WHATEVER MY FATE...

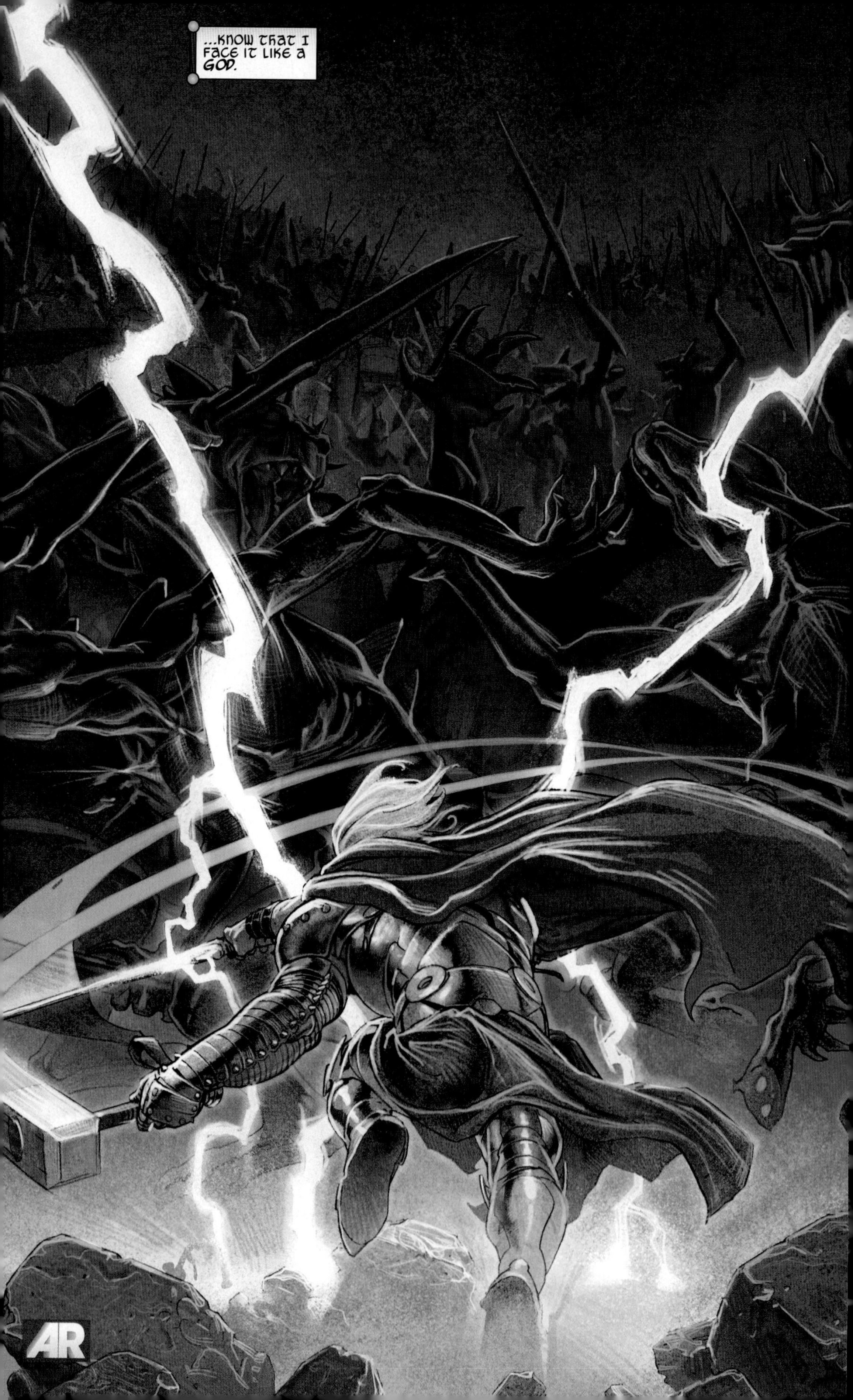
...KNOW THAT I FACE IT LIKE A GOD.

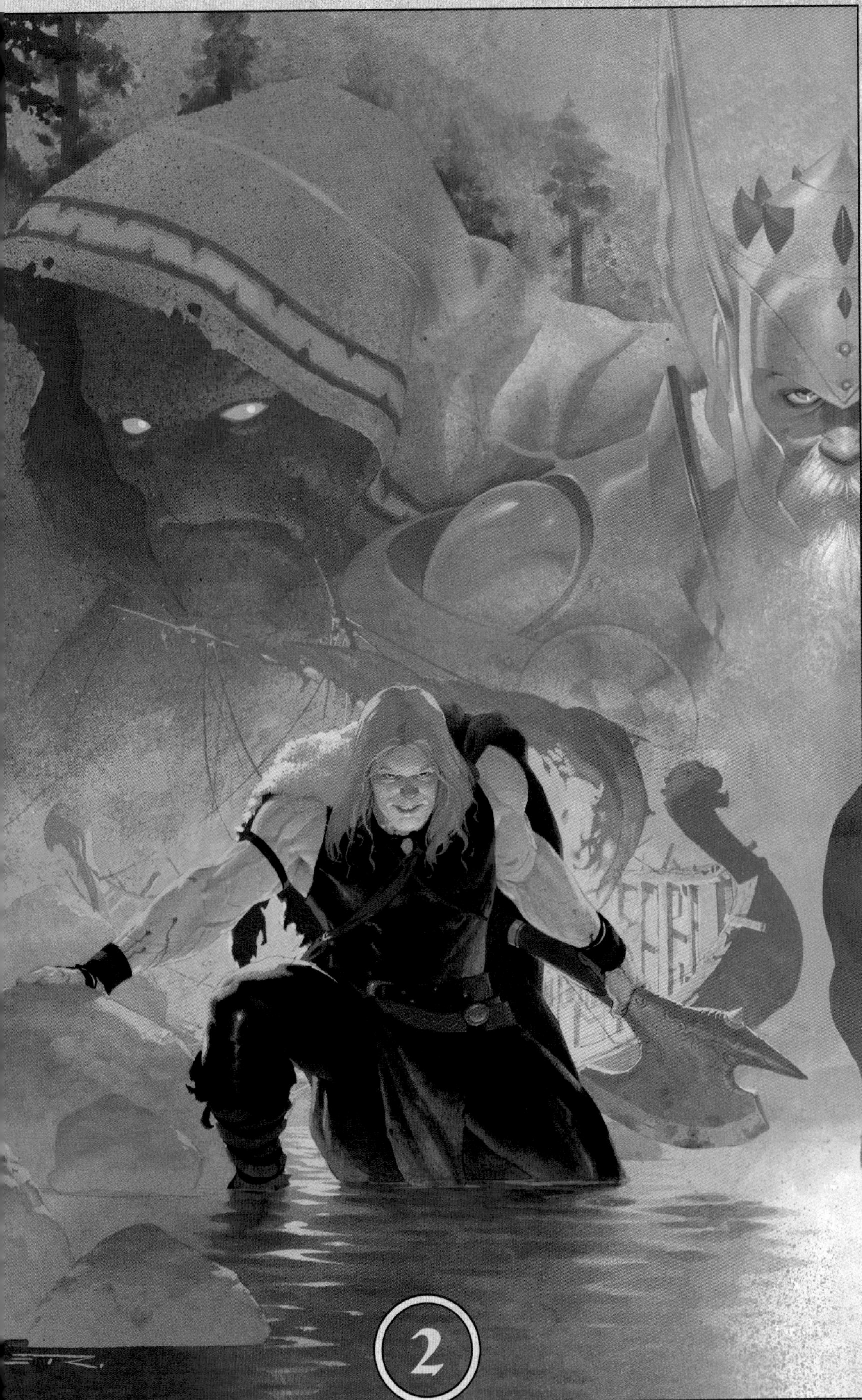
2

Blood in the Clouds

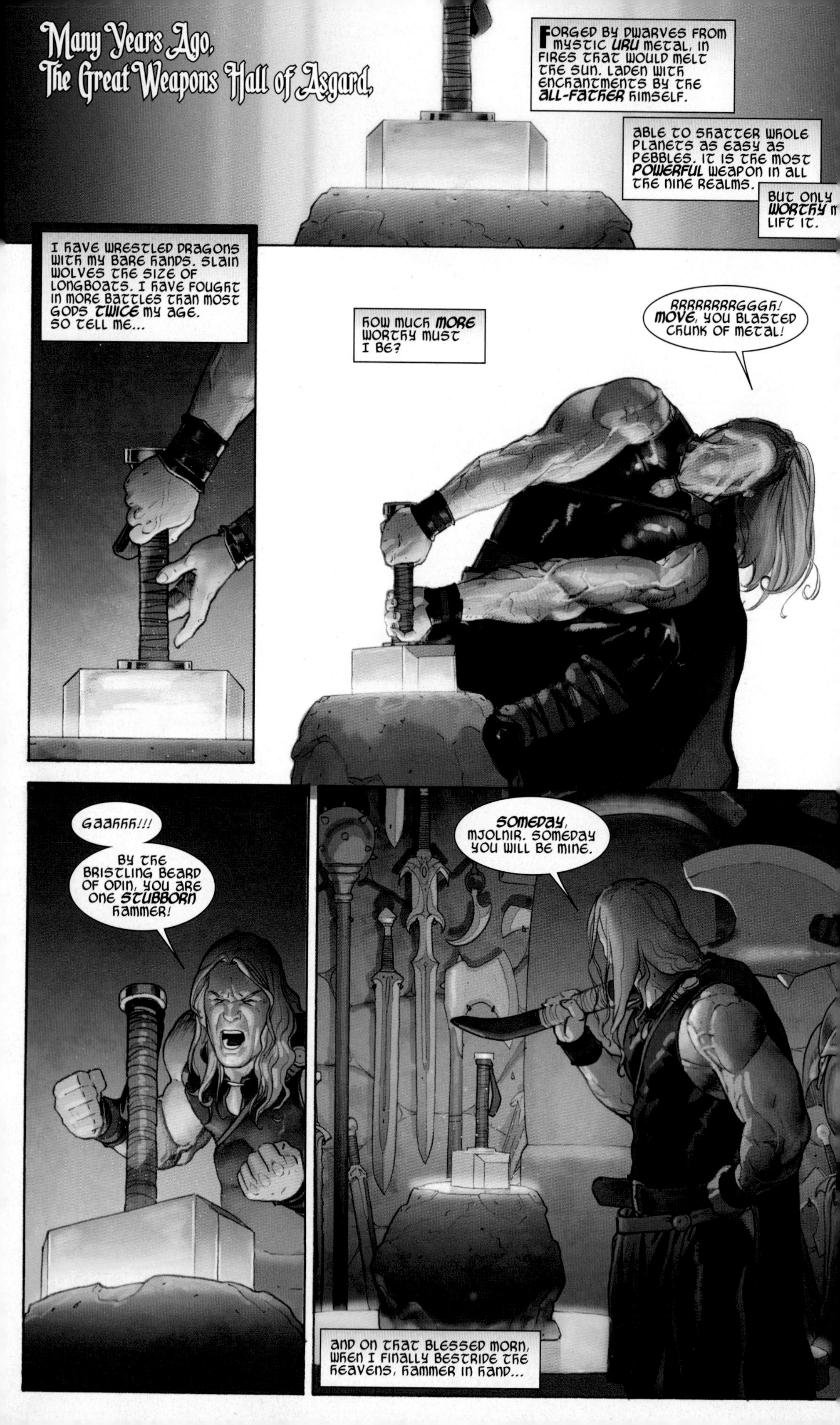
Many Years Ago,
The Great Weapons Hall of Asgard,
FORGED BY DWARVES FROM MYSTIC URU METAL, IN FIRES THAT WOULD MELT THE SUN. LADEN WITH ENCHANTMENTS BY THE ALL-FATHER HIMSELF.
ABLE TO SHATTER WHOLE PLANETS AS EASY AS PEBBLES. IT IS THE MOST POWERFUL WEAPON IN ALL THE NINE REALMS.
BUT ONLY WORTHY LIFT IT.
I HAVE WRESTLED DRAGONS WITH MY BARE HANDS. SLAIN WOLVES THE SIZE OF LONGBOATS. I HAVE FOUGHT IN MORE BATTLES THAN MOST GODS TWICE MY AGE. SO TELL ME...
HOW MUCH MORE WORTHY MUST I BE?
RRRRRRRRGGGH! MOVE, YOU BLASTED CHUNK OF METAL!
GAAHHH!!!
BY THE BRISTLING BEARD OF ODIN, YOU ARE ONE STUBBORN HAMMER!
SOMEDAY, MJOLNIR. SOMEDAY YOU WILL BE MINE.
AND ON THAT BLESSED MORN, WHEN I FINALLY BESTRIDE THE HEAVENS, HAMMER IN HAND...

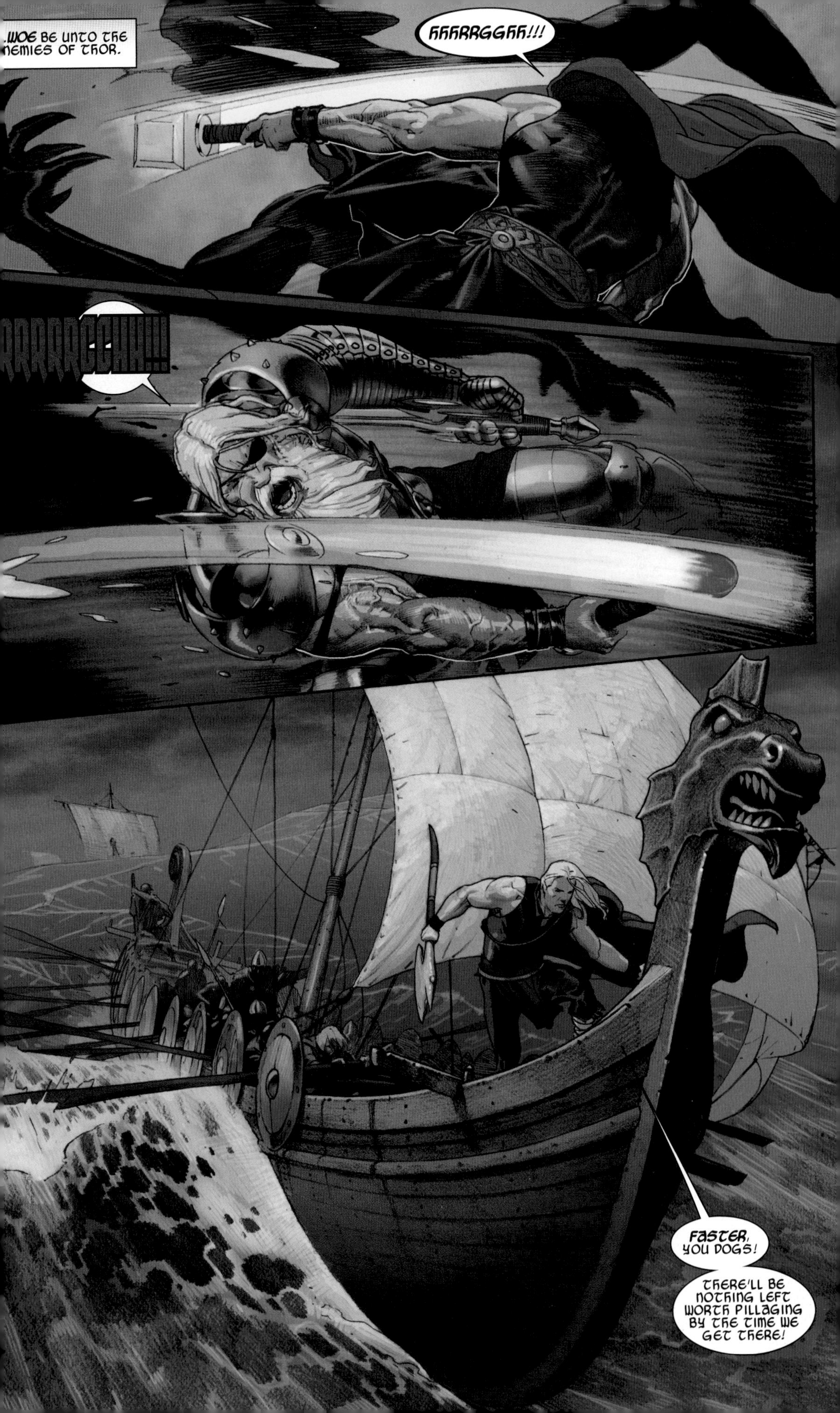
..WOE BE UNTO THE ENEMIES OF THOR.
HHHRRGGHH!!!
RRRRRCCHH!!!
FASTER, YOU DOGS!
THERE'LL BE NOTHING LEFT WORTH PILLAGING BY THE TIME WE GET THERE!

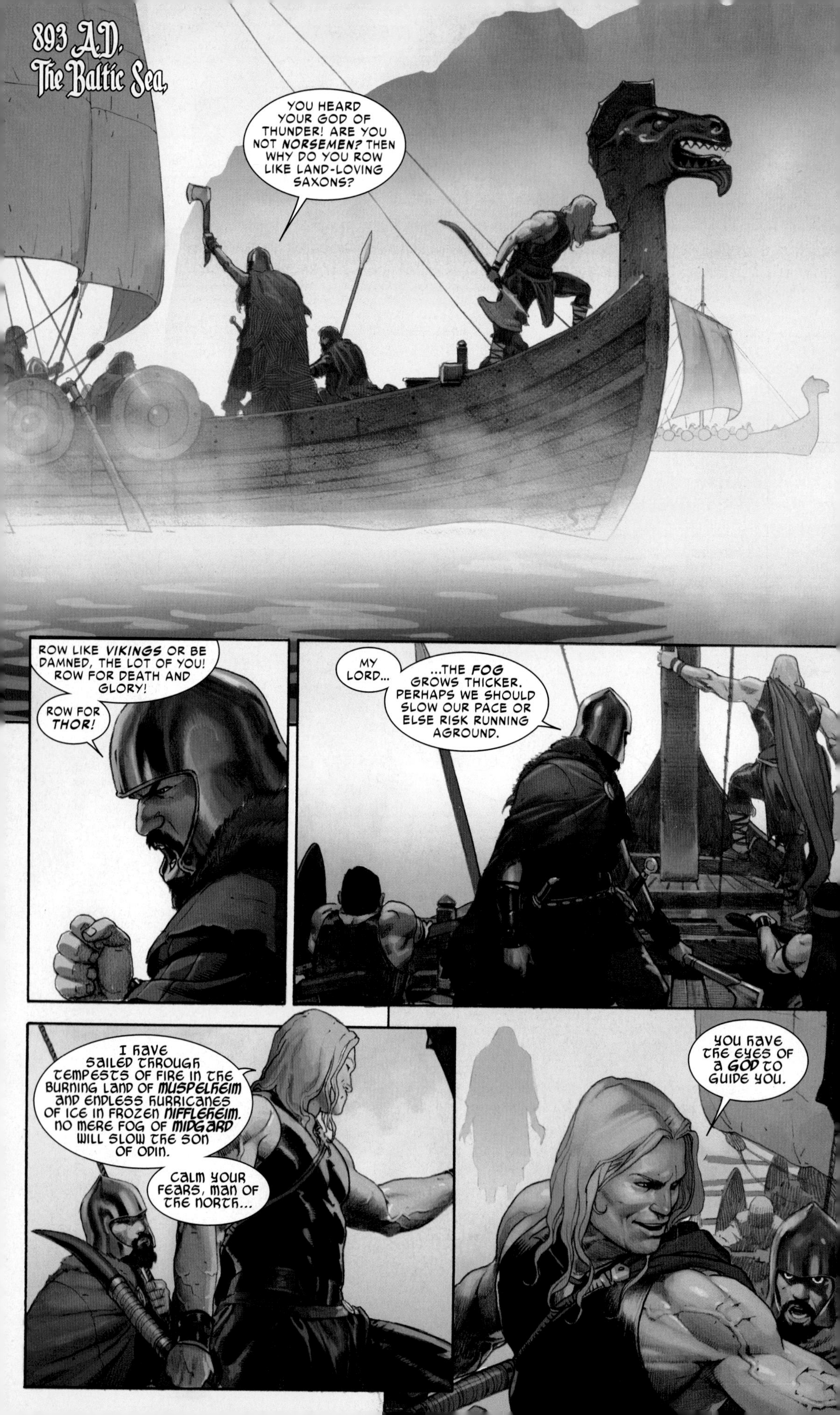
893 A.D.
The Baltic Sea.
YOU HEARD YOUR GOD OF THUNDER! ARE YOU NOT NORSEMEN? THEN WHY DO YOU ROW LIKE LAND-LOVING SAXONS?
ROW LIKE VIKINGS OR BE DAMNED, THE LOT OF YOU! ROW FOR DEATH AND GLORY!
ROW FOR THOR!
MY LORD...
...THE FOG GROWS THICKER. PERHAPS WE SHOULD SLOW OUR PACE OR ELSE RISK RUNNING AGROUND.
I HAVE SAILED THROUGH TEMPESTS OF FIRE IN THE BURNING LAND OF MUSPELHEIM AND ENDLESS HURRICANES OF ICE IN FROZEN NIFFLEHEIM. NO MERE FOG OF MIDGARD WILL SLOW THE SON OF ODIN.
CALM YOUR FEARS, MAN OF THE NORTH...
YOU HAVE THE EYES OF A GOD TO GUIDE YOU.

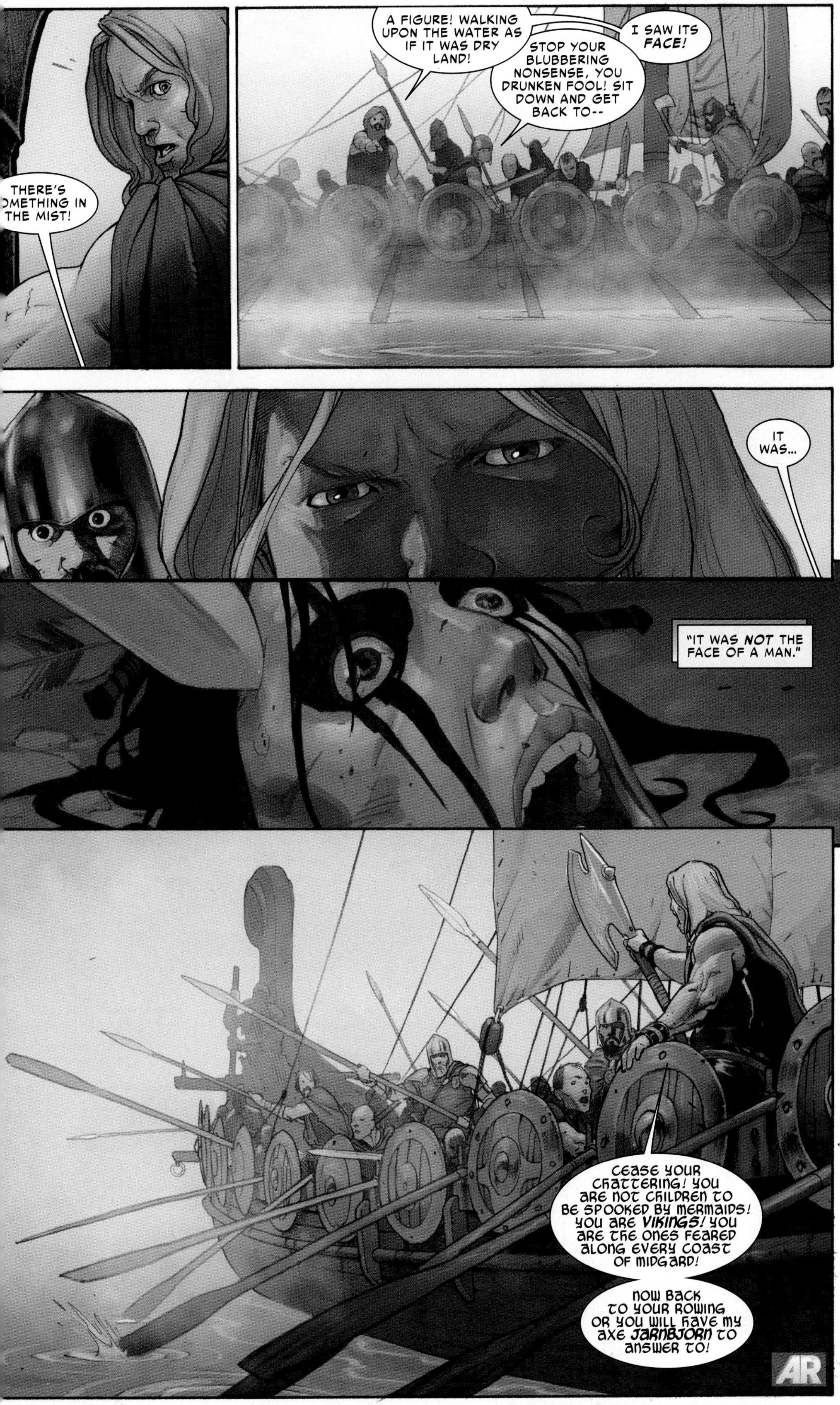
THERE'S
OMETHING IN
THE MIST!
A FIGURE! WALKING
UPON THE WATER AS
IF IT WAS DRY
LAND!
I SAW ITS
FACE!
STOP YOUR
BLUBBERING
NONSENSE, YOU
DRUNKEN FOOL! SIT
DOWN AND GET
BACK TO--
IT
WAS...
"IT WAS *NOT* THE
FACE OF A MAN."
CEASE YOUR
CHATTERING! YOU
ARE NOT CHILDREN TO
BE SPOOKED BY MERMAIDS!
YOU ARE *VIKINGS!* YOU
ARE THE ONES FEARED
ALONG EVERY COAST
OF MIDGARD!
NOW BACK
TO YOUR ROWING
OR YOU WILL HAVE MY
AXE *JARNBJORN* TO
ANSWER TO!

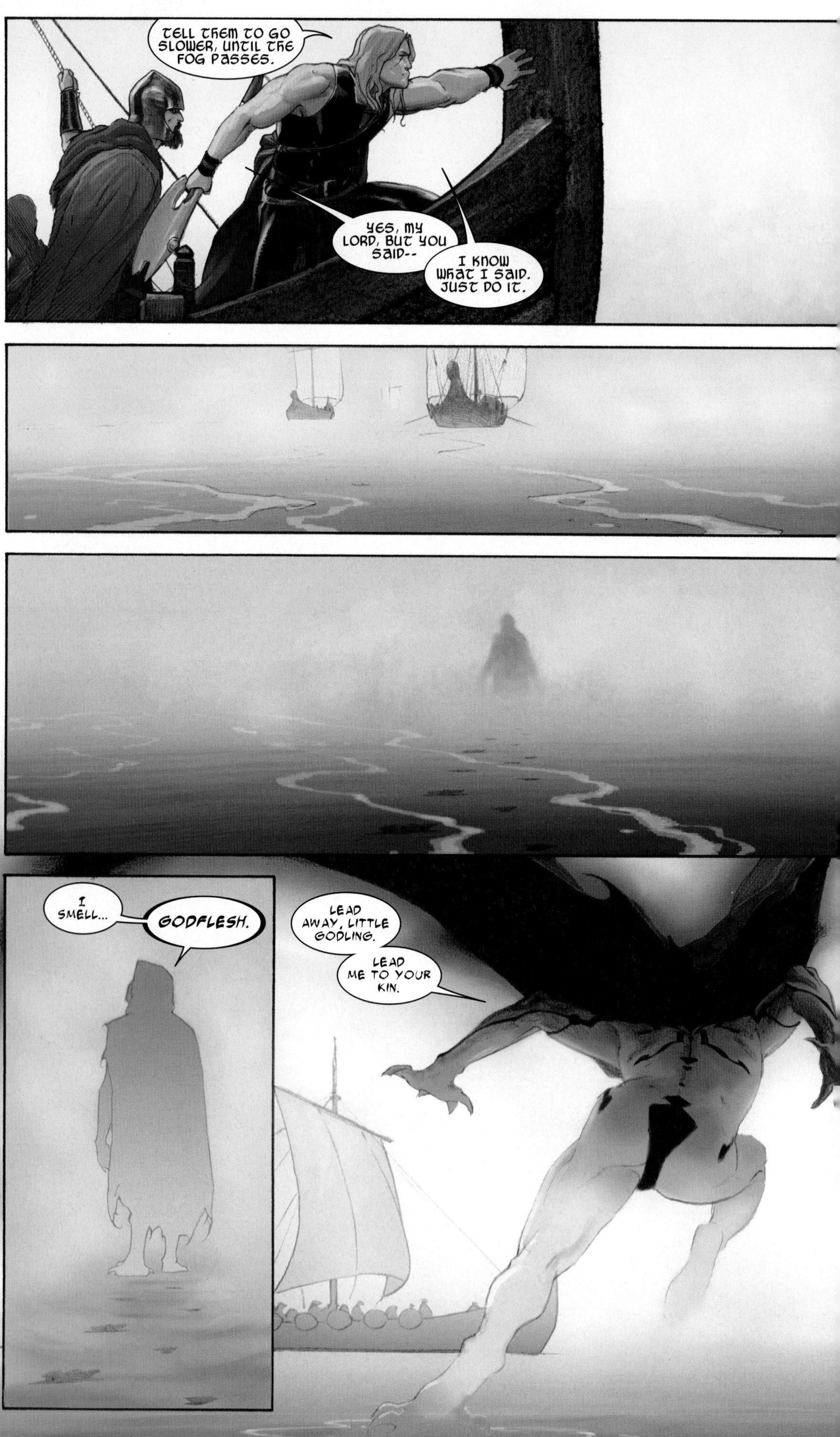
TELL THEM TO GO SLOWER, UNTIL THE FOG PASSES.
YES, MY LORD, BUT YOU SAID--
I KNOW WHAT I SAID. JUST DO IT.
I SMELL...
GODFLESH.
LEAD AWAY, LITTLE GODLING.
LEAD ME TO YOUR KIN.

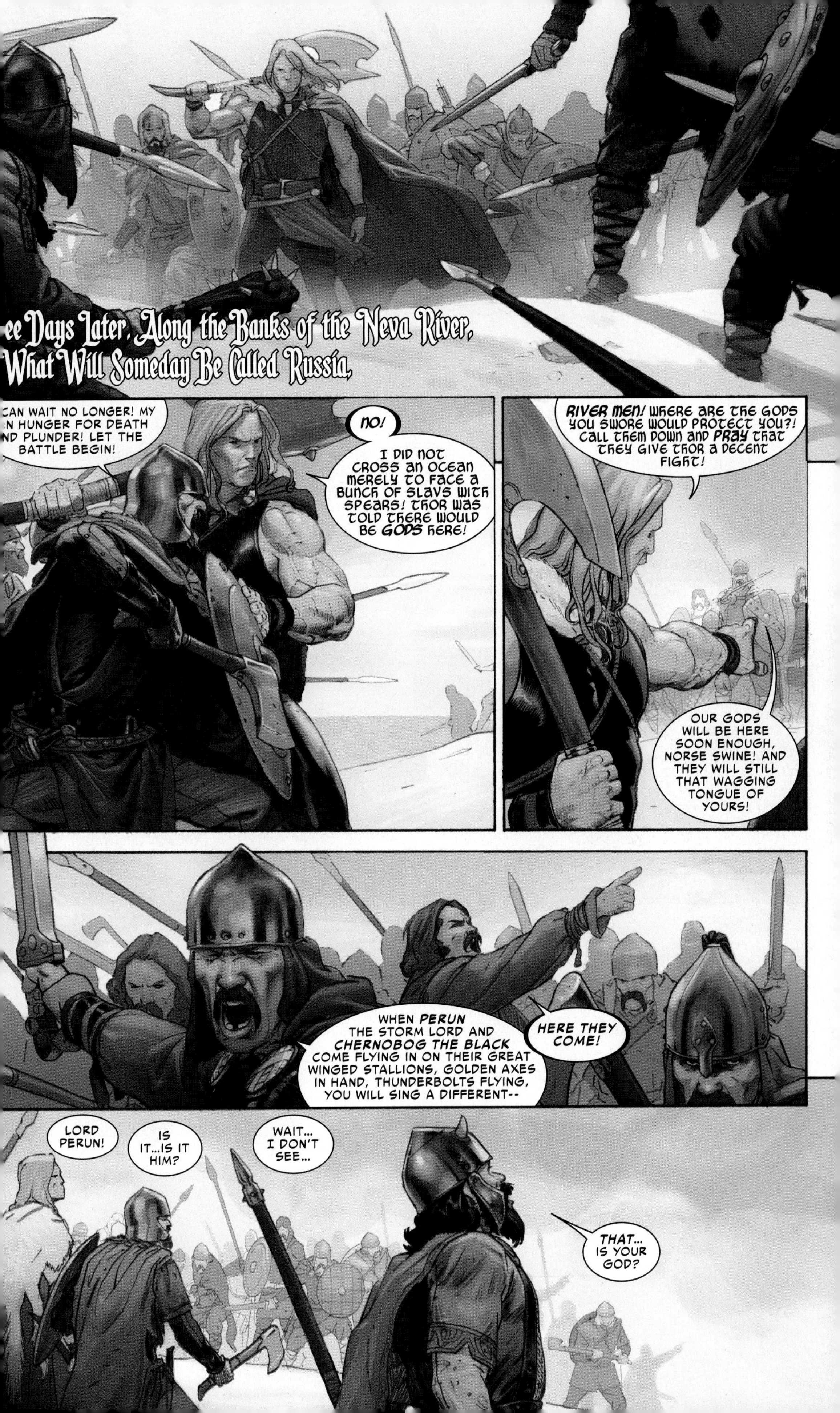
ee Days Later, Along the Banks of the Neva River,
What Will Someday Be Called Russia,
CAN WAIT NO LONGER! MY
N HUNGER FOR DEATH
ND PLUNDER! LET THE
BATTLE BEGIN!
NO!
I DID NOT CROSS AN OCEAN MERELY TO FACE A BUNCH OF SLAVS WITH SPEARS! THOR WAS TOLD THERE WOULD BE GODS HERE!
RIVER MEN! WHERE ARE THE GODS YOU SWORE WOULD PROTECT YOU?! CALL THEM DOWN AND PRAY THAT THEY GIVE THOR A DECENT FIGHT!
OUR GODS WILL BE HERE SOON ENOUGH, NORSE SWINE! AND THEY WILL STILL THAT WAGGING TONGUE OF YOURS!
WHEN PERUN THE STORM LORD AND CHERNOBOG THE BLACK COME FLYING IN ON THEIR GREAT WINGED STALLIONS, GOLDEN AXES IN HAND, THUNDERBOLTS FLYING, YOU WILL SING A DIFFERENT--
HERE THEY COME!
LORD PERUN!
IS IT...IS IT HIM?
WAIT... I DON'T SEE...
THAT... IS YOUR GOD?

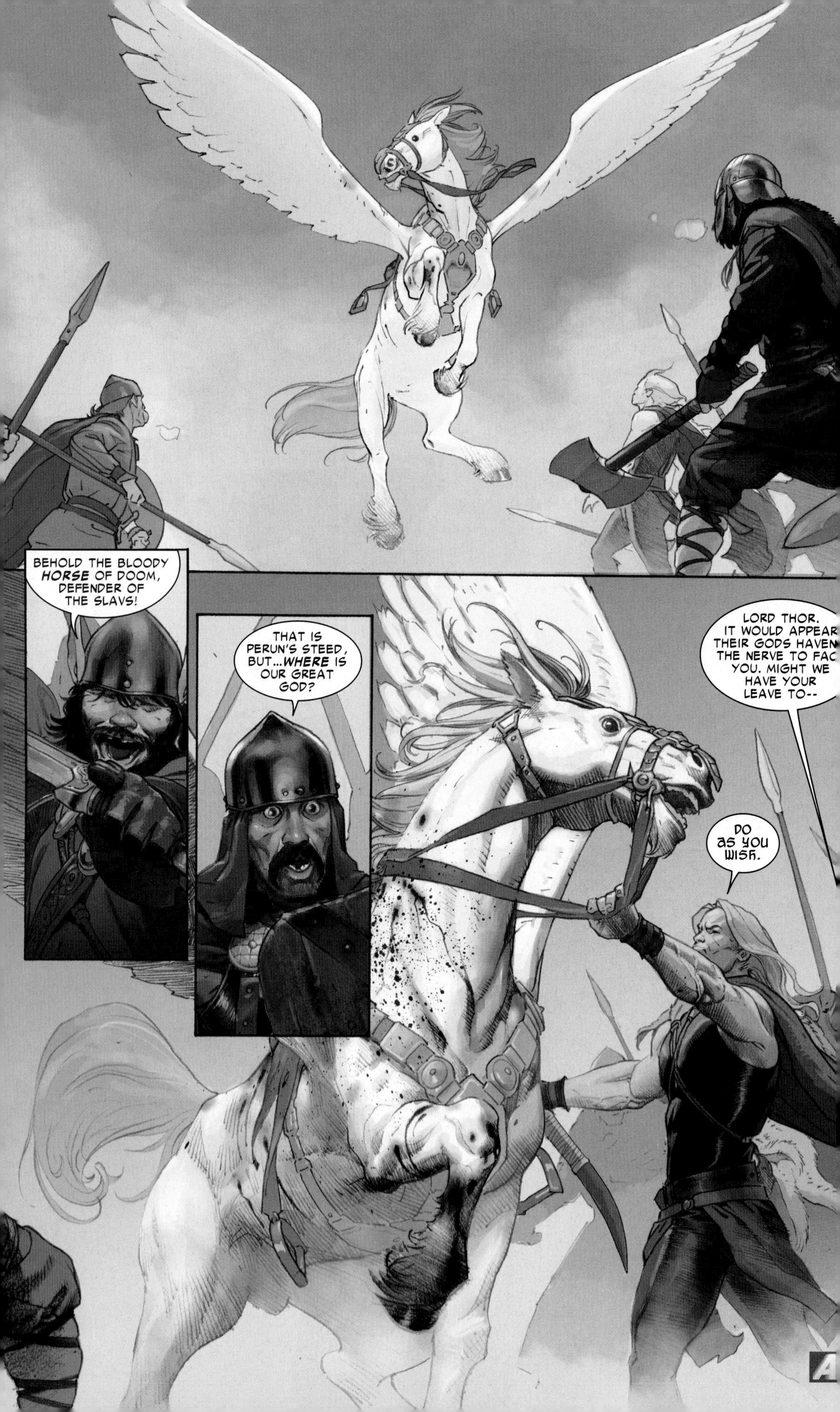
BEHOLD THE BLOODY *HORSE* OF DOOM, DEFENDER OF THE SLAVS!
THAT IS PERUN'S STEED, BUT...*WHERE* IS OUR GREAT GOD?
LORD THOR. IT WOULD APPEAR THEIR GODS HAVEN THE NERVE TO FAC YOU. MIGHT WE HAVE YOUR LEAVE TO--
DO AS YOU WISH.

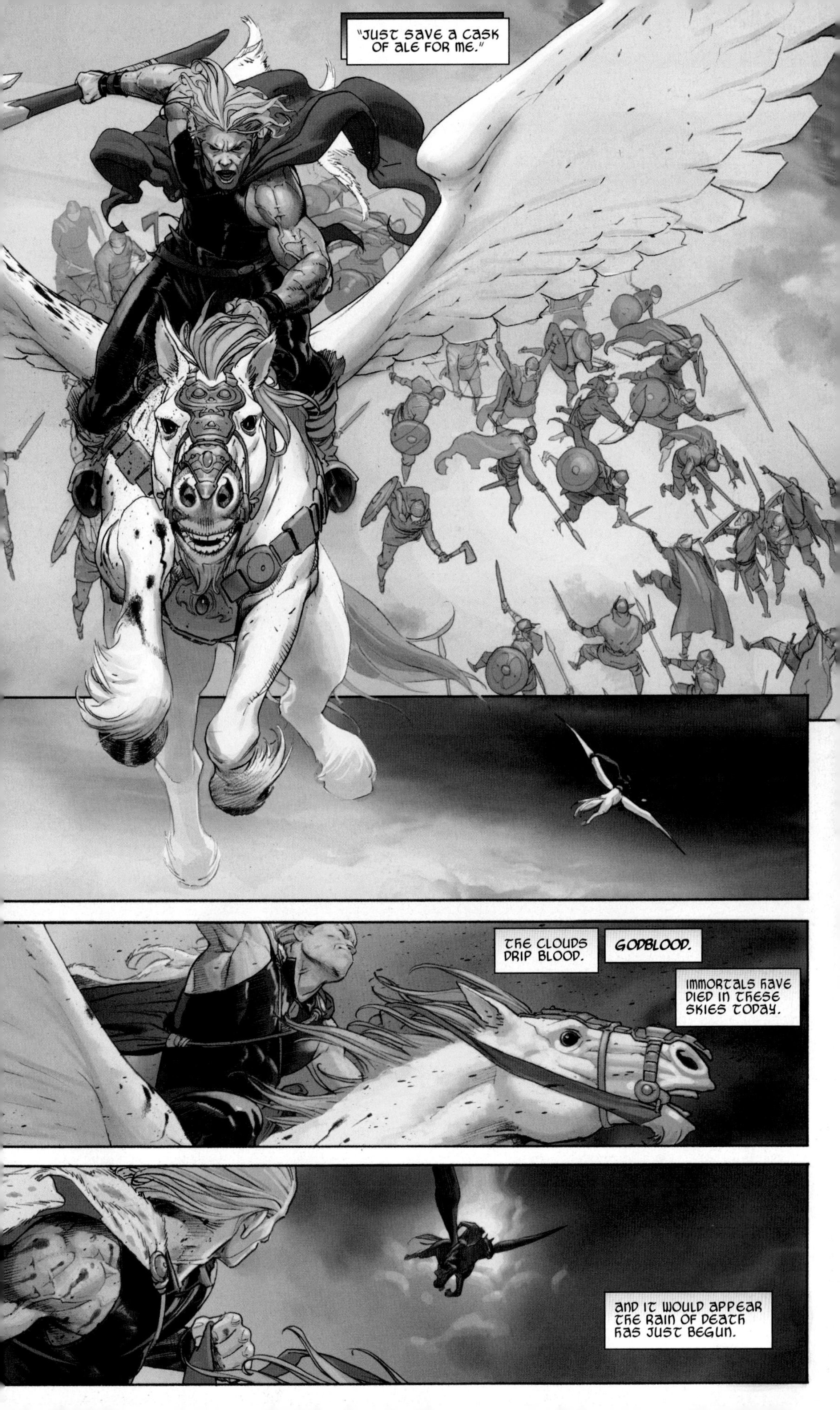
"JUST SAVE A CASK OF ALE FOR ME."
THE CLOUDS DRIP BLOOD.
GODBLOOD.
IMMORTALS HAVE DIED IN THESE SKIES TODAY.
AND IT WOULD APPEAR THE RAIN OF DEATH HAS JUST BEGUN.

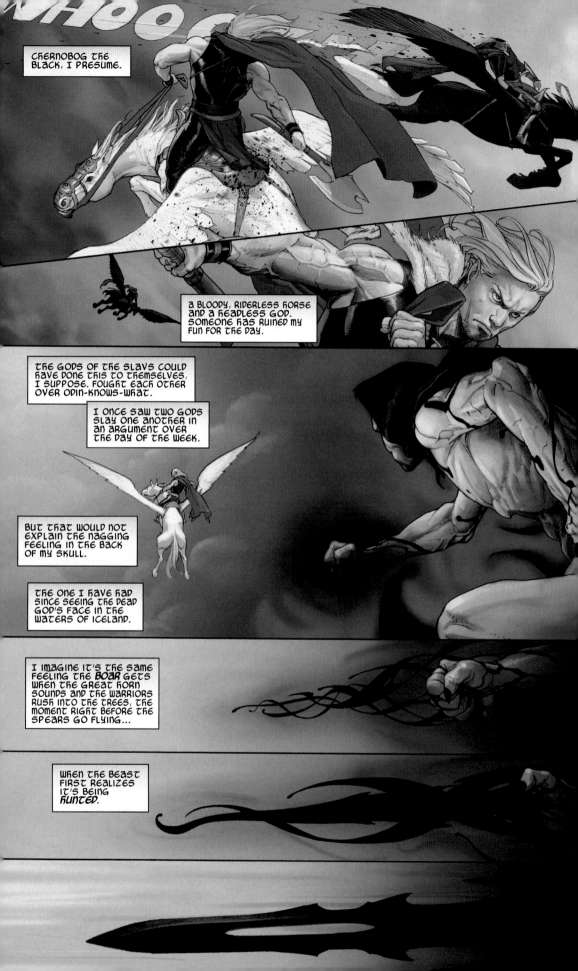

CHERNOBOG THE BLACK, I PRESUME.

A BLOODY, RIDERLESS HORSE AND A HEADLESS GOD. SOMEONE HAS RUINED MY FUN FOR THE DAY.

THE GODS OF THE SLAVS COULD HAVE DONE THIS TO THEMSELVES, I SUPPOSE. FOUGHT EACH OTHER OVER ODIN-KNOWS-WHAT.

I ONCE SAW TWO GODS SLAY ONE ANOTHER IN AN ARGUMENT OVER THE DAY OF THE WEEK.

BUT THAT WOULD NOT EXPLAIN THE NAGGING FEELING IN THE BACK OF MY SKULL.

THE ONE I HAVE HAD SINCE SEEING THE DEAD GOD'S FACE IN THE WATERS OF ICELAND.

I IMAGINE IT'S THE SAME FEELING THE BOAR GETS WHEN THE GREAT HORN SOUNDS AND THE WARRIORS RUSH INTO THE TREES, THE MOMENT RIGHT BEFORE THE SPEARS GO FLYING...

WHEN THE BEAST FIRST REALIZES IT'S BEING HUNTED.

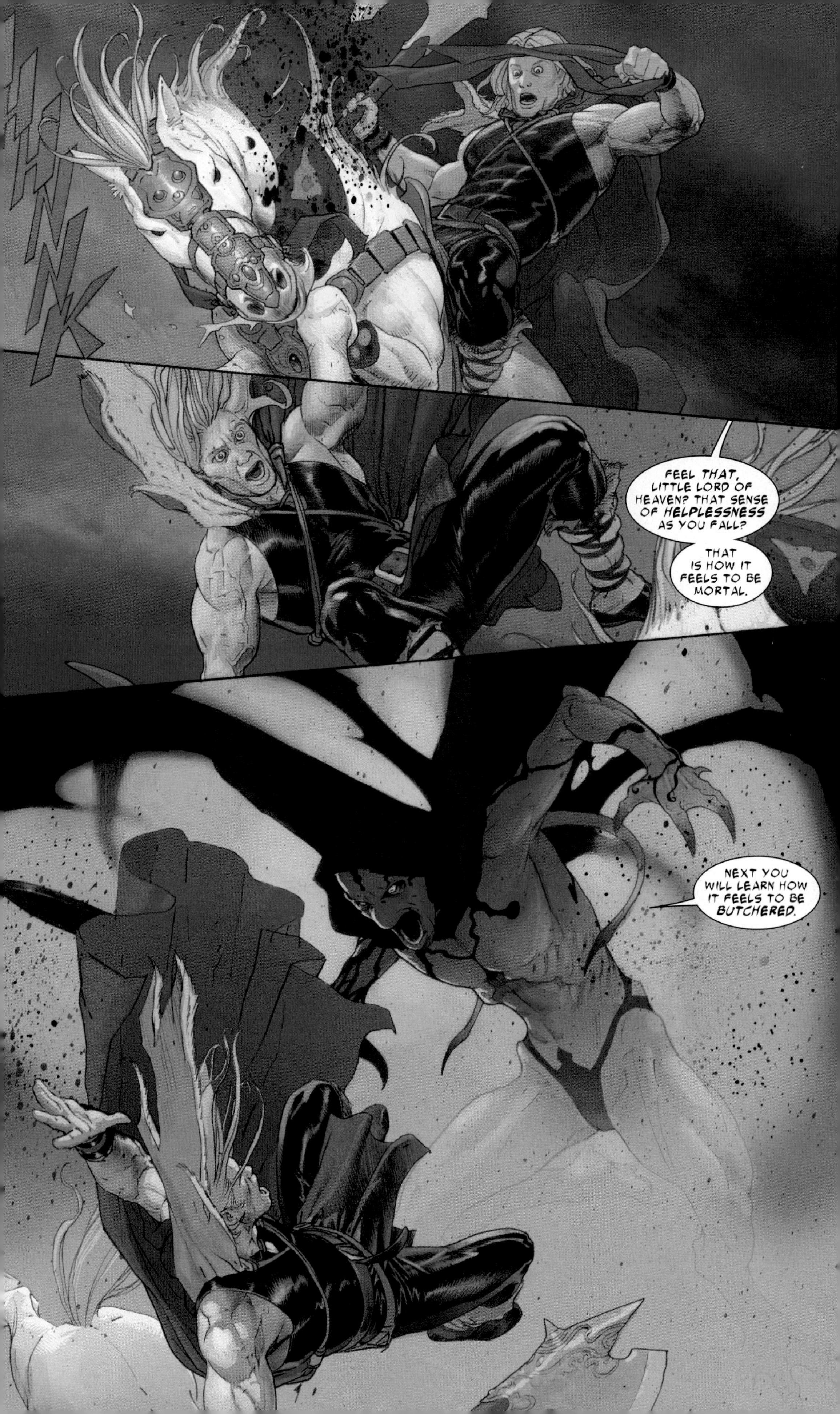
HHNNK
FEEL THAT, LITTLE LORD OF HEAVEN? THAT SENSE OF HELPLESSNESS AS YOU FALL?
THAT IS HOW IT FEELS TO BE MORTAL.
NEXT YOU WILL LEARN HOW IT FEELS TO BE BUTCHERED.

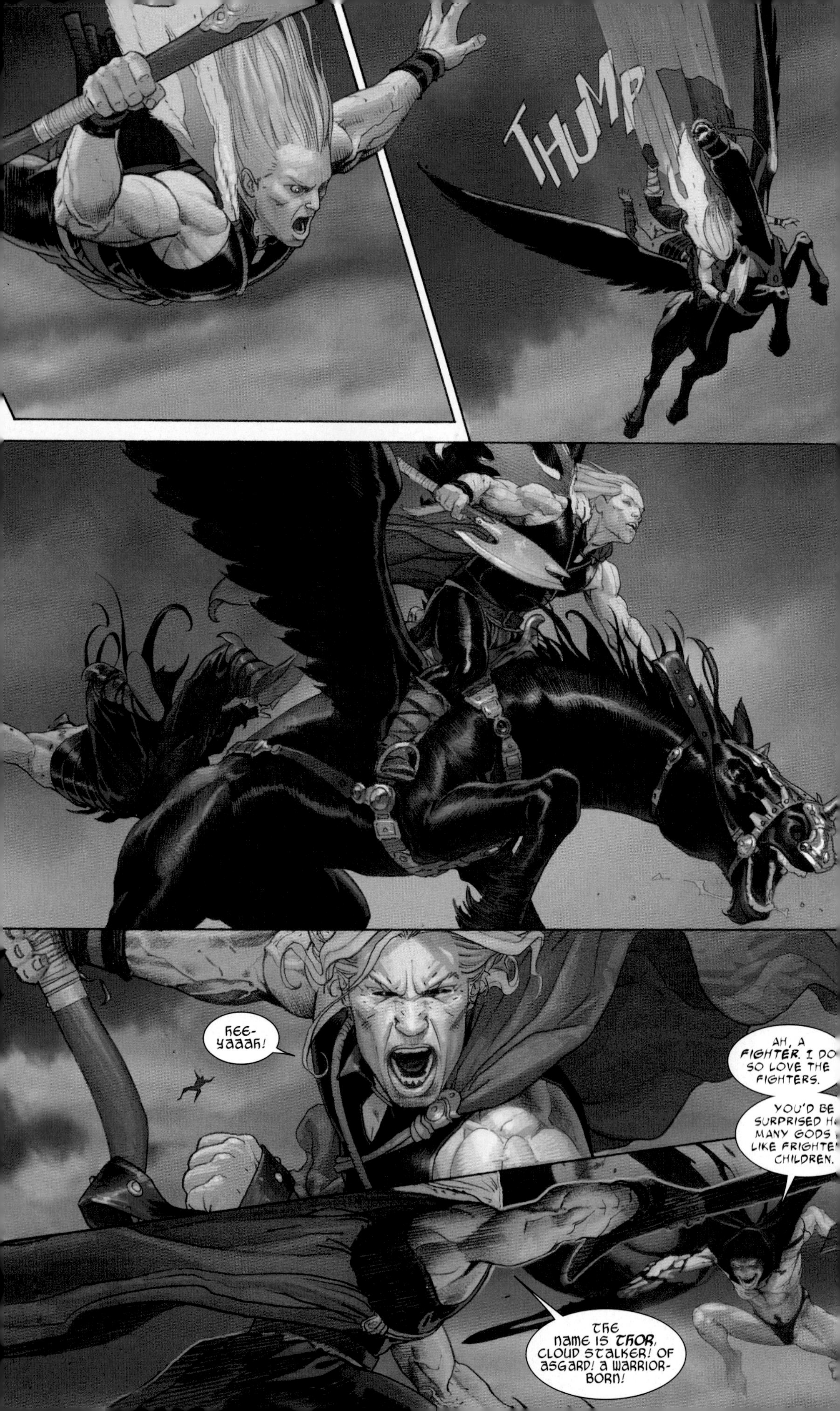
THUMP
HEE-YAAAH!
AH, A FIGHTER. I DO SO LOVE THE FIGHTERS.
THE NAME IS THOR, CLOUD STALKER! OF ASGARD! A WARRIOR-BORN!

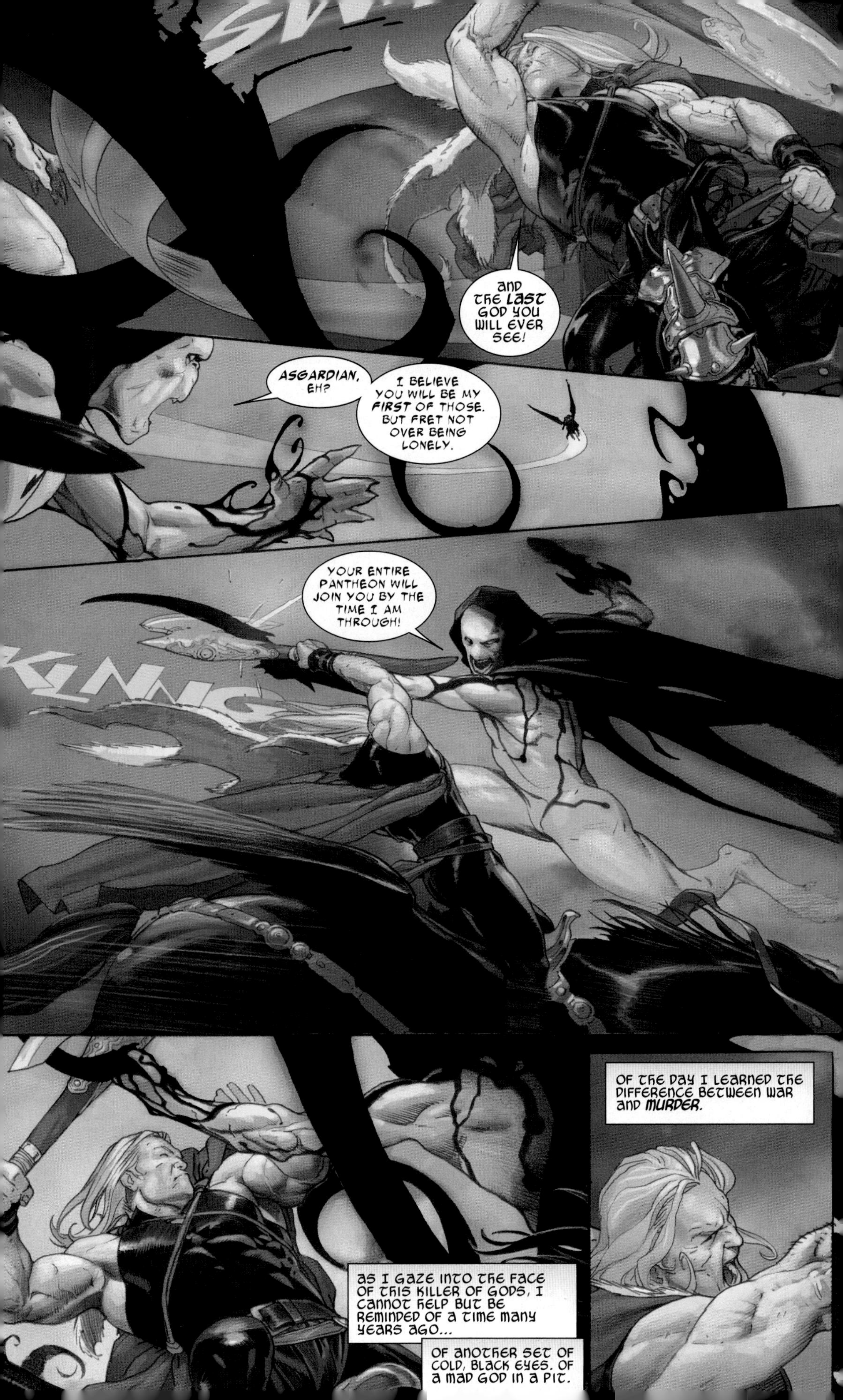
AND THE LAST GOD YOU WILL EVER SEE!
ASGARDIAN, EH?
I BELIEVE YOU WILL BE MY FIRST OF THOSE. BUT FRET NOT OVER BEING LONELY.
YOUR ENTIRE PANTHEON WILL JOIN YOU BY THE TIME I AM THROUGH!
KLNNG
AS I GAZE INTO THE FACE OF THIS KILLER OF GODS, I CANNOT HELP BUT BE REMINDED OF A TIME MANY YEARS AGO...
OF ANOTHER SET OF COLD, BLACK EYES. OF A MAD GOD IN A PIT.
OF THE DAY I LEARNED THE DIFFERENCE BETWEEN WAR AND MURDER.

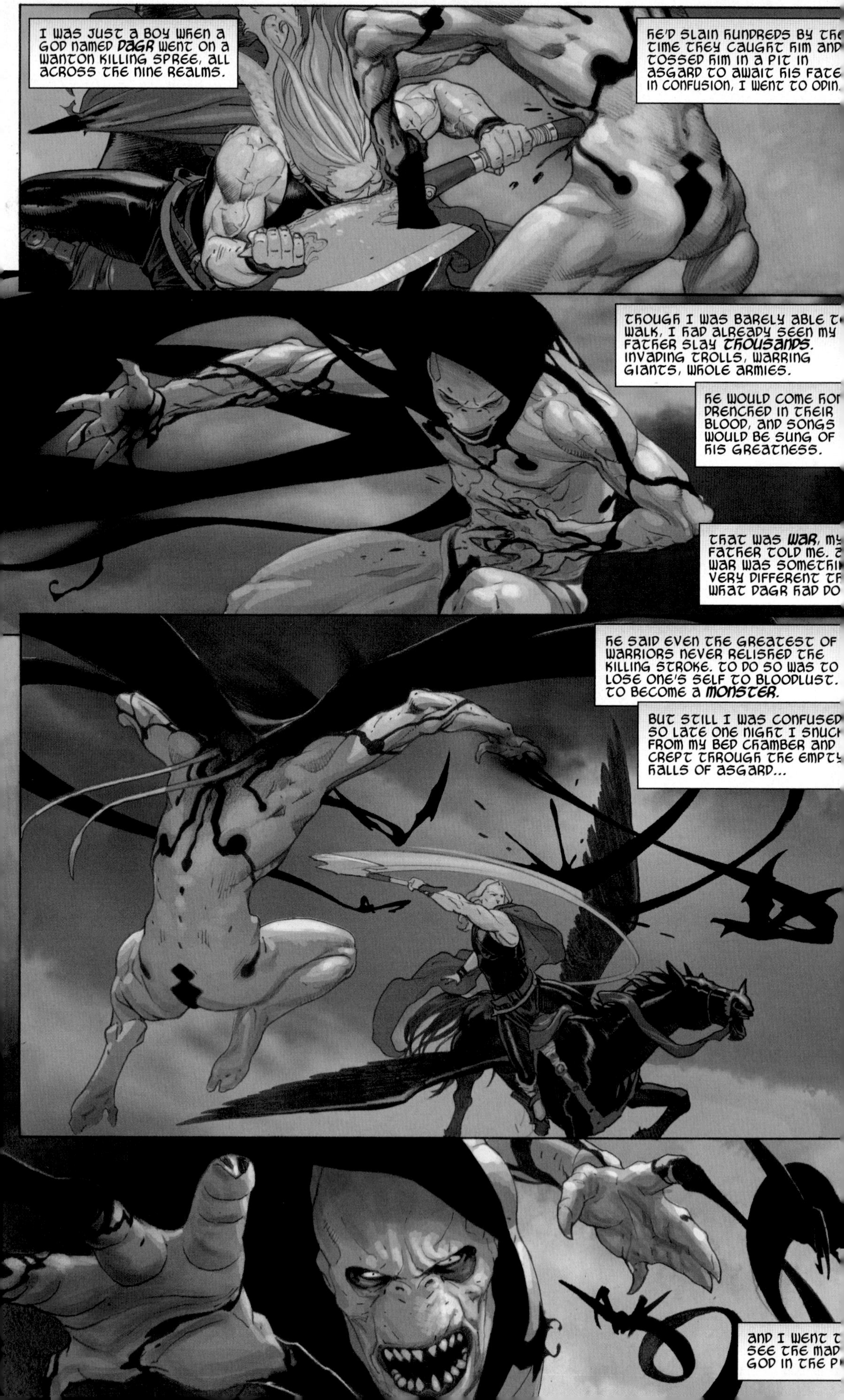
I WAS JUST A BOY WHEN A GOD NAMED DAGR WENT ON A WANTON KILLING SPREE, ALL ACROSS THE NINE REALMS.
HE'D SLAIN HUNDREDS BY THE TIME THEY CAUGHT HIM AND TOSSED HIM IN A PIT IN ASGARD TO AWAIT HIS FATE. IN CONFUSION, I WENT TO ODIN.
THOUGH I WAS BARELY ABLE T WALK, I HAD ALREADY SEEN MY FATHER SLAY THOUSANDS. INVADING TROLLS, WARRING GIANTS, WHOLE ARMIES.
HE WOULD COME HO DRENCHED IN THEIR BLOOD, AND SONGS WOULD BE SUNG OF HIS GREATNESS.
THAT WAS WAR, MY FATHER TOLD ME. WAR WAS SOMETHI VERY DIFFERENT TH WHAT DAGR HAD DO
HE SAID EVEN THE GREATEST OF WARRIORS NEVER RELISHED THE KILLING STROKE. TO DO SO WAS TO LOSE ONE'S SELF TO BLOODLUST. TO BECOME A MONSTER.
BUT STILL I WAS CONFUSED SO LATE ONE NIGHT I SNUC FROM MY BED CHAMBER AND CREPT THROUGH THE EMPTY HALLS OF ASGARD...
AND I WENT T SEE THE MAD GOD IN THE P

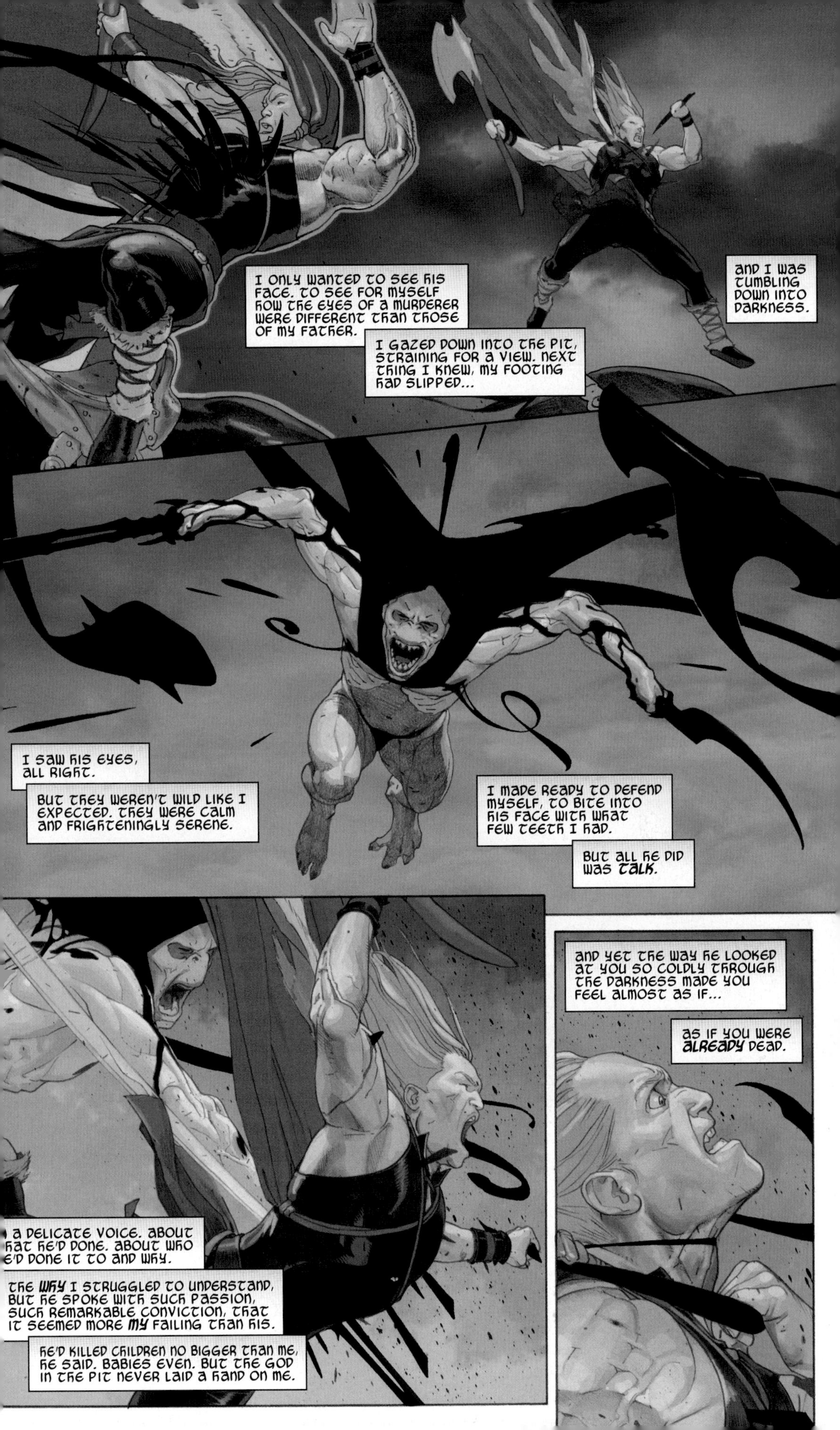
I ONLY WANTED TO SEE HIS FACE. TO SEE FOR MYSELF HOW THE EYES OF A MURDERER WERE DIFFERENT THAN THOSE OF MY FATHER.
I GAZED DOWN INTO THE PIT, STRAINING FOR A VIEW. NEXT THING I KNEW, MY FOOTING HAD SLIPPED...
AND I WAS TUMBLING DOWN INTO DARKNESS.
I SAW HIS EYES, ALL RIGHT.
BUT THEY WEREN'T WILD LIKE I EXPECTED. THEY WERE CALM AND FRIGHTENINGLY SERENE.
I MADE READY TO DEFEND MYSELF, TO BITE INTO HIS FACE WITH WHAT FEW TEETH I HAD.
BUT ALL HE DID WAS TALK.
A DELICATE VOICE. ABOUT HAT HE'D DONE. ABOUT WHO E'D DONE IT TO AND WHY.
THE WHY I STRUGGLED TO UNDERSTAND, BUT HE SPOKE WITH SUCH PASSION, SUCH REMARKABLE CONVICTION, THAT IT SEEMED MORE MY FAILING THAN HIS.
HE'D KILLED CHILDREN NO BIGGER THAN ME, HE SAID. BABIES EVEN. BUT THE GOD IN THE PIT NEVER LAID A HAND ON ME.
AND YET THE WAY HE LOOKED AT YOU SO COLDLY THROUGH THE DARKNESS MADE YOU FEEL ALMOST AS IF...
AS IF YOU WERE ALREADY DEAD.

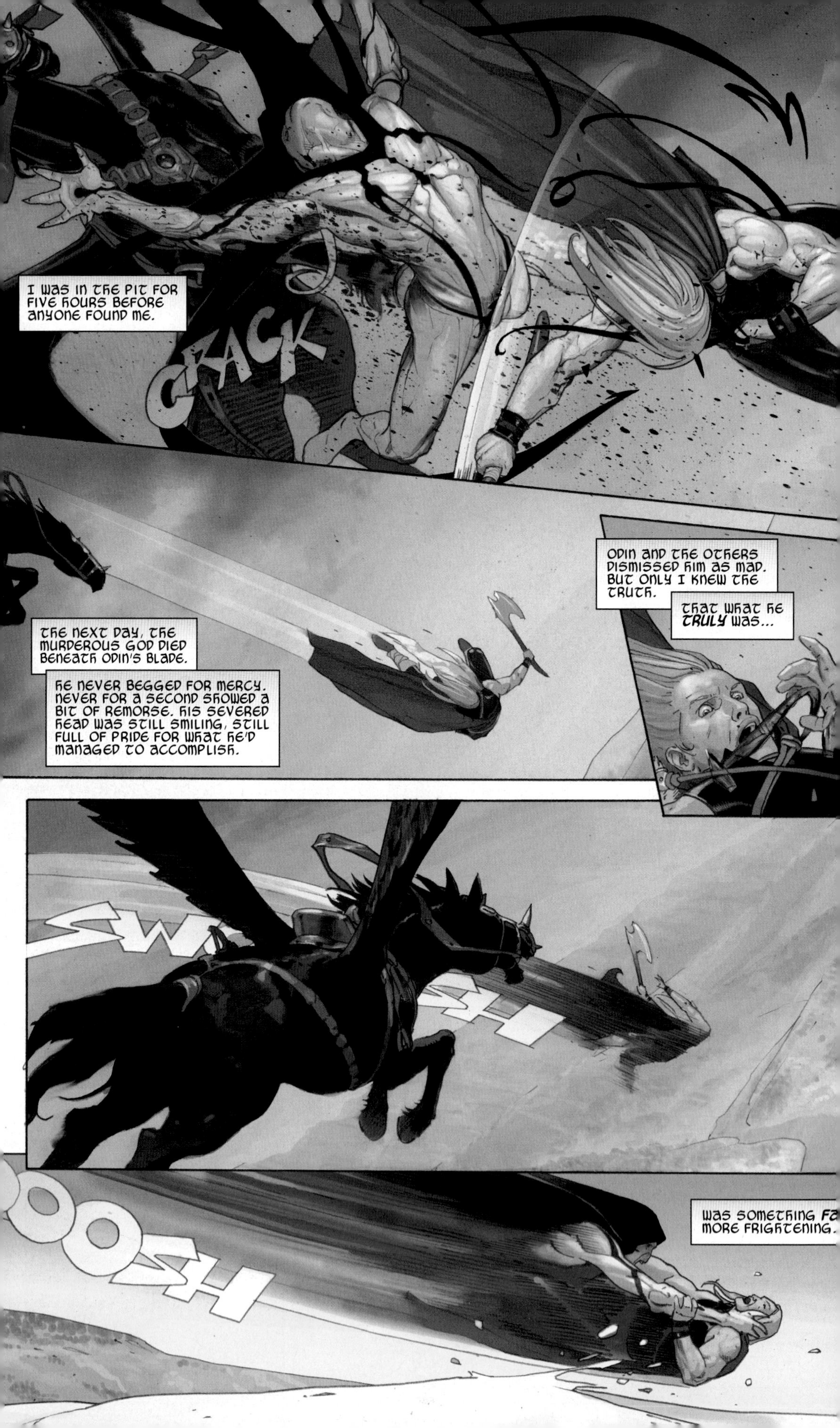
I WAS IN THE PIT FOR FIVE HOURS BEFORE ANYONE FOUND ME.
CRACK
THE NEXT DAY, THE MURDEROUS GOD DIED BENEATH ODIN'S BLADE.
HE NEVER BEGGED FOR MERCY. NEVER FOR A SECOND SHOWED A BIT OF REMORSE. HIS SEVERED HEAD WAS STILL SMILING, STILL FULL OF PRIDE FOR WHAT HE'D MANAGED TO ACCOMPLISH.
ODIN AND THE OTHERS DISMISSED HIM AS MAD. BUT ONLY I KNEW THE TRUTH.
THAT WHAT HE TRULY WAS...
SWASH
WAS SOMETHING FA
MORE FRIGHTENING.
WHOOOOSH

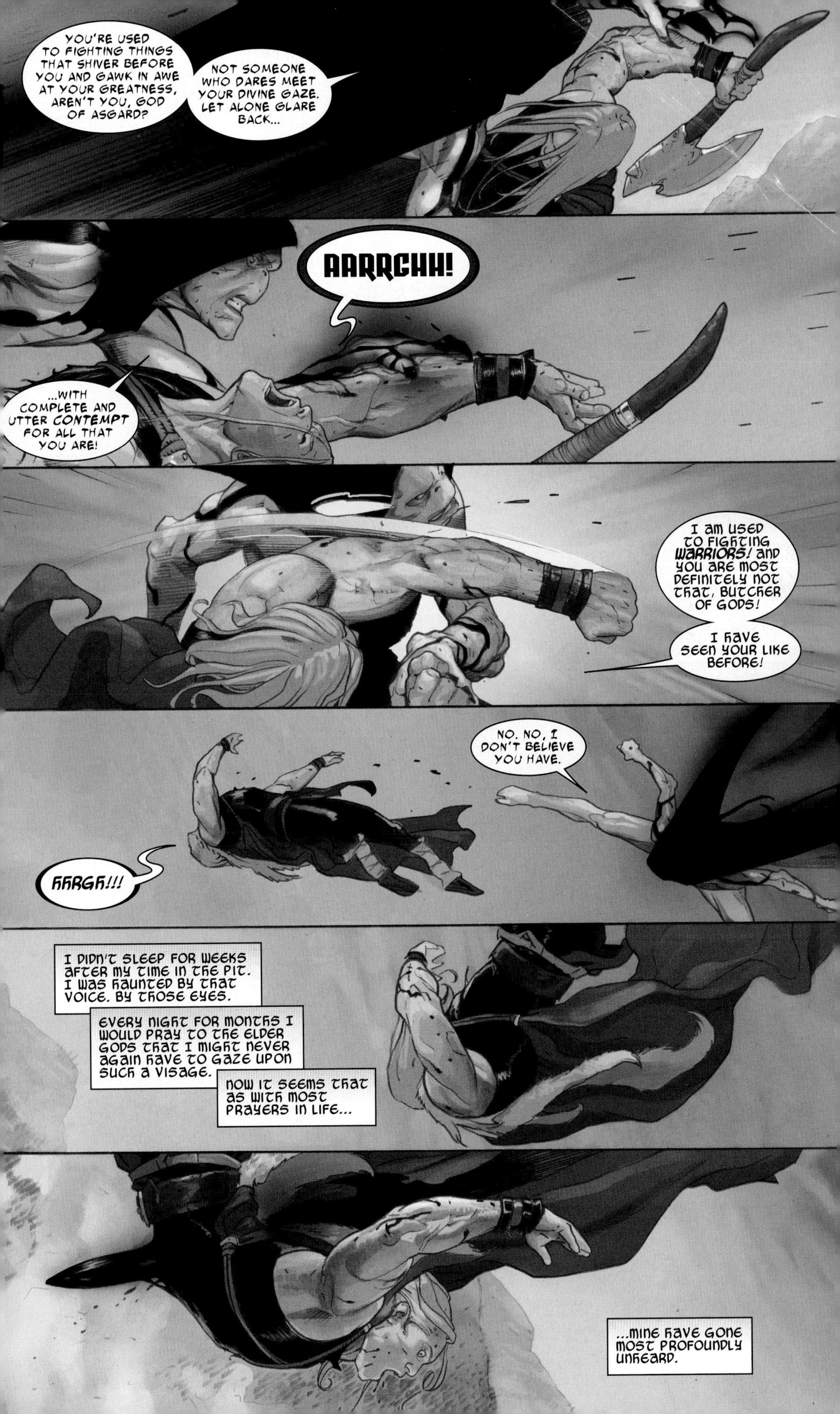

YOU'RE USED TO FIGHTING THINGS THAT SHIVER BEFORE YOU AND GAWK IN AWE AT YOUR GREATNESS, AREN'T YOU, GOD OF ASGARD?
NOT SOMEONE WHO DARES MEET YOUR DIVINE GAZE. LET ALONE GLARE BACK...
AARRGHH!
...WITH COMPLETE AND UTTER CONTEMPT FOR ALL THAT YOU ARE!
I AM USED TO FIGHTING WARRIORS! AND YOU ARE MOST DEFINITELY NOT THAT, BUTCHER OF GODS!
I HAVE SEEN YOUR LIKE BEFORE!
NO. NO, I DON'T BELIEVE YOU HAVE.
HHRGH!!!
I DIDN'T SLEEP FOR WEEKS AFTER MY TIME IN THE PIT. I WAS HAUNTED BY THAT VOICE. BY THOSE EYES.
EVERY NIGHT FOR MONTHS I WOULD PRAY TO THE ELDER GODS THAT I MIGHT NEVER AGAIN HAVE TO GAZE UPON SUCH A VISAGE.
NOW IT SEEMS THAT AS WITH MOST PRAYERS IN LIFE...
...MINE HAVE GONE MOST PROFOUNDLY UNHEARD.

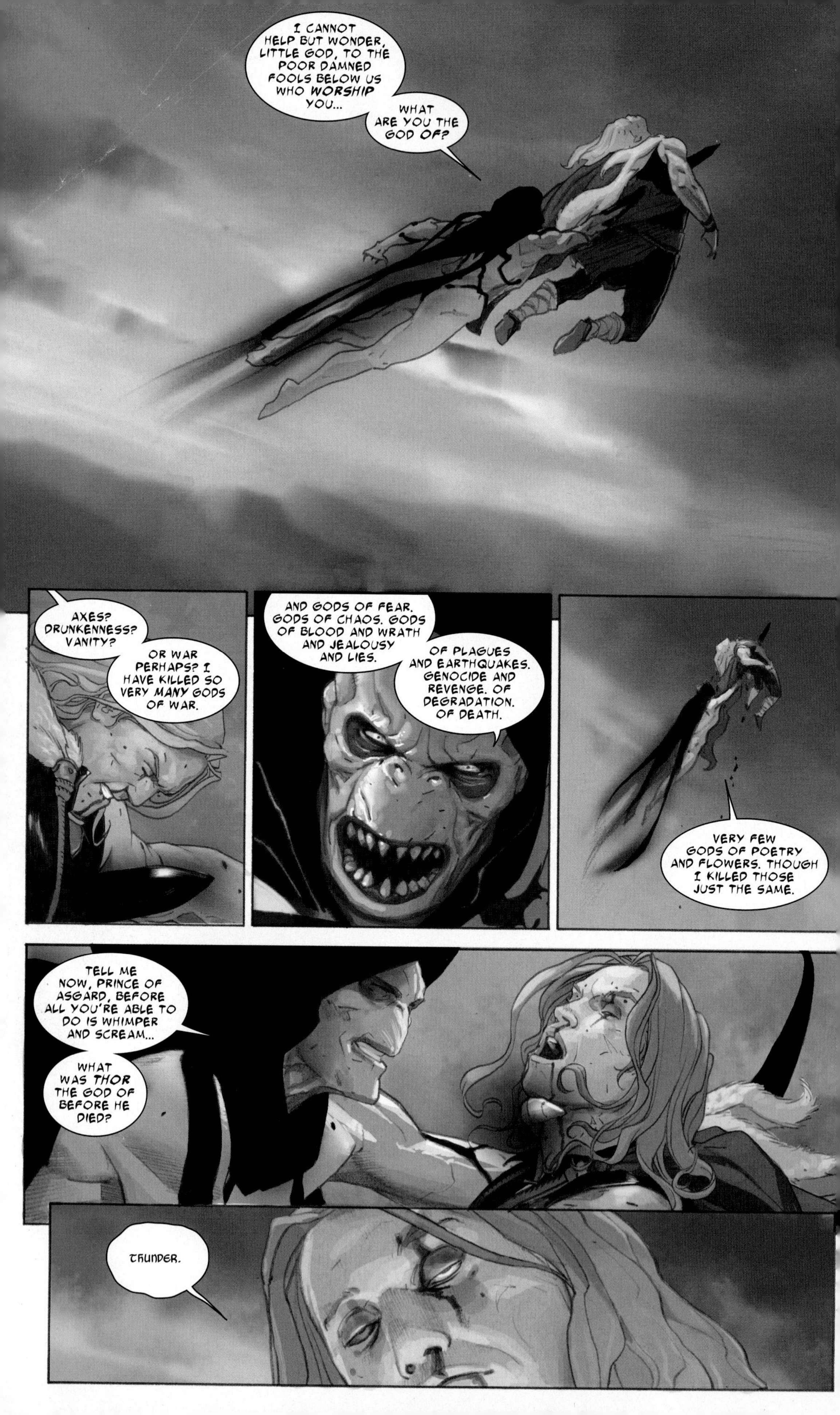
I CANNOT HELP BUT WONDER, LITTLE GOD, TO THE POOR DAMNED FOOLS BELOW US WHO WORSHIP YOU...
WHAT ARE YOU THE GOD OF?
AXES? DRUNKENNESS? VANITY?
OR WAR PERHAPS? I HAVE KILLED SO VERY MANY GODS OF WAR.
AND GODS OF FEAR. GODS OF CHAOS. GODS OF BLOOD AND WRATH AND JEALOUSY AND LIES.
OF PLAGUES AND EARTHQUAKES. GENOCIDE AND REVENGE. OF DEGRADATION. OF DEATH.
VERY FEW GODS OF POETRY AND FLOWERS. THOUGH I KILLED THOSE JUST THE SAME.
TELL ME NOW, PRINCE OF ASGARD, BEFORE ALL YOU'RE ABLE TO DO IS WHIMPER AND SCREAM...
WHAT WAS THOR THE GOD OF BEFORE HE DIED?
THUNDER.

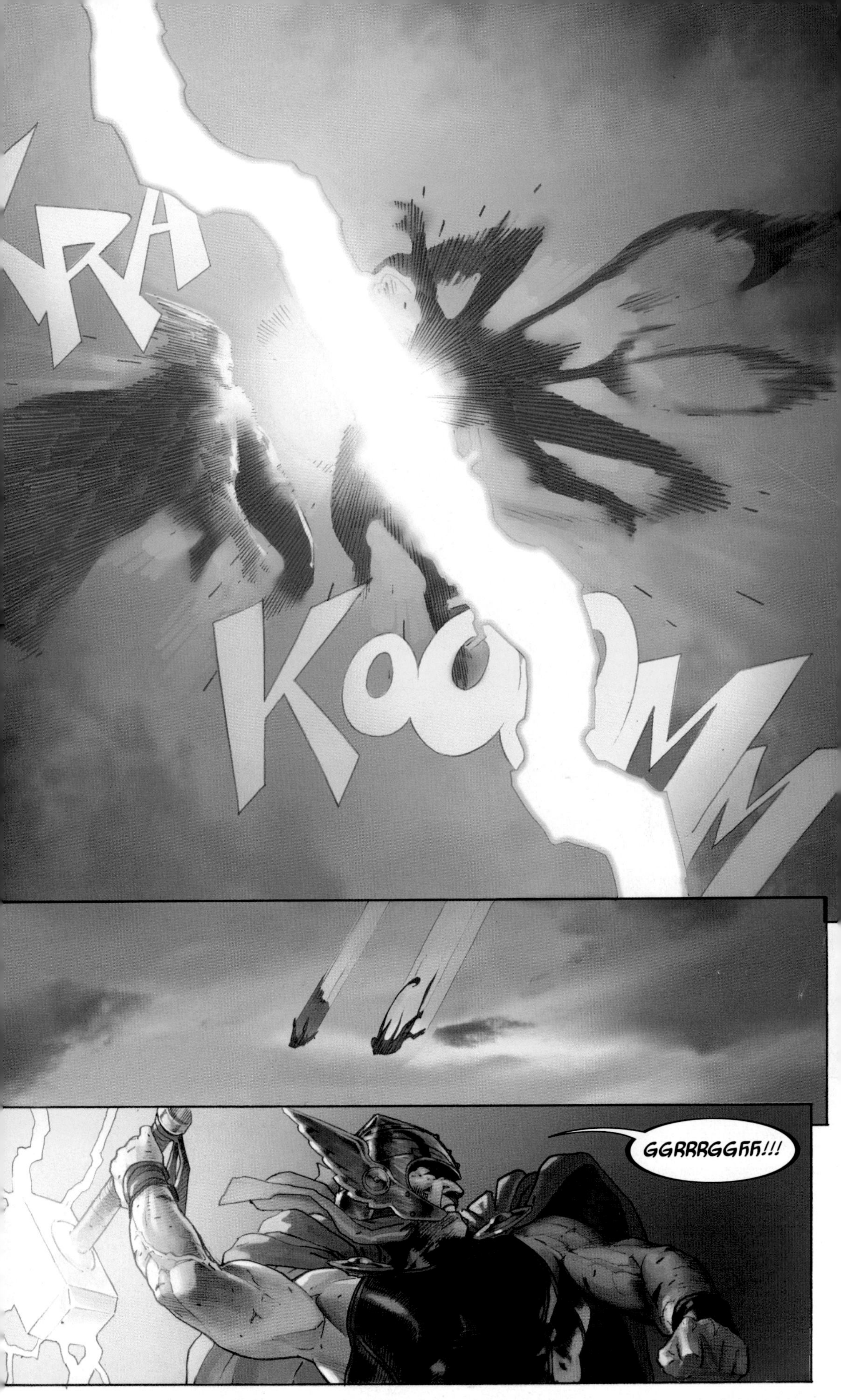

KRA
KOOOMM
GGRRRGGHH!!!

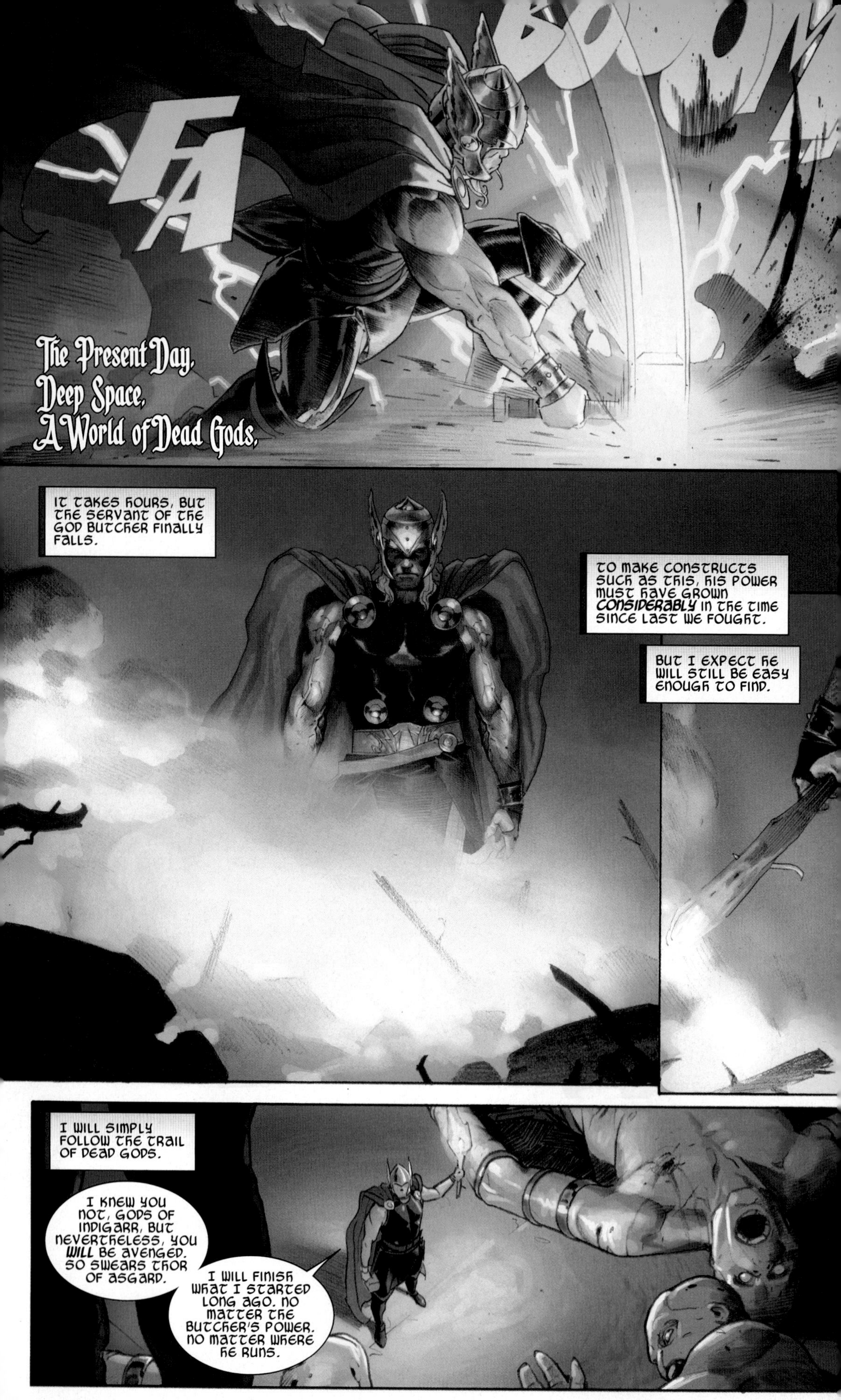
BOOOM
FA
The Present Day,
Deep Space,
A World of Dead Gods,
IT TAKES HOURS, BUT THE SERVANT OF THE GOD BUTCHER FINALLY FALLS.
TO MAKE CONSTRUCTS SUCH AS THIS, HIS POWER MUST HAVE GROWN CONSIDERABLY IN THE TIME SINCE LAST WE FOUGHT.
BUT I EXPECT HE WILL STILL BE EASY ENOUGH TO FIND.
I WILL SIMPLY FOLLOW THE TRAIL OF DEAD GODS.
I KNEW YOU NOT, GODS OF INDIGARR, BUT NEVERTHELESS, YOU WILL BE AVENGED. SO SWEARS THOR OF ASGARD.
I WILL FINISH WHAT I STARTED LONG AGO. NO MATTER THE BUTCHER'S POWER. NO MATTER WHERE HE RUNS.

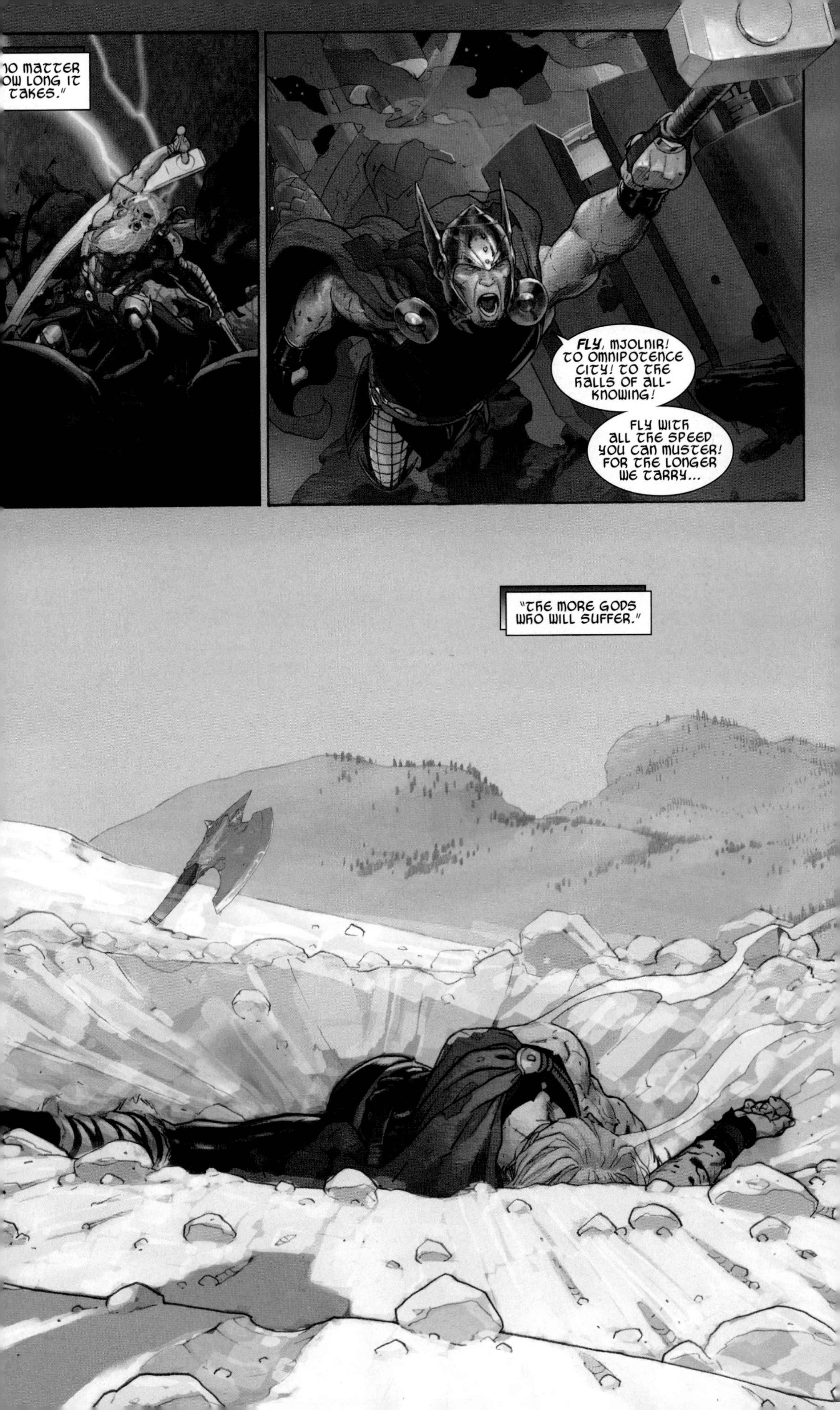

NO MATTER HOW LONG IT TAKES."
FLY, MJOLNIR! TO OMNIPOTENCE CITY! TO THE HALLS OF ALL-KNOWING!
FLY WITH ALL THE SPEED YOU CAN MUSTER! FOR THE LONGER WE TARRY...
"THE MORE GODS WHO WILL SUFFER."

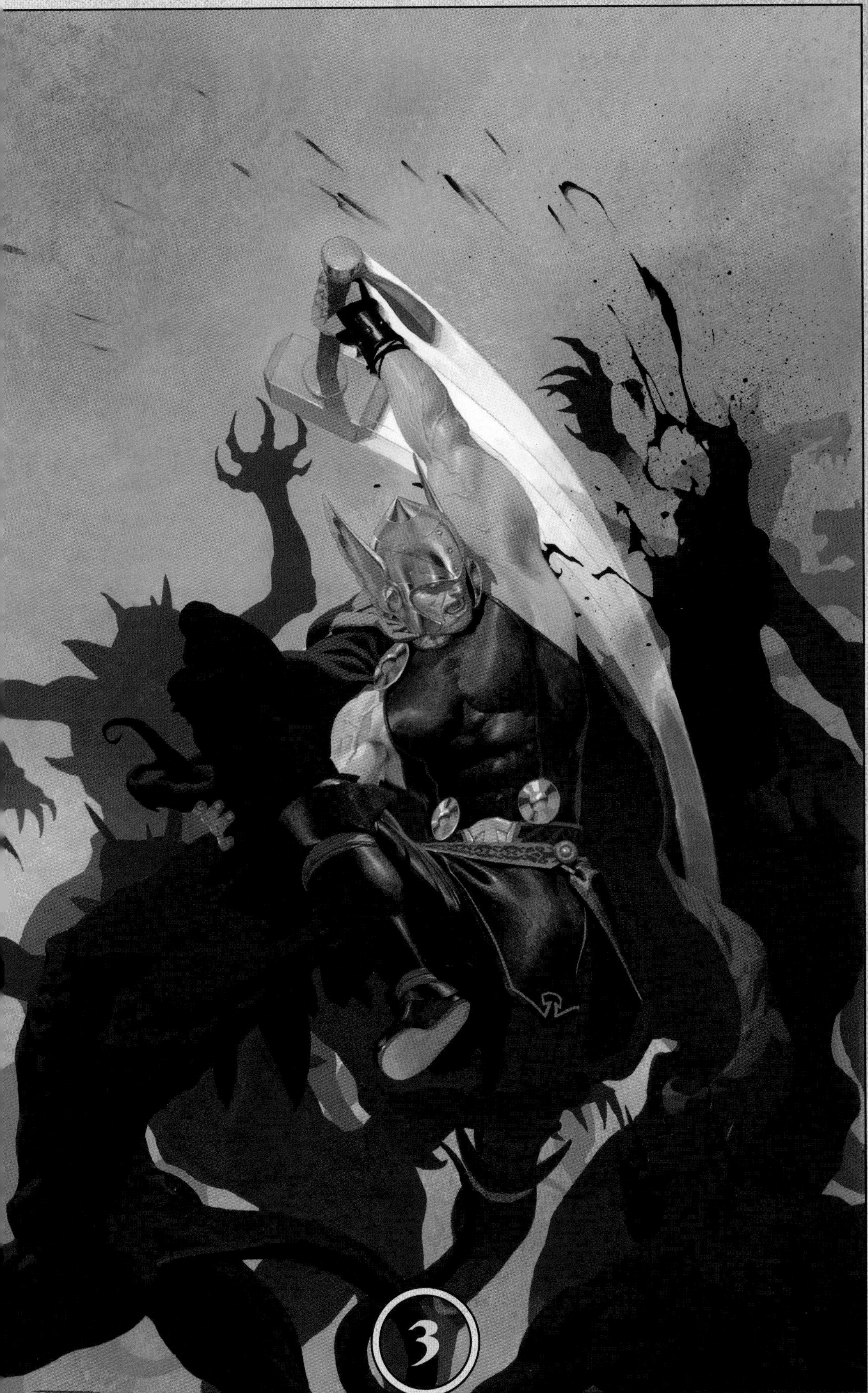
3

THE HALL OF THE LOST

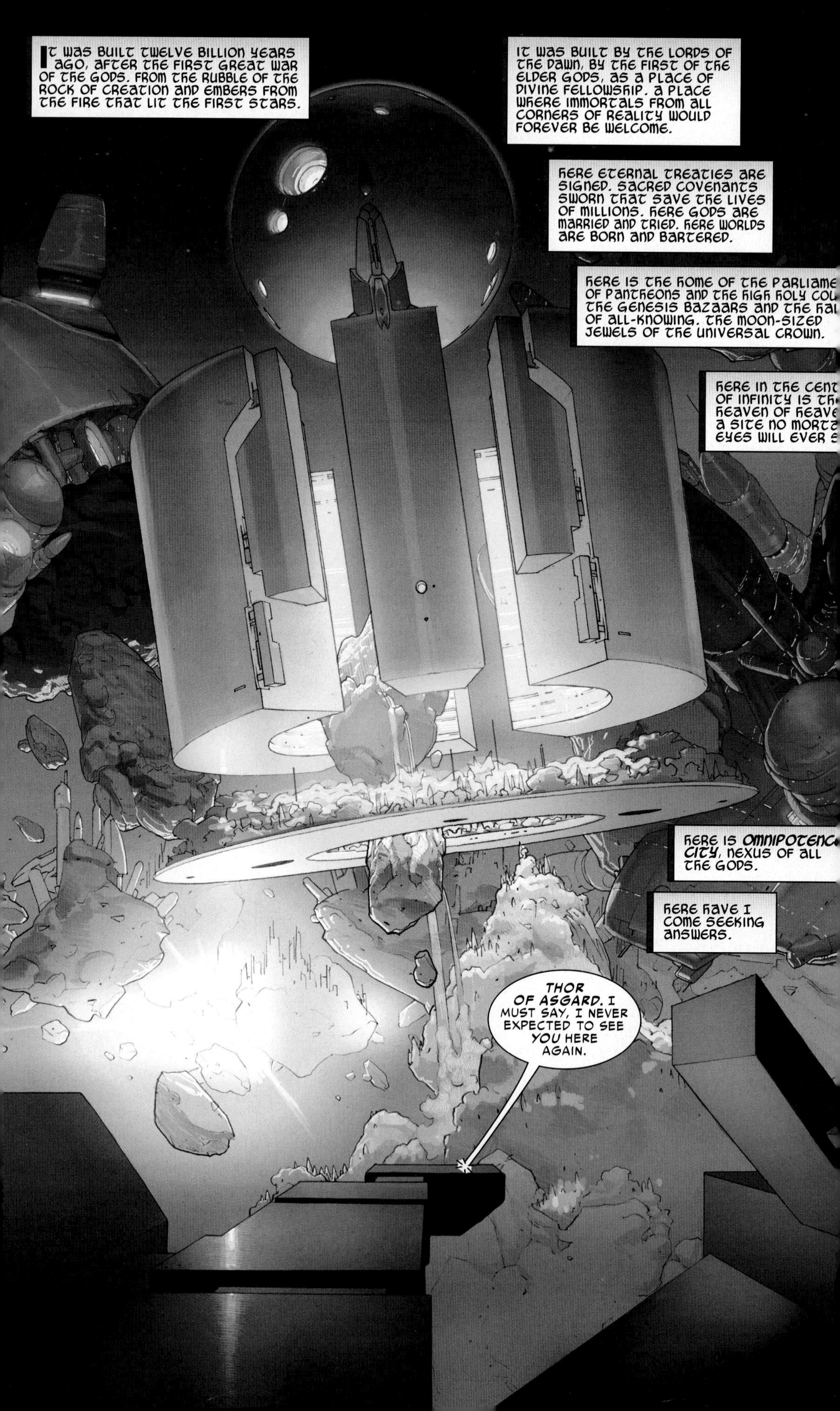

IT WAS BUILT TWELVE BILLION YEARS AGO, AFTER THE FIRST GREAT WAR OF THE GODS. FROM THE RUBBLE OF THE ROCK OF CREATION AND EMBERS FROM THE FIRE THAT LIT THE FIRST STARS.
IT WAS BUILT BY THE LORDS OF THE DAWN, BY THE FIRST OF THE ELDER GODS, AS A PLACE OF DIVINE FELLOWSHIP. A PLACE WHERE IMMORTALS FROM ALL CORNERS OF REALITY WOULD FOREVER BE WELCOME.
HERE ETERNAL TREATIES ARE SIGNED. SACRED COVENANTS SWORN THAT SAVE THE LIVES OF MILLIONS. HERE GODS ARE MARRIED AND TRIED. HERE WORLDS ARE BORN AND BARTERED.
HERE IS THE HOME OF THE PARLIAME OF PANTHEONS AND THE HIGH HOLY COU THE GENESIS BAZAARS AND THE HAL OF ALL-KNOWING. THE MOON-SIZED JEWELS OF THE UNIVERSAL CROWN.
HERE IN THE CENT OF INFINITY IS TH HEAVEN OF HEAVE A SITE NO MORTA EYES WILL EVER S
HERE IS OMNIPOTENC CITY, NEXUS OF ALL THE GODS.
HERE HAVE I COME SEEKING ANSWERS.
THOR OF ASGARD. I MUST SAY, I NEVER EXPECTED TO SEE YOU HERE AGAIN.

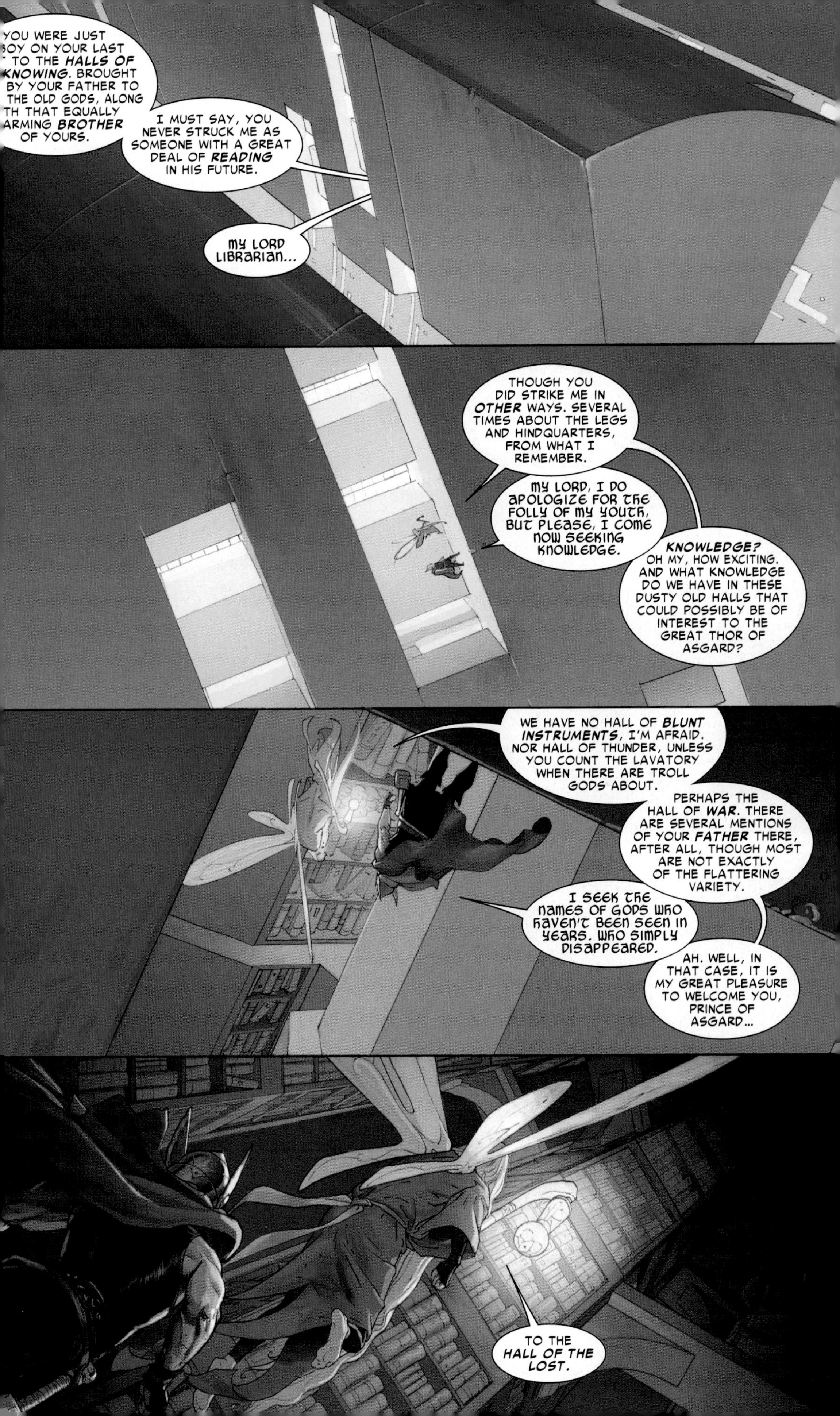
YOU WERE JUST BOY ON YOUR LAST TO THE HALLS OF KNOWING. BROUGHT BY YOUR FATHER TO THE OLD GODS, ALONG TH THAT EQUALLY ARMING BROTHER OF YOURS.
I MUST SAY, YOU NEVER STRUCK ME AS SOMEONE WITH A GREAT DEAL OF READING IN HIS FUTURE.
MY LORD LIBRARIAN...
THOUGH YOU DID STRIKE ME IN OTHER WAYS. SEVERAL TIMES ABOUT THE LEGS AND HINDQUARTERS, FROM WHAT I REMEMBER.
MY LORD, I DO APOLOGIZE FOR THE FOLLY OF MY YOUTH, BUT PLEASE, I COME NOW SEEKING KNOWLEDGE.
KNOWLEDGE? OH MY, HOW EXCITING. AND WHAT KNOWLEDGE DO WE HAVE IN THESE DUSTY OLD HALLS THAT COULD POSSIBLY BE OF INTEREST TO THE GREAT THOR OF ASGARD?
WE HAVE NO HALL OF BLUNT INSTRUMENTS, I'M AFRAID. NOR HALL OF THUNDER, UNLESS YOU COUNT THE LAVATORY WHEN THERE ARE TROLL GODS ABOUT.
PERHAPS THE HALL OF WAR. THERE ARE SEVERAL MENTIONS OF YOUR FATHER THERE, AFTER ALL, THOUGH MOST ARE NOT EXACTLY OF THE FLATTERING VARIETY.
I SEEK THE NAMES OF GODS WHO HAVEN'T BEEN SEEN IN YEARS. WHO SIMPLY DISAPPEARED.
AH. WELL, IN THAT CASE, IT IS MY GREAT PLEASURE TO WELCOME YOU, PRINCE OF ASGARD...
TO THE HALL OF THE LOST.

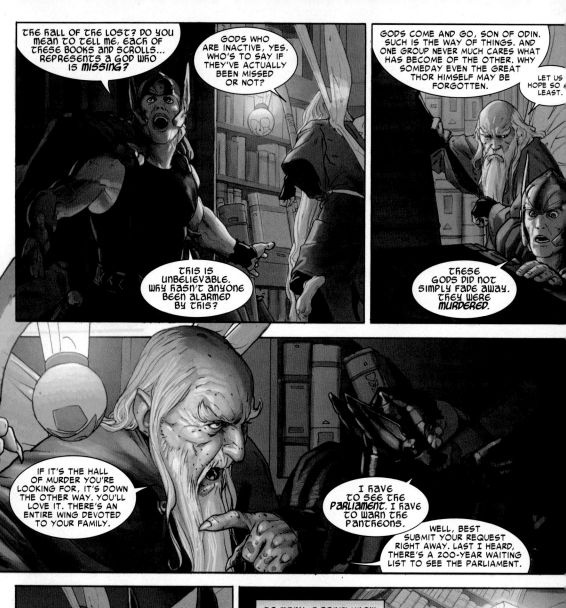

THE HALL OF THE LOST? DO YOU MEAN TO TELL ME, EACH OF THESE BOOKS AND SCROLLS... REPRESENTS A GOD WHO IS *MISSING?*

GODS WHO ARE INACTIVE, YES. WHO'S TO SAY IF THEY'VE ACTUALLY BEEN MISSED OR NOT?

GODS COME AND GO, SON OF ODIN. SUCH IS THE WAY OF THINGS. AND ONE GROUP NEVER MUCH CARES WHAT HAS BECOME OF THE OTHER. WHY SOMEDAY EVEN THE GREAT THOR HIMSELF MAY BE FORGOTTEN.

LET US HOPE SO AT LEAST.

THIS IS UNBELIEVABLE. WHY HASN'T ANYONE BEEN ALARMED BY THIS?

THESE GODS DID NOT SIMPLY FADE AWAY. THEY WERE *MURDERED.*

IF IT'S THE HALL OF MURDER YOU'RE LOOKING FOR, IT'S DOWN THE OTHER WAY. YOU'LL LOVE IT. THERE'S AN ENTIRE WING DEVOTED TO YOUR FAMILY.

I HAVE TO SEE THE *PARLIAMENT.* I HAVE TO WARN THE PANTHEONS.

WELL, BEST SUBMIT YOUR REQUEST RIGHT AWAY. LAST I HEARD, THERE'S A 200-YEAR WAITING LIST TO SEE THE PARLIAMENT.

AND BEFORE YOU ASK, *NO,* YOU MAY NOT WAIT HERE.

SO MANY. I DON'T KNOW WHERE TO START. COULD ALL OF THESE GODS REALLY HAVE BEEN MURDERED BY ONE MAN?

I SUPPOSE THERE'S ONLY ONE WAY TO FIND OUT.

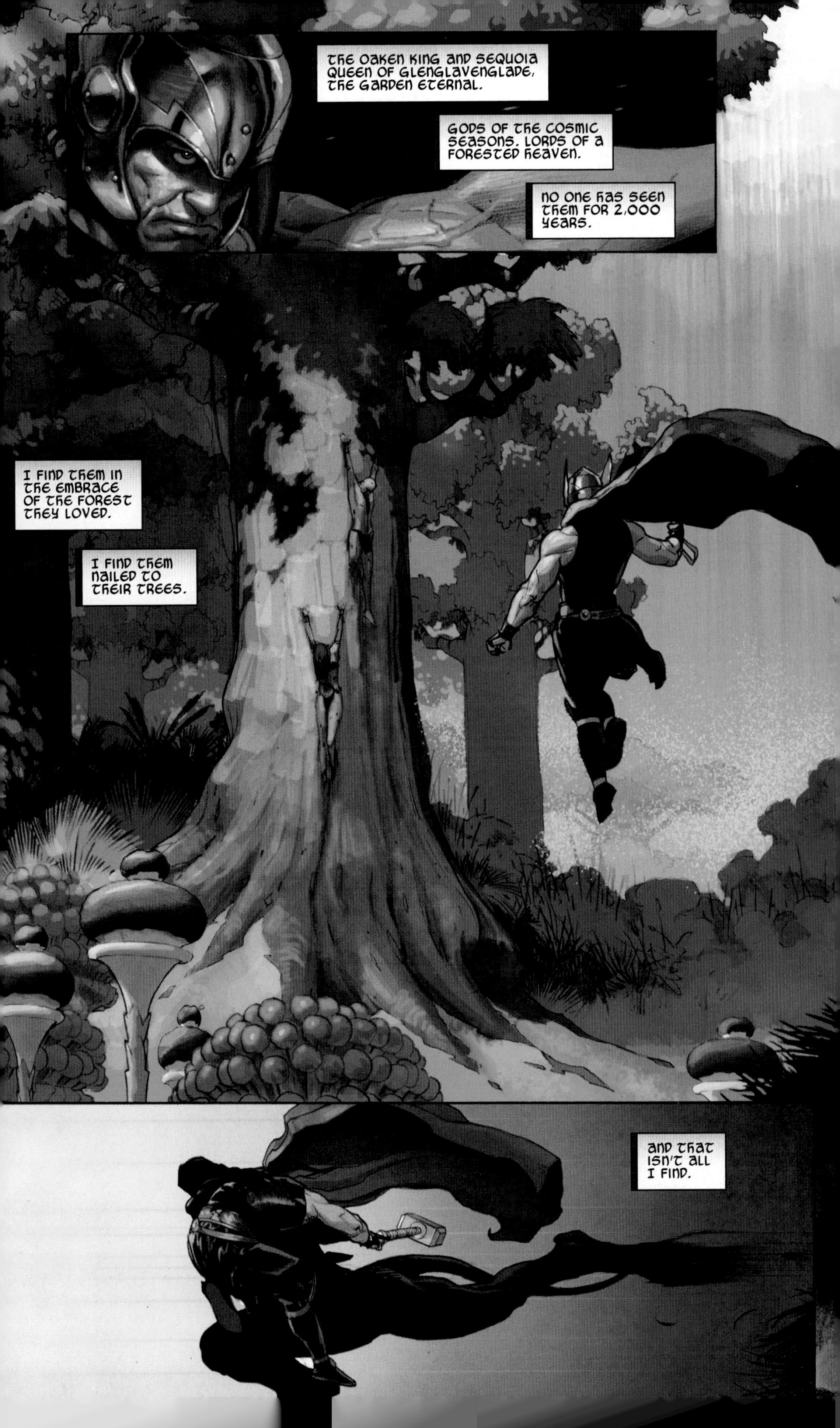
THE OAKEN KING AND SEQUOIA QUEEN OF GLENGLAVENGLADE, THE GARDEN ETERNAL.
GODS OF THE COSMIC SEASONS. LORDS OF A FORESTED HEAVEN.
NO ONE HAS SEEN THEM FOR 2,000 YEARS.
I FIND THEM IN THE EMBRACE OF THE FOREST THEY LOVED.
I FIND THEM NAILED TO THEIR TREES.
AND THAT ISN'T ALL I FIND.

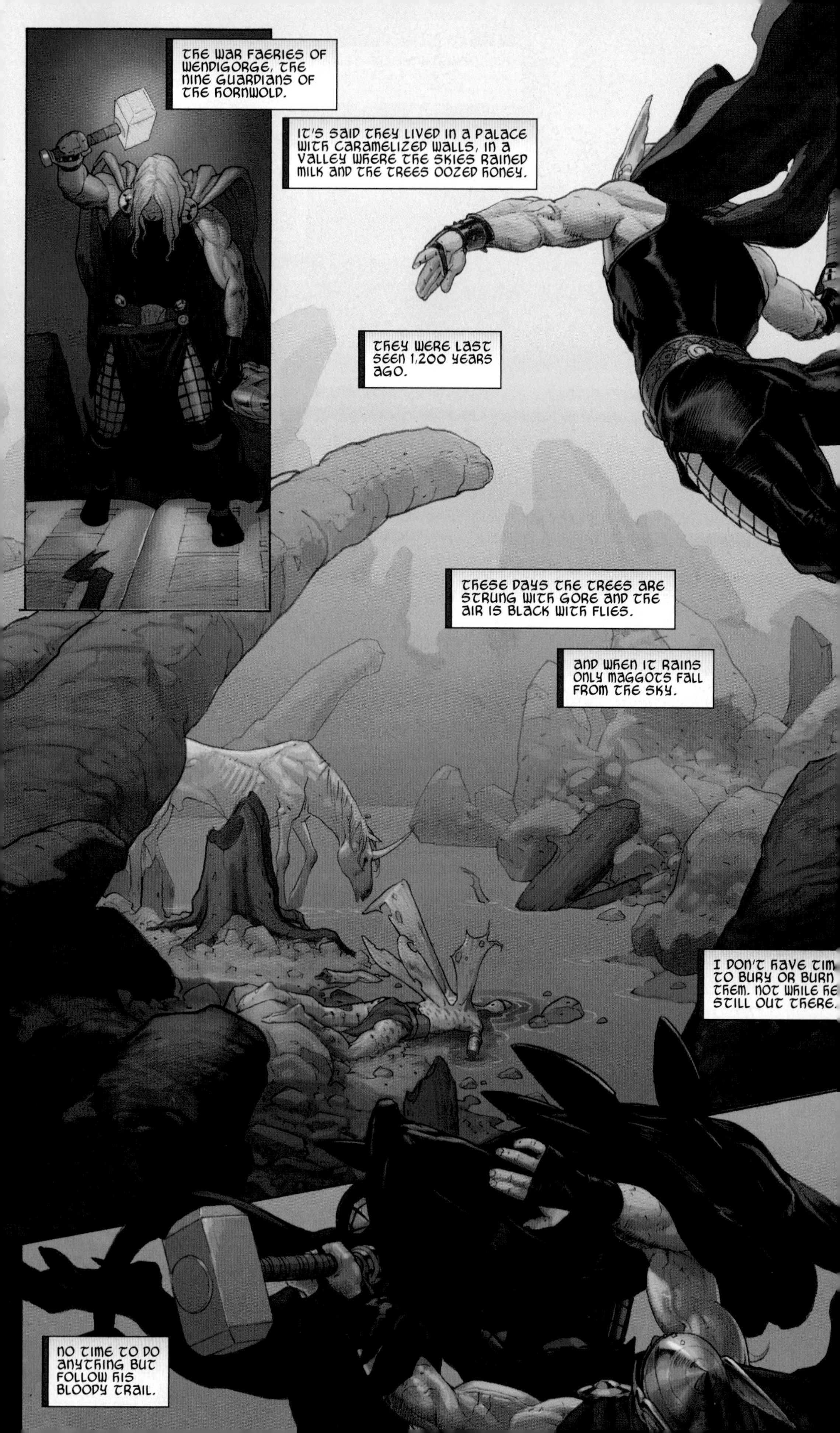
THE WAR FAERIES OF WENDIGORGE, THE NINE GUARDIANS OF THE HORNWOLD.
IT'S SAID THEY LIVED IN A PALACE WITH CARAMELIZED WALLS, IN A VALLEY WHERE THE SKIES RAINED MILK AND THE TREES OOZED HONEY.
THEY WERE LAST SEEN 1,200 YEARS AGO.
THESE DAYS THE TREES ARE STRUNG WITH GORE AND THE AIR IS BLACK WITH FLIES.
AND WHEN IT RAINS ONLY MAGGOTS FALL FROM THE SKY.
I DON'T HAVE TIM TO BURY OR BURN THEM. NOT WHILE HE STILL OUT THERE.
NO TIME TO DO ANYTHING BUT FOLLOW HIS BLOODY TRAIL.

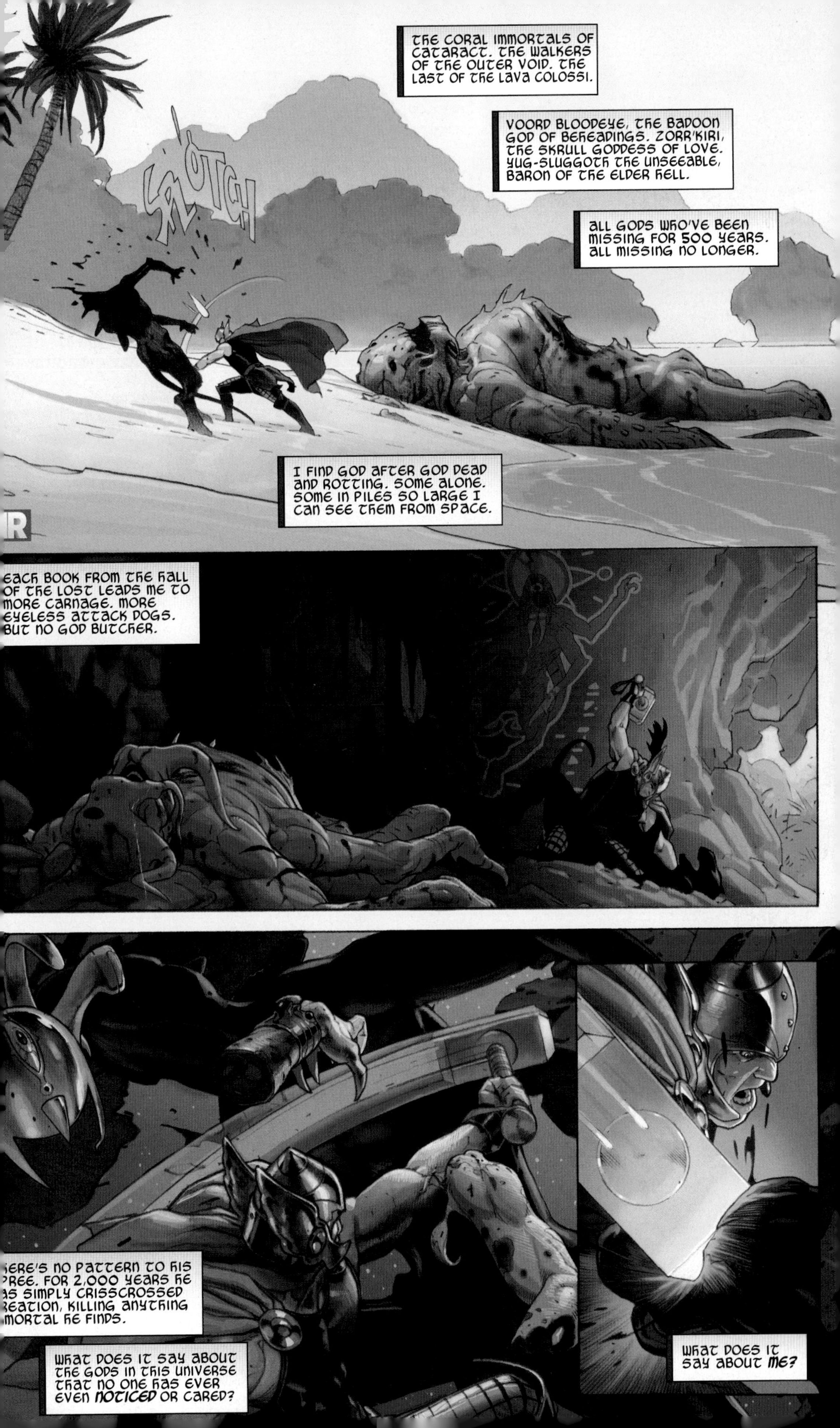
THE CORAL IMMORTALS OF CATARACT. THE WALKERS OF THE OUTER VOID. THE LAST OF THE LAVA COLOSSI.
SKLOTCH
VOORD BLOODEYE, THE BADOON GOD OF BEHEADINGS. ZORR'KIRI, THE SKRULL GODDESS OF LOVE. YUG-SLUGGOTH THE UNSEEABLE, BARON OF THE ELDER HELL.
ALL GODS WHO'VE BEEN MISSING FOR 500 YEARS. ALL MISSING NO LONGER.
I FIND GOD AFTER GOD DEAD AND ROTTING. SOME ALONE. SOME IN PILES SO LARGE I CAN SEE THEM FROM SPACE.
EACH BOOK FROM THE HALL OF THE LOST LEADS ME TO MORE CARNAGE. MORE EYELESS ATTACK DOGS. BUT NO GOD BUTCHER.
HERE'S NO PATTERN TO HIS PREE. FOR 2,000 YEARS HE AS SIMPLY CRISSCROSSED REATION, KILLING ANYTHING MORTAL HE FINDS.
WHAT DOES IT SAY ABOUT THE GODS IN THIS UNIVERSE THAT NO ONE HAS EVER EVEN NOTICED OR CARED?
WHAT DOES IT SAY ABOUT ME?

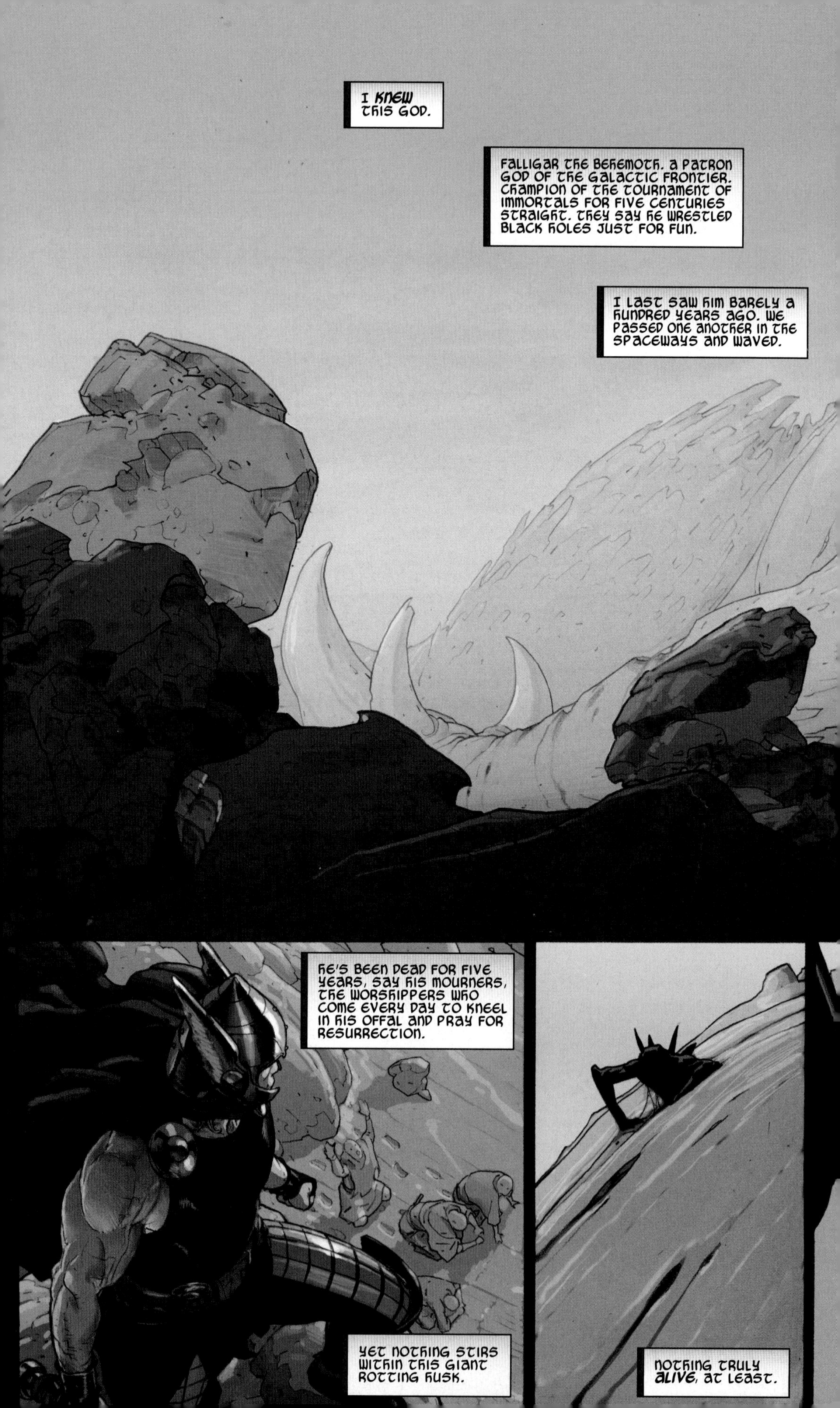
I KNEW THIS GOD.
FALLIGAR THE BEHEMOTH. A PATRON GOD OF THE GALACTIC FRONTIER. CHAMPION OF THE TOURNAMENT OF IMMORTALS FOR FIVE CENTURIES STRAIGHT. THEY SAY HE WRESTLED BLACK HOLES JUST FOR FUN.
I LAST SAW HIM BARELY A HUNDRED YEARS AGO. WE PASSED ONE ANOTHER IN THE SPACEWAYS AND WAVED.
HE'S BEEN DEAD FOR FIVE YEARS, SAY HIS MOURNERS, THE WORSHIPPERS WHO COME EVERY DAY TO KNEEL IN HIS OFFAL AND PRAY FOR RESURRECTION.
YET NOTHING STIRS WITHIN THIS GIANT ROTTING HUSK.
NOTHING TRULY ALIVE, AT LEAST.

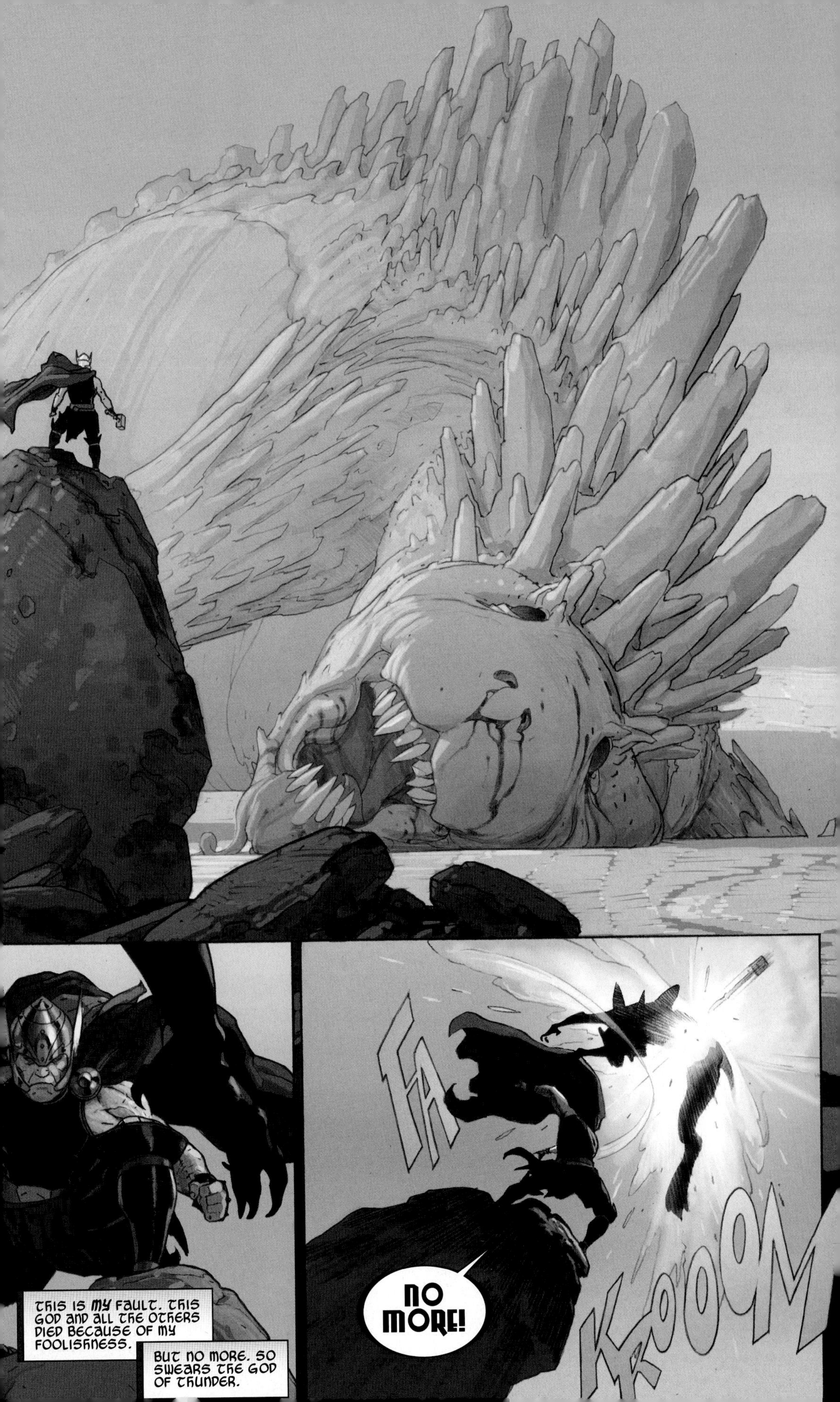

THIS IS MY FAULT. THIS GOD AND ALL THE OTHERS DIED BECAUSE OF MY FOOLISHNESS.
BUT NO MORE. SO SWEARS THE GOD OF THUNDER.
FA
NO MORE!
KROOOM

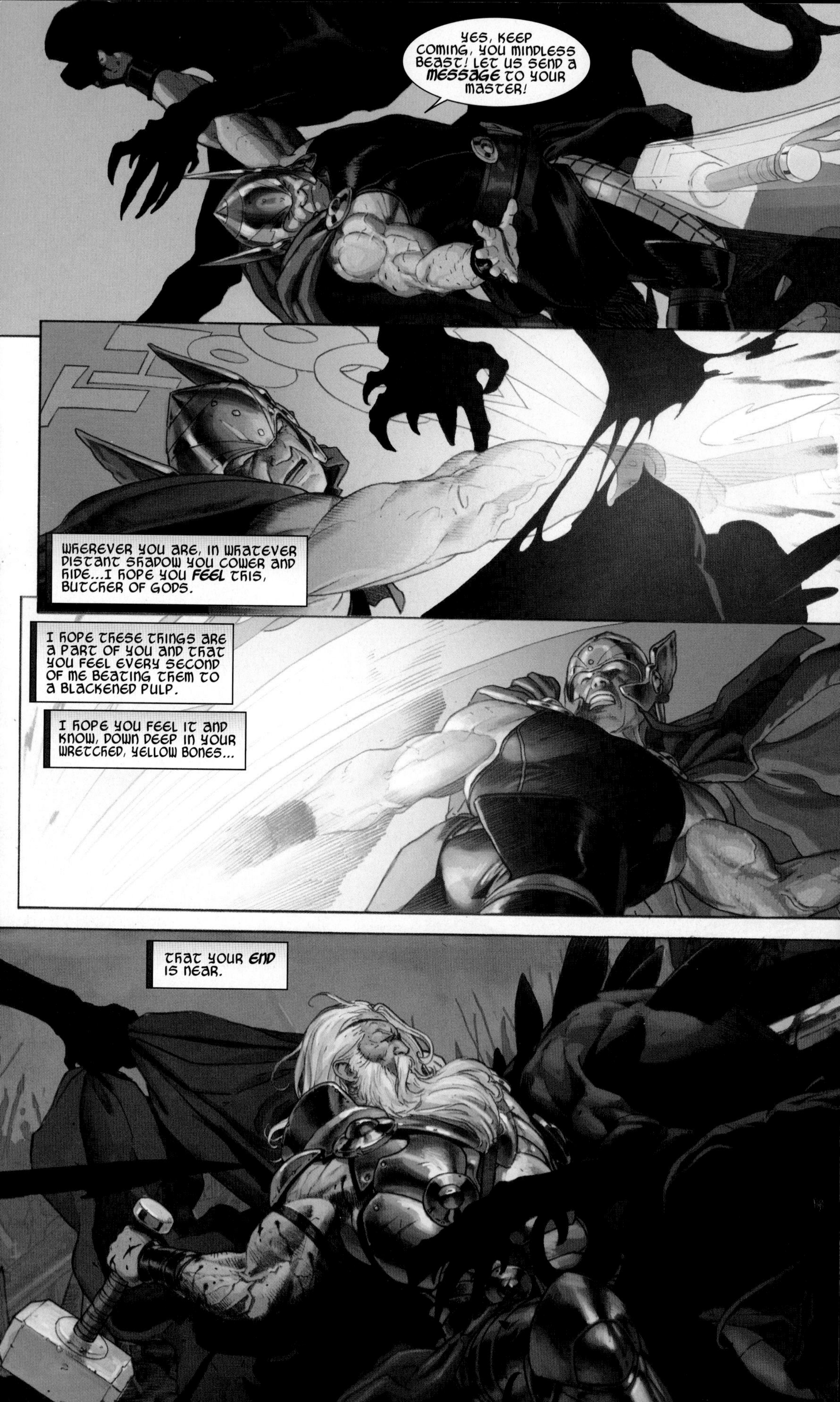
YES, KEEP COMING, YOU MINDLESS BEAST! LET US SEND A MESSAGE TO YOUR MASTER!
WHEREVER YOU ARE, IN WHATEVER DISTANT SHADOW YOU COWER AND HIDE...I HOPE YOU FEEL THIS, BUTCHER OF GODS.
I HOPE THESE THINGS ARE A PART OF YOU AND THAT YOU FEEL EVERY SECOND OF ME BEATING THEM TO A BLACKENED PULP.
I HOPE YOU FEEL IT AND KNOW, DOWN DEEP IN YOUR WRETCHED, YELLOW BONES...
THAT YOUR END IS NEAR.

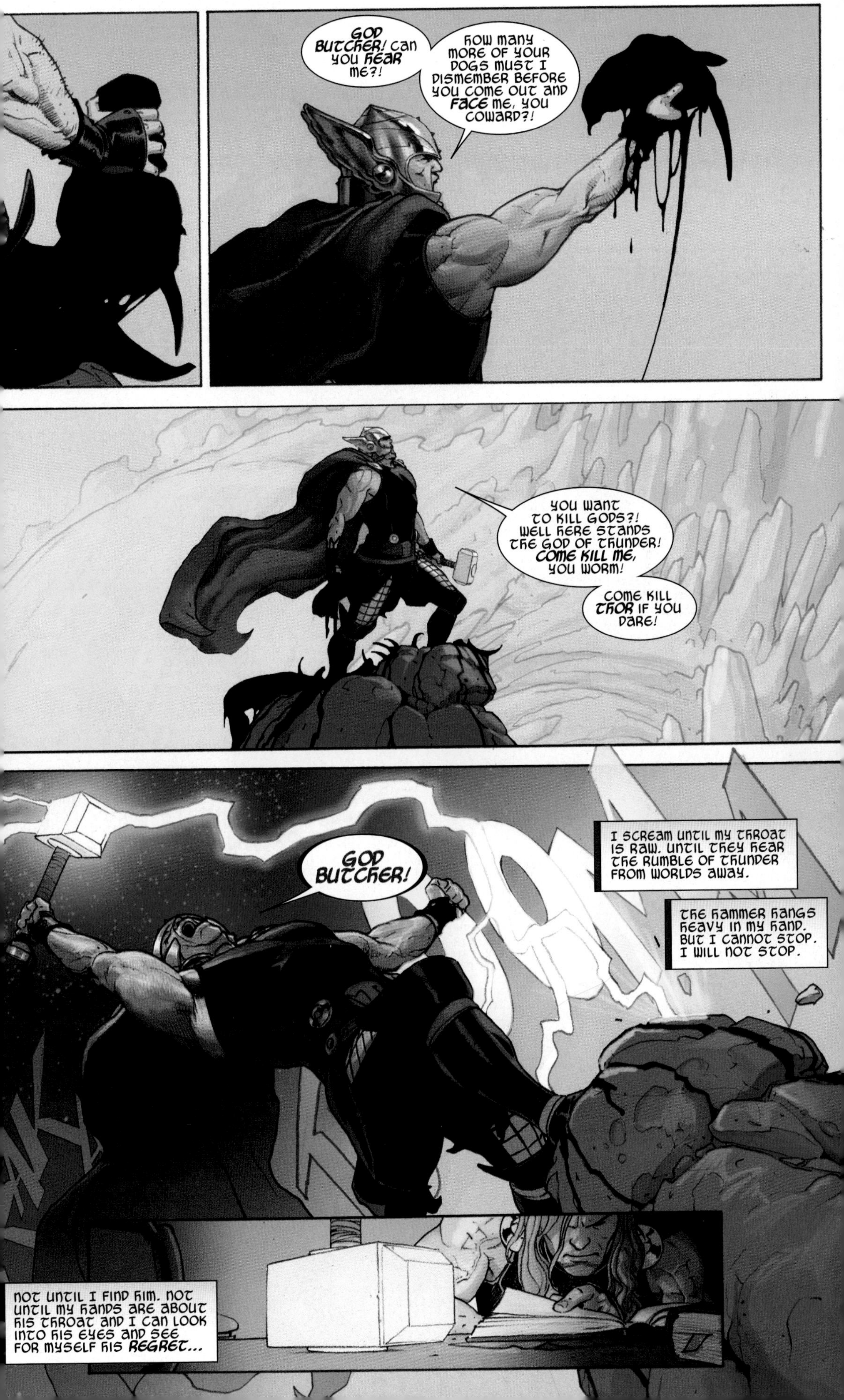
GOD BUTCHER! CAN YOU HEAR ME?!
HOW MANY MORE OF YOUR DOGS MUST I DISMEMBER BEFORE YOU COME OUT AND FACE ME, YOU COWARD?!
YOU WANT TO KILL GODS?! WELL HERE STANDS THE GOD OF THUNDER! COME KILL ME, YOU WORM!
COME KILL THOR IF YOU DARE!
GOD BUTCHER!
I SCREAM UNTIL MY THROAT IS RAW. UNTIL THEY HEAR THE RUMBLE OF THUNDER FROM WORLDS AWAY.
THE HAMMER HANGS HEAVY IN MY HAND. BUT I CANNOT STOP. I WILL NOT STOP.
NOT UNTIL I FIND HIM. NOT UNTIL MY HANDS ARE ABOUT HIS THROAT AND I CAN LOOK INTO HIS EYES AND SEE FOR MYSELF HIS REGRET...

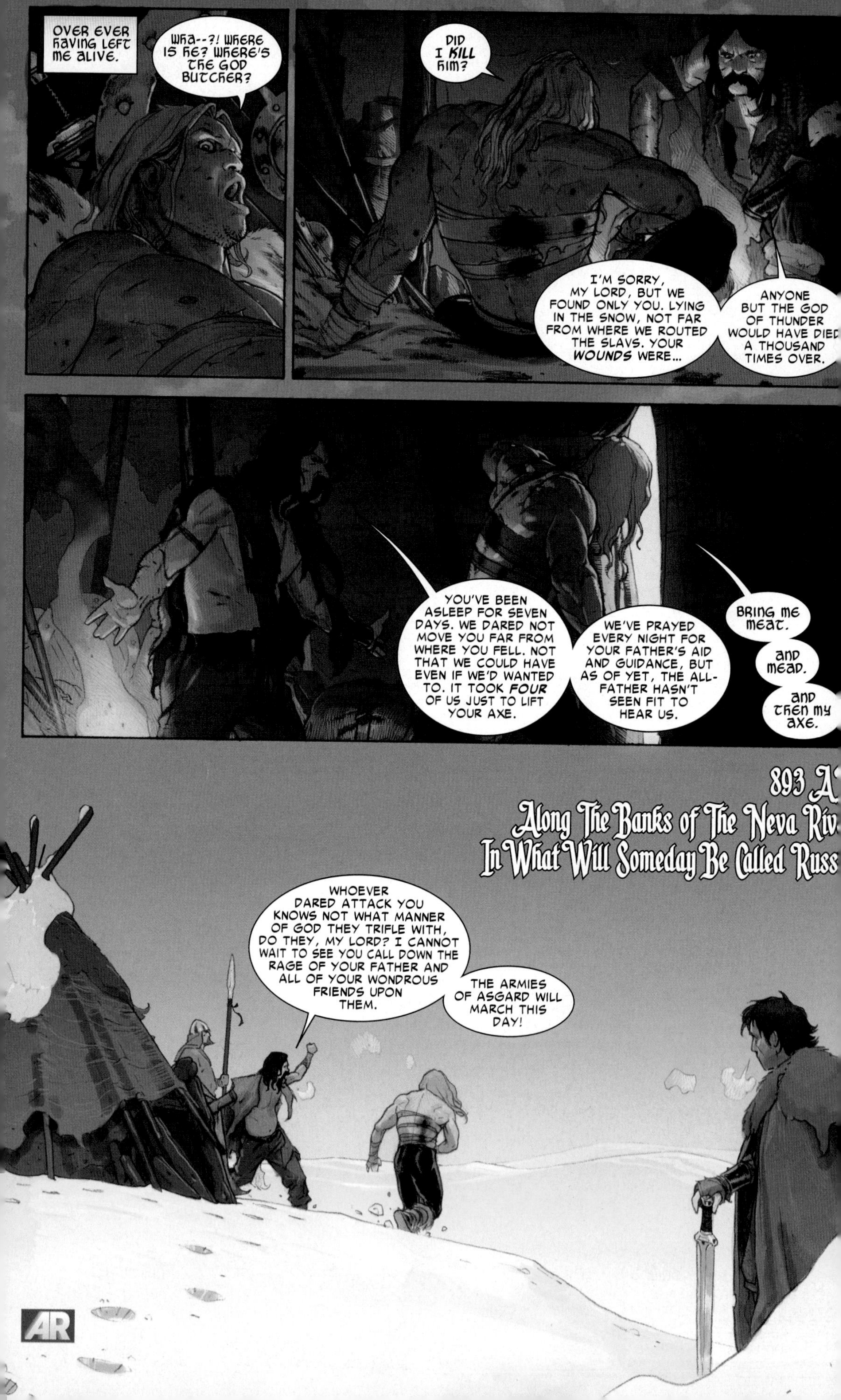
OVER EVER HAVING LEFT ME ALIVE.
WHA--?! WHERE IS HE? WHERE'S THE GOD BUTCHER?
DID I KILL HIM?
I'M SORRY, MY LORD, BUT WE FOUND ONLY YOU. LYING IN THE SNOW, NOT FAR FROM WHERE WE ROUTED THE SLAVS. YOUR WOUNDS WERE...
ANYONE BUT THE GOD OF THUNDER WOULD HAVE DIED A THOUSAND TIMES OVER.
YOU'VE BEEN ASLEEP FOR SEVEN DAYS. WE DARED NOT MOVE YOU FAR FROM WHERE YOU FELL. NOT THAT WE COULD HAVE EVEN IF WE'D WANTED TO. IT TOOK FOUR OF US JUST TO LIFT YOUR AXE.
WE'VE PRAYED EVERY NIGHT FOR YOUR FATHER'S AID AND GUIDANCE, BUT AS OF YET, THE ALL-FATHER HASN'T SEEN FIT TO HEAR US.
BRING ME MEAT.
AND MEAD.
AND THEN MY AXE.
893 A
Along The Banks of The Neva Riv
In What Will Someday Be Called Russ
WHOEVER DARED ATTACK YOU KNOWS NOT WHAT MANNER OF GOD THEY TRIFLE WITH, DO THEY, MY LORD? I CANNOT WAIT TO SEE YOU CALL DOWN THE RAGE OF YOUR FATHER AND ALL OF YOUR WONDROUS FRIENDS UPON THEM.
THE ARMIES OF ASGARD WILL MARCH THIS DAY!

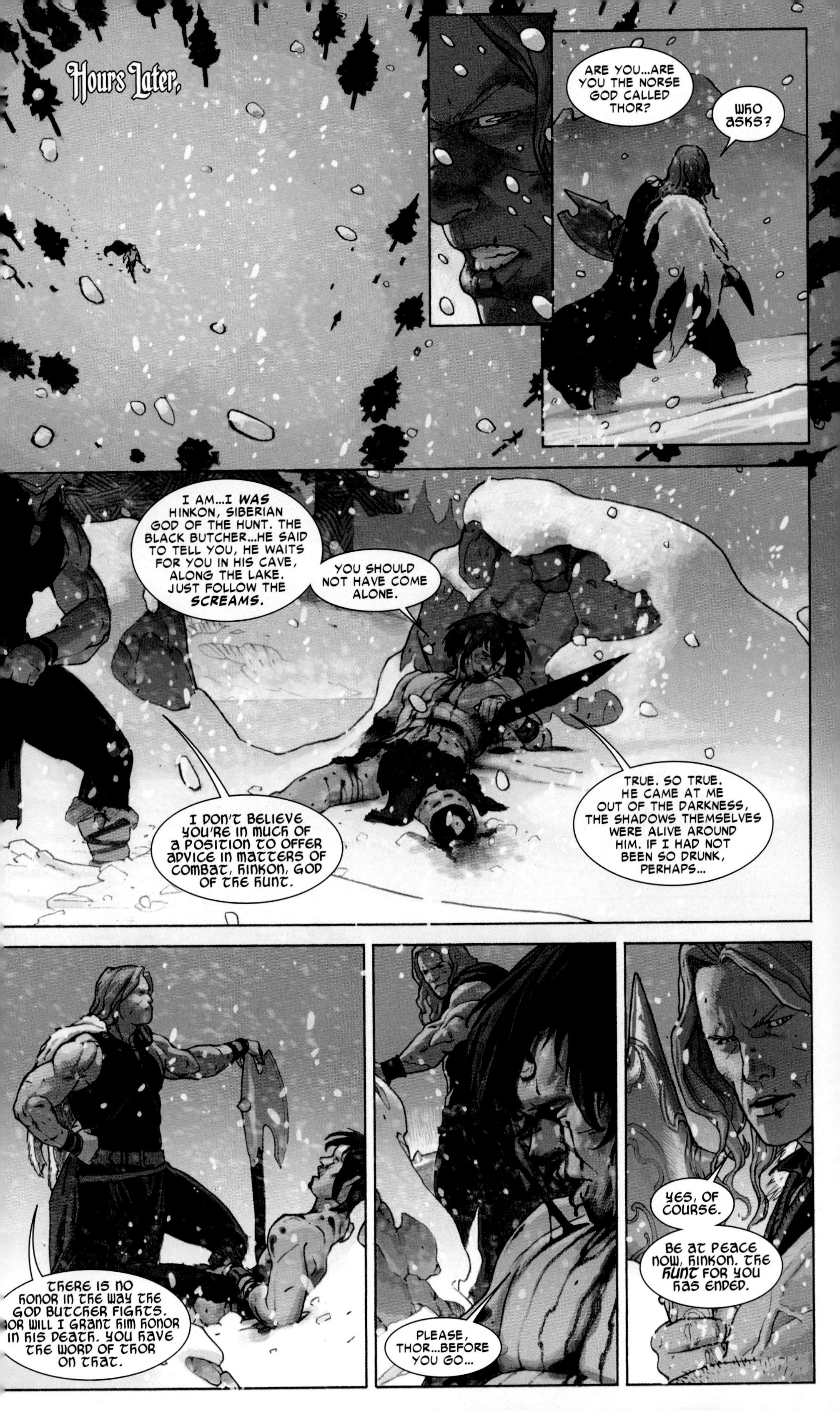
Hours Later,
ARE YOU...ARE YOU THE NORSE GOD CALLED THOR?
WHO ASKS?
I AM...I WAS HINKON, SIBERIAN GOD OF THE HUNT. THE BLACK BUTCHER...HE SAID TO TELL YOU, HE WAITS FOR YOU IN HIS CAVE, ALONG THE LAKE. JUST FOLLOW THE SCREAMS.
YOU SHOULD NOT HAVE COME ALONE.
I DON'T BELIEVE YOU'RE IN MUCH OF A POSITION TO OFFER ADVICE IN MATTERS OF COMBAT, HINKON, GOD OF THE HUNT.
TRUE. SO TRUE. HE CAME AT ME OUT OF THE DARKNESS, THE SHADOWS THEMSELVES WERE ALIVE AROUND HIM. IF I HAD NOT BEEN SO DRUNK, PERHAPS...
THERE IS NO HONOR IN THE WAY THE GOD BUTCHER FIGHTS. NOR WILL I GRANT HIM HONOR IN HIS DEATH. YOU HAVE THE WORD OF THOR ON THAT.
PLEASE, THOR...BEFORE YOU GO...
YES, OF COURSE.
BE AT PEACE NOW, HINKON. THE HUNT FOR YOU HAS ENDED.

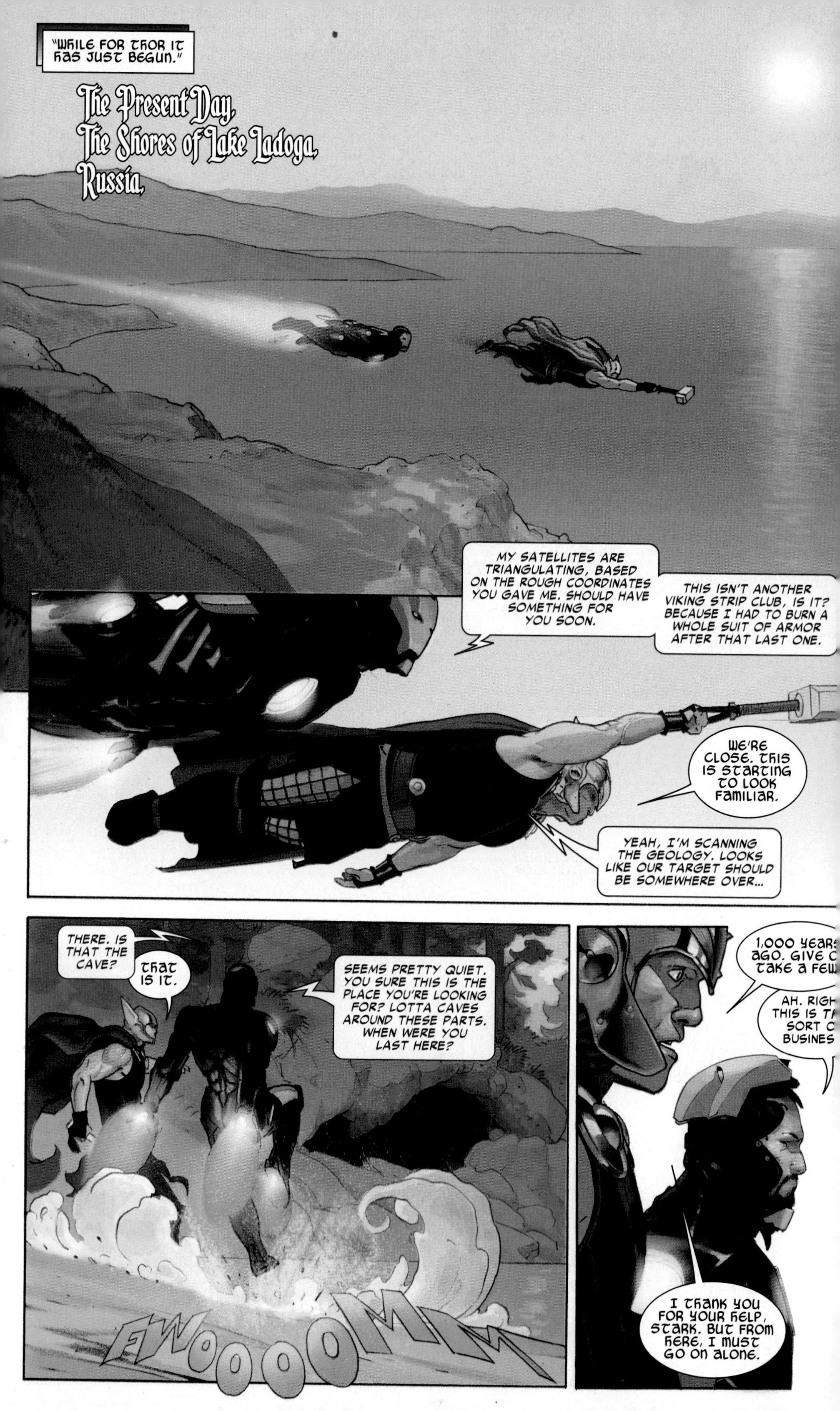

"WHILE FOR THOR IT HAS JUST BEGUN."
The Present Day, The Shores of Lake Ladoga, Russia.
MY SATELLITES ARE TRIANGULATING, BASED ON THE ROUGH COORDINATES YOU GAVE ME. SHOULD HAVE SOMETHING FOR YOU SOON.
THIS ISN'T ANOTHER VIKING STRIP CLUB, IS IT? BECAUSE I HAD TO BURN A WHOLE SUIT OF ARMOR AFTER THAT LAST ONE.
WE'RE CLOSE. THIS IS STARTING TO LOOK FAMILIAR.
YEAH, I'M SCANNING THE GEOLOGY. LOOKS LIKE OUR TARGET SHOULD BE SOMEWHERE OVER...
THERE. IS THAT THE CAVE?
THAT IS IT.
SEEMS PRETTY QUIET. YOU SURE THIS IS THE PLACE YOU'RE LOOKING FOR? LOTTA CAVES AROUND THESE PARTS. WHEN WERE YOU LAST HERE?
FWOOOOMM
1,000 YEAR AGO. GIVE O TAKE A FEW
AH. RIGH THIS IS T SORT O BUSINES
I THANK YOU FOR YOUR HELP, STARK. BUT FROM HERE, I MUST GO ON ALONE.

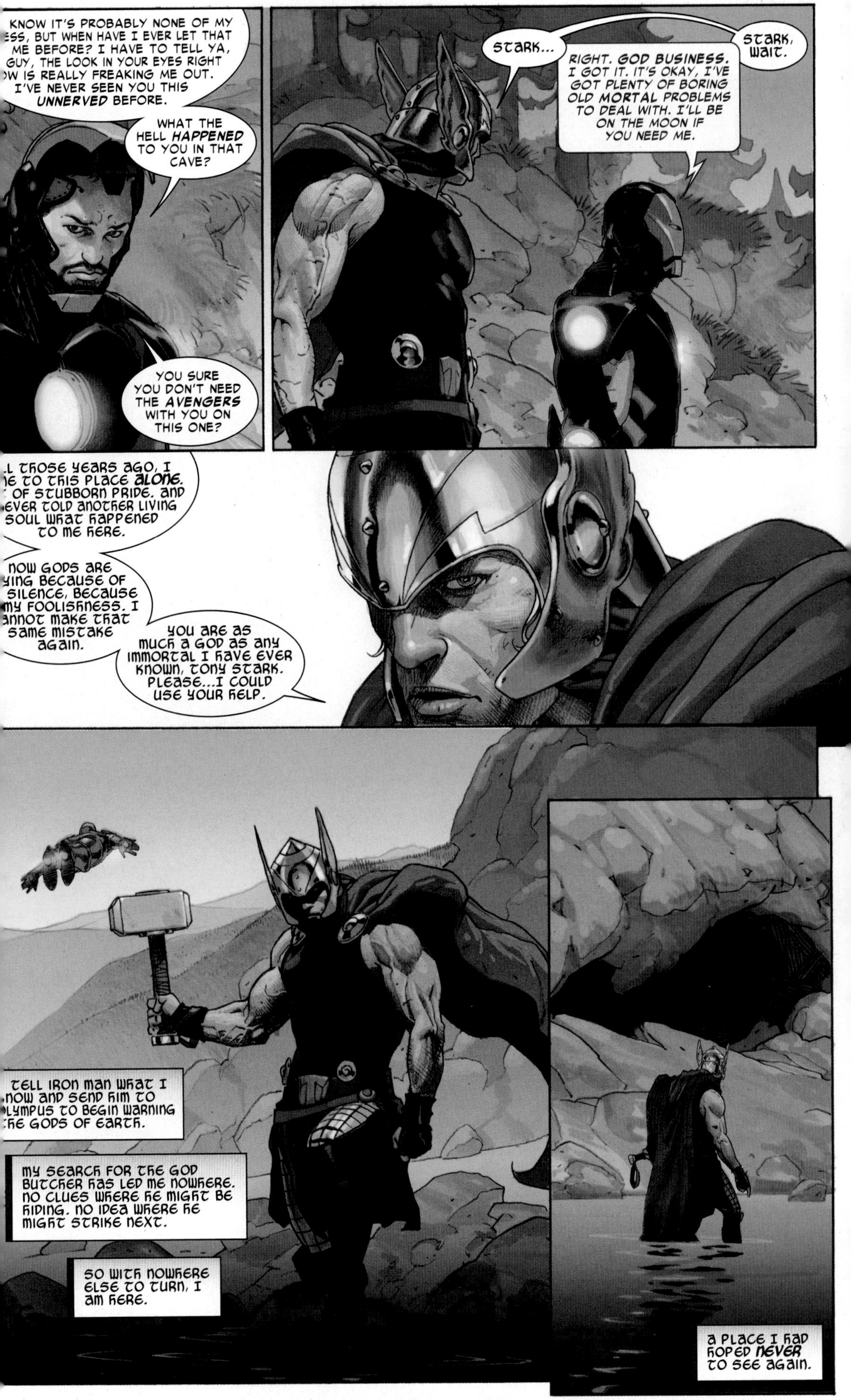

KNOW IT'S PROBABLY NONE OF MY
ESS, BUT WHEN HAVE I EVER LET THAT
ME BEFORE? I HAVE TO TELL YA,
GUY, THE LOOK IN YOUR EYES RIGHT
OW IS REALLY FREAKING ME OUT.
I'VE NEVER SEEN YOU THIS
UNNERVED BEFORE.
WHAT THE HELL HAPPENED TO YOU IN THAT CAVE?
YOU SURE YOU DON'T NEED THE AVENGERS WITH YOU ON THIS ONE?
STARK...
STARK, WAIT.
RIGHT. GOD BUSINESS. I GOT IT. IT'S OKAY, I'VE GOT PLENTY OF BORING OLD MORTAL PROBLEMS TO DEAL WITH. I'LL BE ON THE MOON IF YOU NEED ME.
L THOSE YEARS AGO, I
E TO THIS PLACE ALONE.
OF STUBBORN PRIDE. AND
EVER TOLD ANOTHER LIVING
SOUL WHAT HAPPENED
TO ME HERE.
NOW GODS ARE
YING BECAUSE OF
SILENCE, BECAUSE
MY FOOLISHNESS. I
ANNOT MAKE THAT
SAME MISTAKE
AGAIN.
YOU ARE AS MUCH A GOD AS ANY IMMORTAL I HAVE EVER KNOWN, TONY STARK. PLEASE...I COULD USE YOUR HELP.
TELL IRON MAN WHAT I
NOW AND SEND HIM TO
LYMPUS TO BEGIN WARNING
HE GODS OF EARTH.
MY SEARCH FOR THE GOD BUTCHER HAS LED ME NOWHERE. NO CLUES WHERE HE MIGHT BE HIDING. NO IDEA WHERE HE MIGHT STRIKE NEXT.
SO WITH NOWHERE ELSE TO TURN, I AM HERE.
A PLACE I HAD HOPED NEVER TO SEE AGAIN.

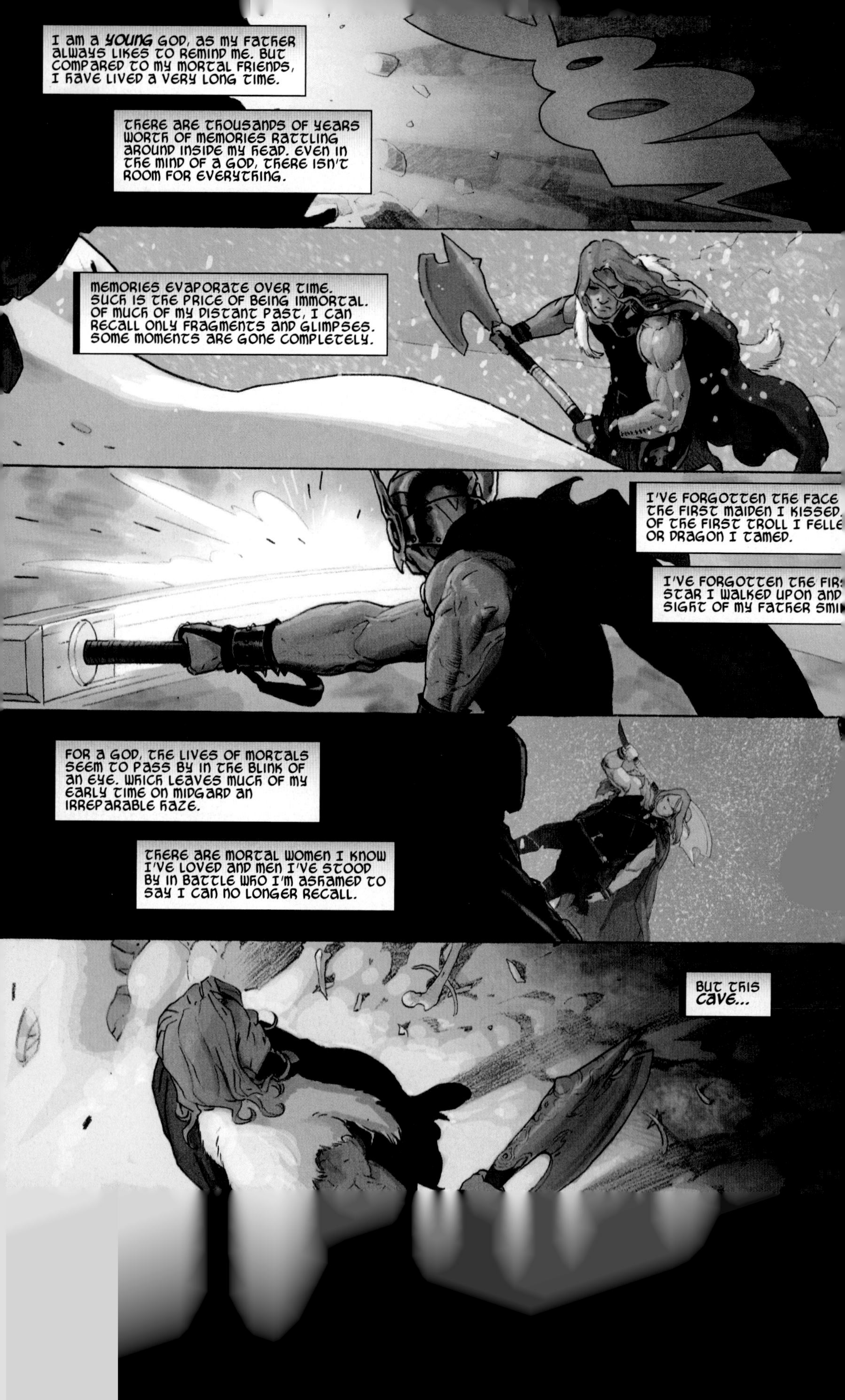
I am a YOUNG GOD, AS MY FATHER ALWAYS LIKES TO REMIND ME. BUT COMPARED TO MY MORTAL FRIENDS, I HAVE LIVED A VERY LONG TIME.
THERE ARE THOUSANDS OF YEARS WORTH OF MEMORIES RATTLING AROUND INSIDE MY HEAD. EVEN IN THE MIND OF A GOD, THERE ISN'T ROOM FOR EVERYTHING.
MEMORIES EVAPORATE OVER TIME. SUCH IS THE PRICE OF BEING IMMORTAL. OF MUCH OF MY DISTANT PAST, I CAN RECALL ONLY FRAGMENTS AND GLIMPSES. SOME MOMENTS ARE GONE COMPLETELY.
I'VE FORGOTTEN THE FACE THE FIRST MAIDEN I KISSED. OF THE FIRST TROLL I FELLE OR DRAGON I TAMED.
I'VE FORGOTTEN THE FIR STAR I WALKED UPON AND SIGHT OF MY FATHER SMI
FOR A GOD, THE LIVES OF MORTALS SEEM TO PASS BY IN THE BLINK OF AN EYE. WHICH LEAVES MUCH OF MY EARLY TIME ON MIDGARD AN IRREPARABLE HAZE.
THERE ARE MORTAL WOMEN I KNOW I'VE LOVED AND MEN I'VE STOOD BY IN BATTLE WHO I'M ASHAMED TO SAY I CAN NO LONGER RECALL.
BUT THIS CAVE...

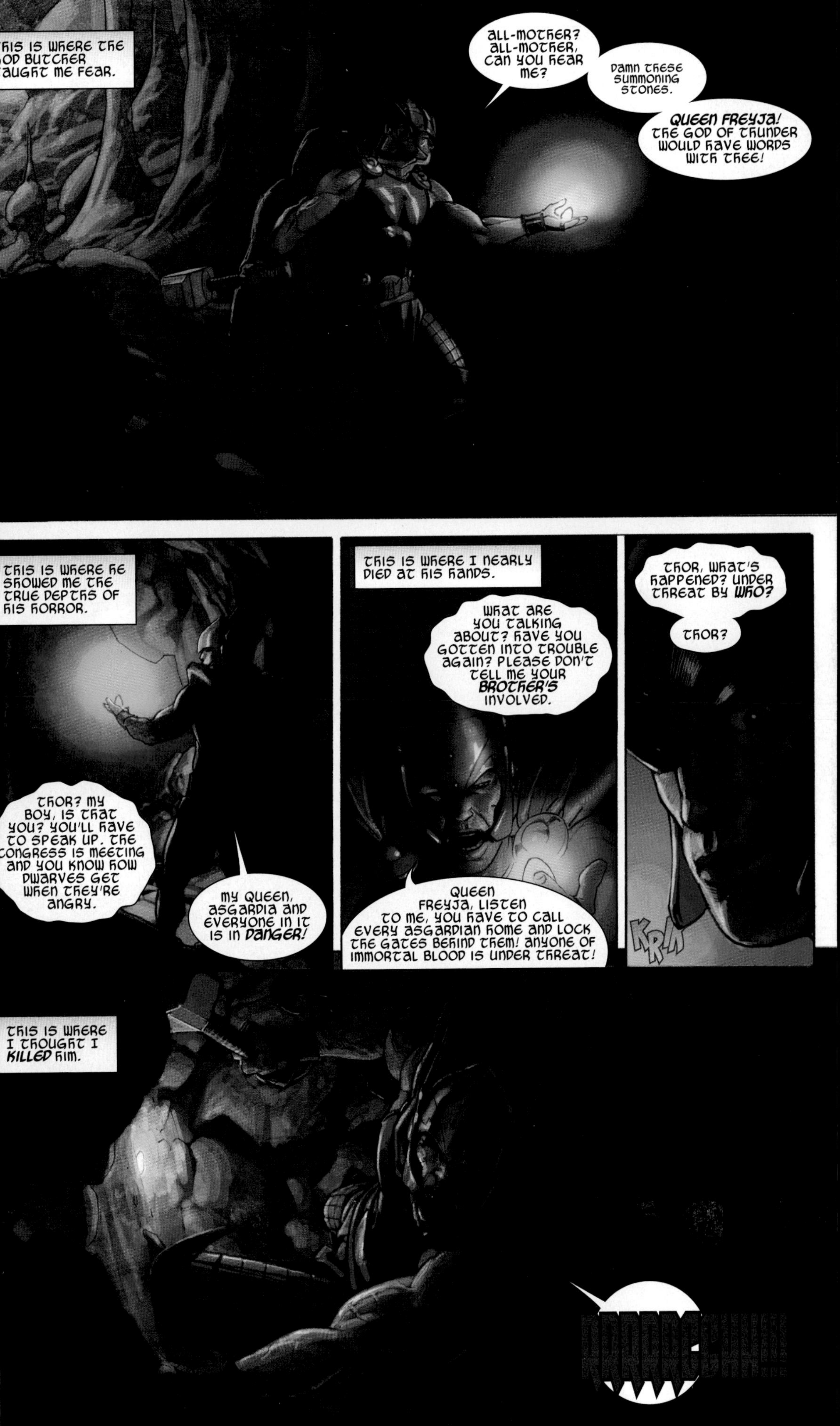

HIS IS WHERE THE OD BUTCHER TAUGHT ME FEAR.
ALL-MOTHER? ALL-MOTHER, CAN YOU HEAR ME?
DAMN THESE SUMMONING STONES.
QUEEN FREYJA! THE GOD OF THUNDER WOULD HAVE WORDS WITH THEE!
THIS IS WHERE HE SHOWED ME THE TRUE DEPTHS OF HIS HORROR.
THOR? MY BOY, IS THAT YOU? YOU'LL HAVE TO SPEAK UP. THE CONGRESS IS MEETING AND YOU KNOW HOW DWARVES GET WHEN THEY'RE ANGRY.
MY QUEEN, ASGARDIA AND EVERYONE IN IT IS IN DANGER!
THIS IS WHERE I NEARLY DIED AT HIS HANDS.
WHAT ARE YOU TALKING ABOUT? HAVE YOU GOTTEN INTO TROUBLE AGAIN? PLEASE DON'T TELL ME YOUR BROTHER'S INVOLVED.
QUEEN FREYJA, LISTEN TO ME, YOU HAVE TO CALL EVERY ASGARDIAN HOME AND LOCK THE GATES BEHIND THEM! ANYONE OF IMMORTAL BLOOD IS UNDER THREAT!
THOR, WHAT'S HAPPENED? UNDER THREAT BY WHO?
THOR?
THIS IS WHERE I THOUGHT I KILLED HIM.

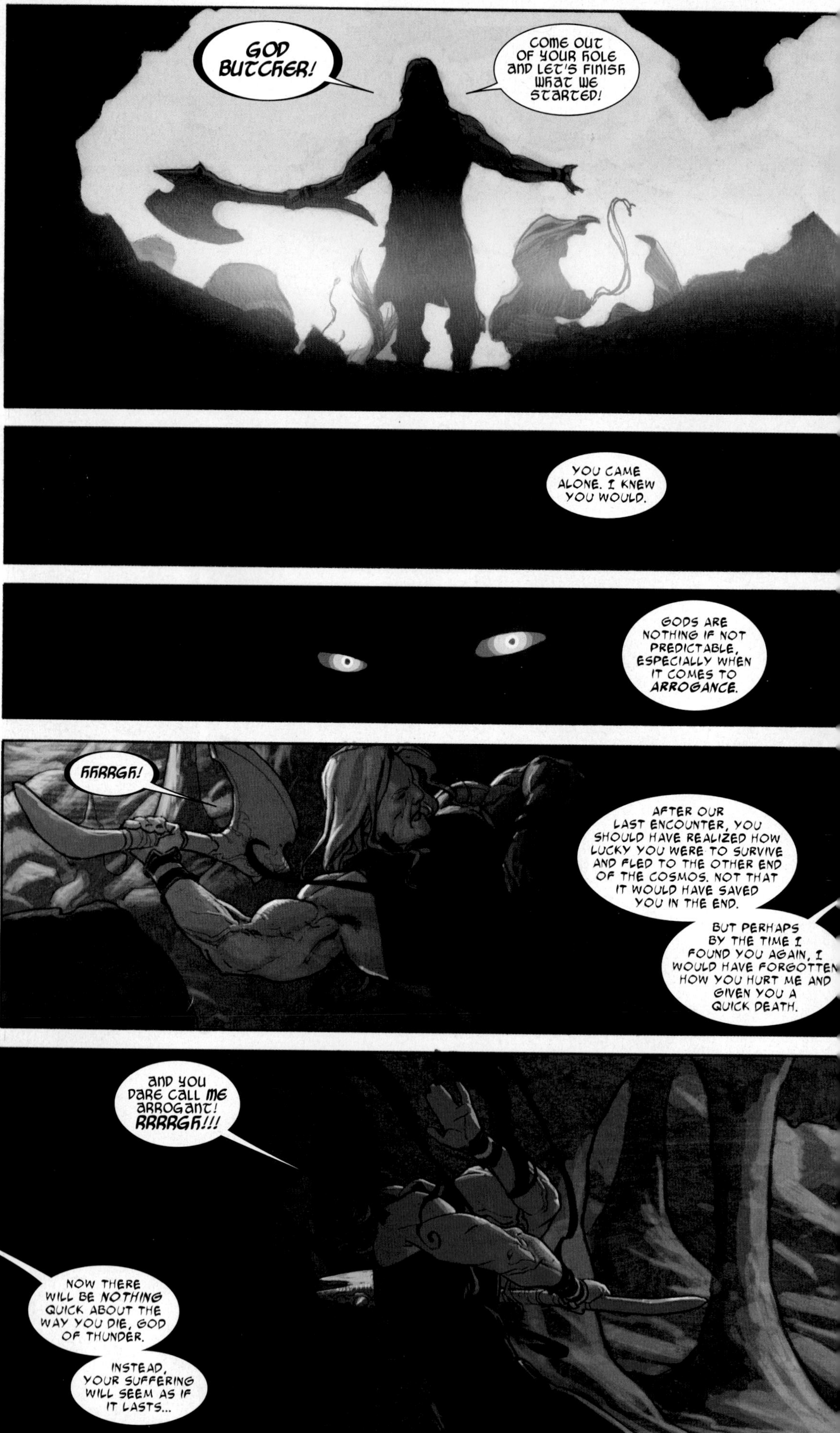
GOD BUTCHER!
COME OUT OF YOUR HOLE AND LET'S FINISH WHAT WE STARTED!
YOU CAME ALONE. I KNEW YOU WOULD.
GODS ARE NOTHING IF NOT PREDICTABLE, ESPECIALLY WHEN IT COMES TO ARROGANCE.
HHRRGH!
AFTER OUR LAST ENCOUNTER, YOU SHOULD HAVE REALIZED HOW LUCKY YOU WERE TO SURVIVE AND FLED TO THE OTHER END OF THE COSMOS. NOT THAT IT WOULD HAVE SAVED YOU IN THE END.
BUT PERHAPS BY THE TIME I FOUND YOU AGAIN, I WOULD HAVE FORGOTTEN HOW YOU HURT ME AND GIVEN YOU A QUICK DEATH.
AND YOU DARE CALL ME ARROGANT! RRRRGH!!!
NOW THERE WILL BE NOTHING QUICK ABOUT THE WAY YOU DIE, GOD OF THUNDER.
INSTEAD, YOUR SUFFERING WILL SEEM AS IF IT LASTS...

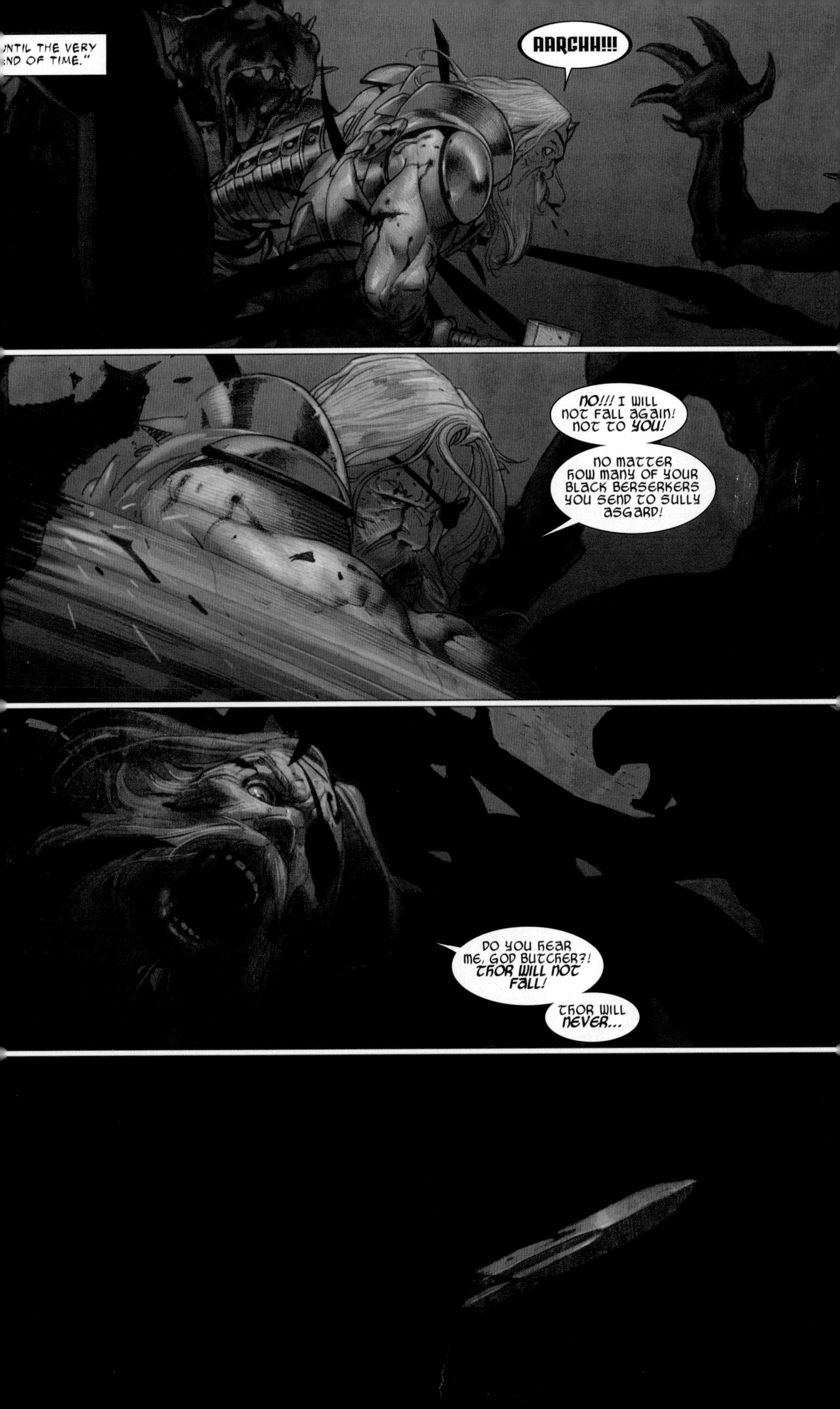

UNTIL THE VERY END OF TIME."
AARCHH!!!
NO!!! I WILL NOT FALL AGAIN! NOT TO YOU!
NO MATTER HOW MANY OF YOUR BLACK BERSERKERS YOU SEND TO SULLY ASGARD!
DO YOU HEAR ME, GOD BUTCHER?! THOR WILL NOT FALL!
THOR WILL NEVER...

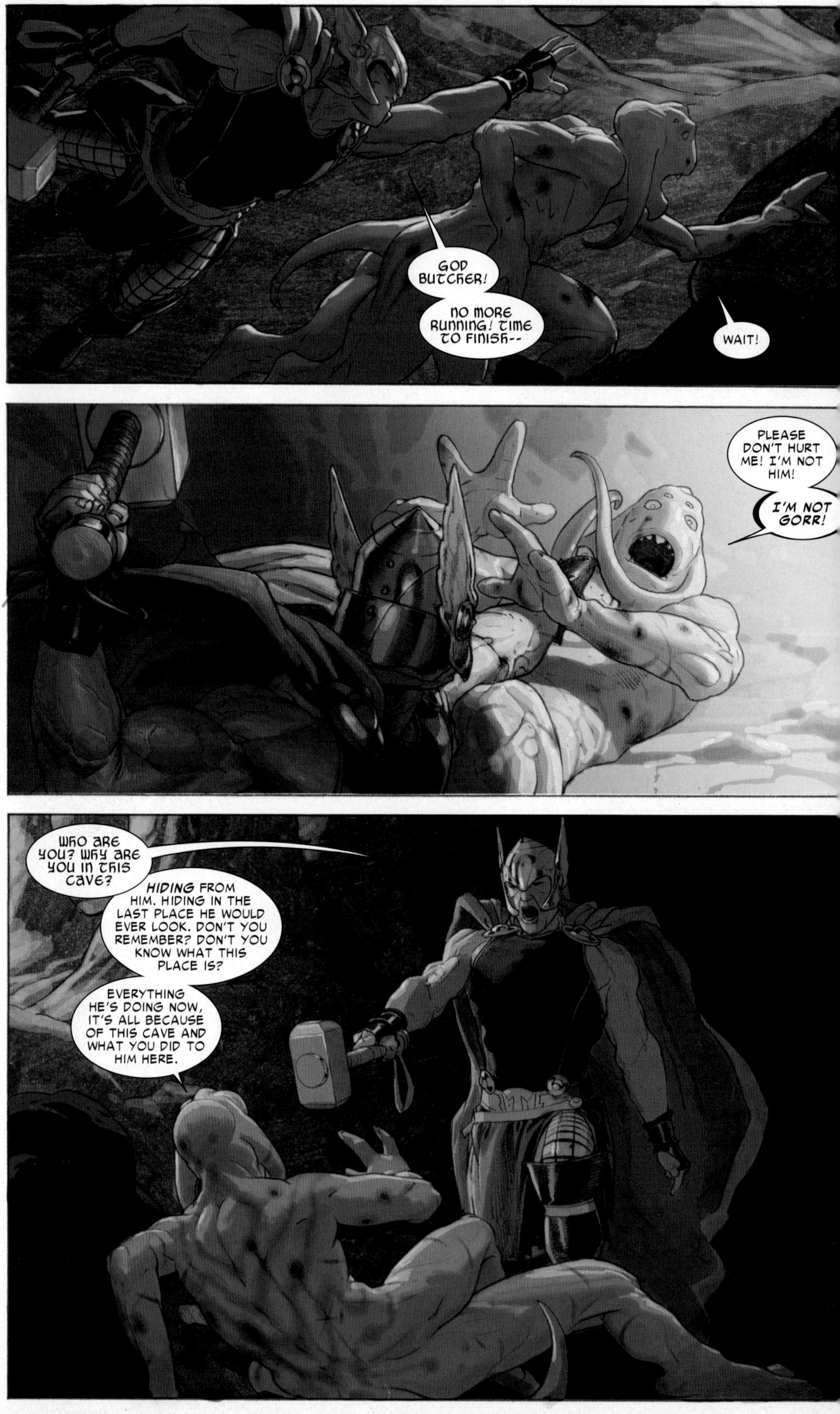
GOD BUTCHER!
NO MORE RUNNING! TIME TO FINISH--
WAIT!
PLEASE DON'T HURT ME! I'M NOT HIM!
I'M NOT GORR!
WHO ARE YOU? WHY ARE YOU IN THIS CAVE?
HIDING FROM HIM. HIDING IN THE LAST PLACE HE WOULD EVER LOOK. DON'T YOU REMEMBER? DON'T YOU KNOW WHAT THIS PLACE IS?
EVERYTHING HE'S DOING NOW, IT'S ALL BECAUSE OF THIS CAVE AND WHAT YOU DID TO HIM HERE.

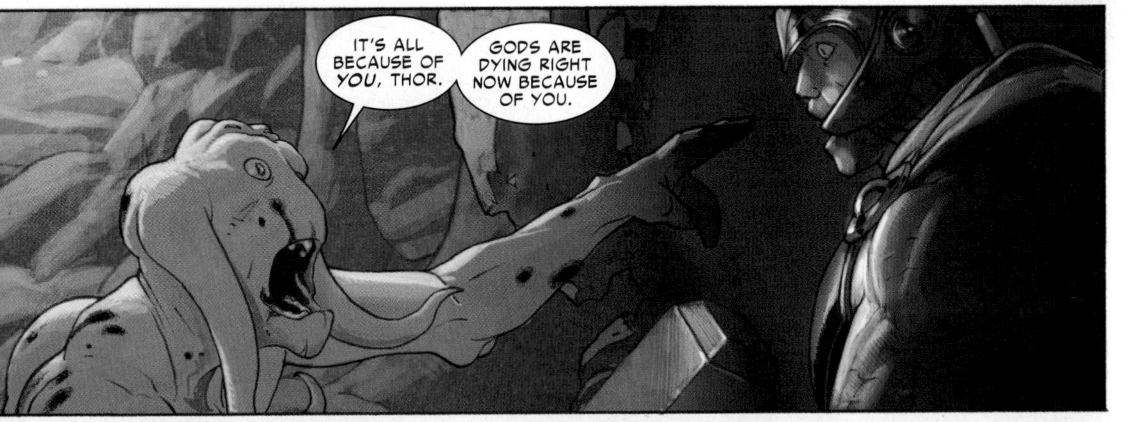
IT'S ALL BECAUSE OF YOU, THOR.
GODS ARE DYING RIGHT NOW BECAUSE OF YOU.

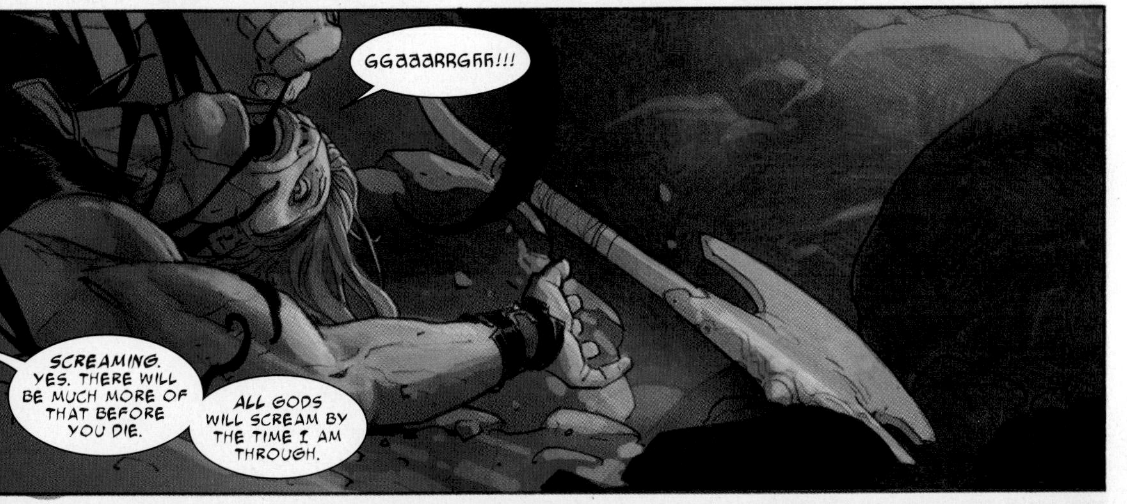
GGAAARRGHH!!!
SCREAMING. YES. THERE WILL BE MUCH MORE OF THAT BEFORE YOU DIE.
ALL GODS WILL SCREAM BY THE TIME I AM THROUGH.

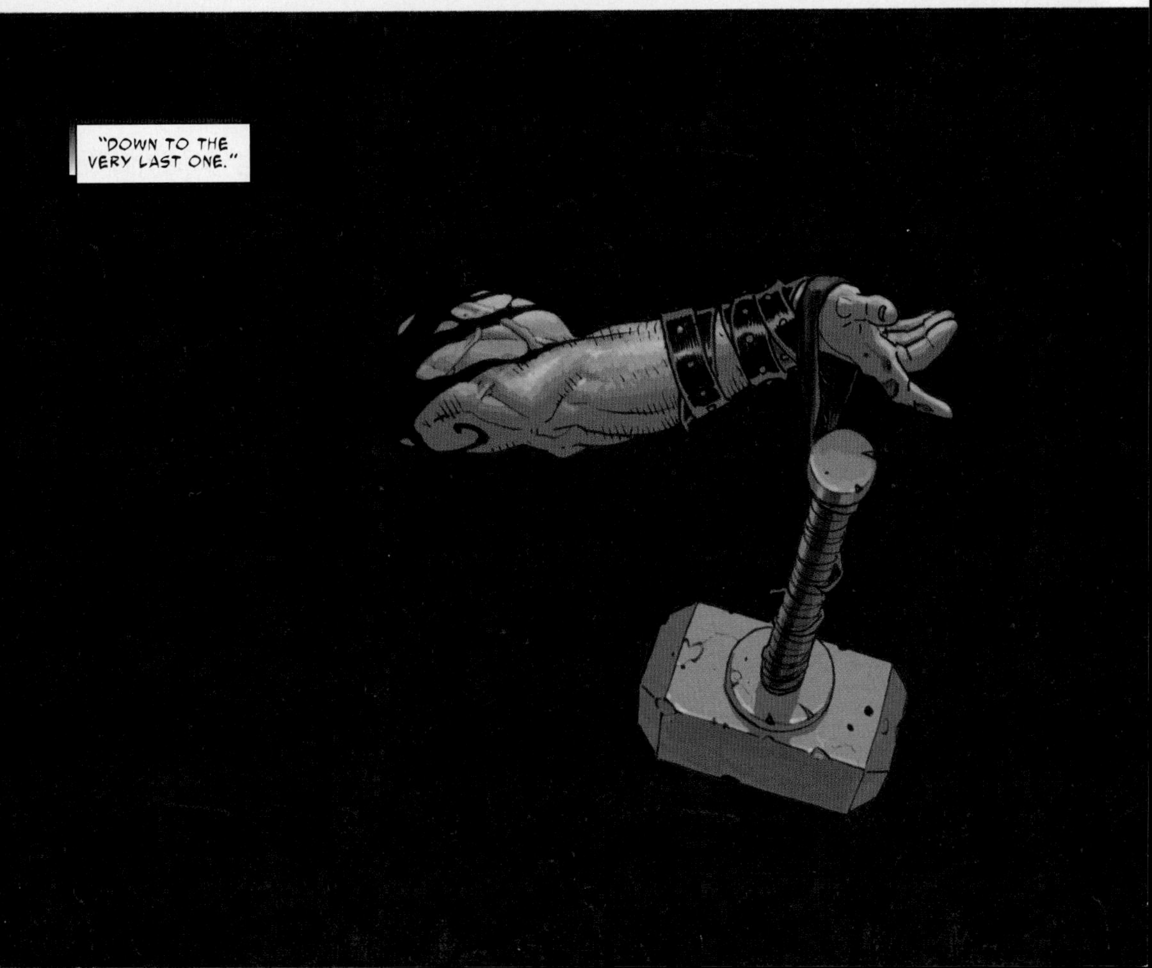
"DOWN TO THE VERY LAST ONE."

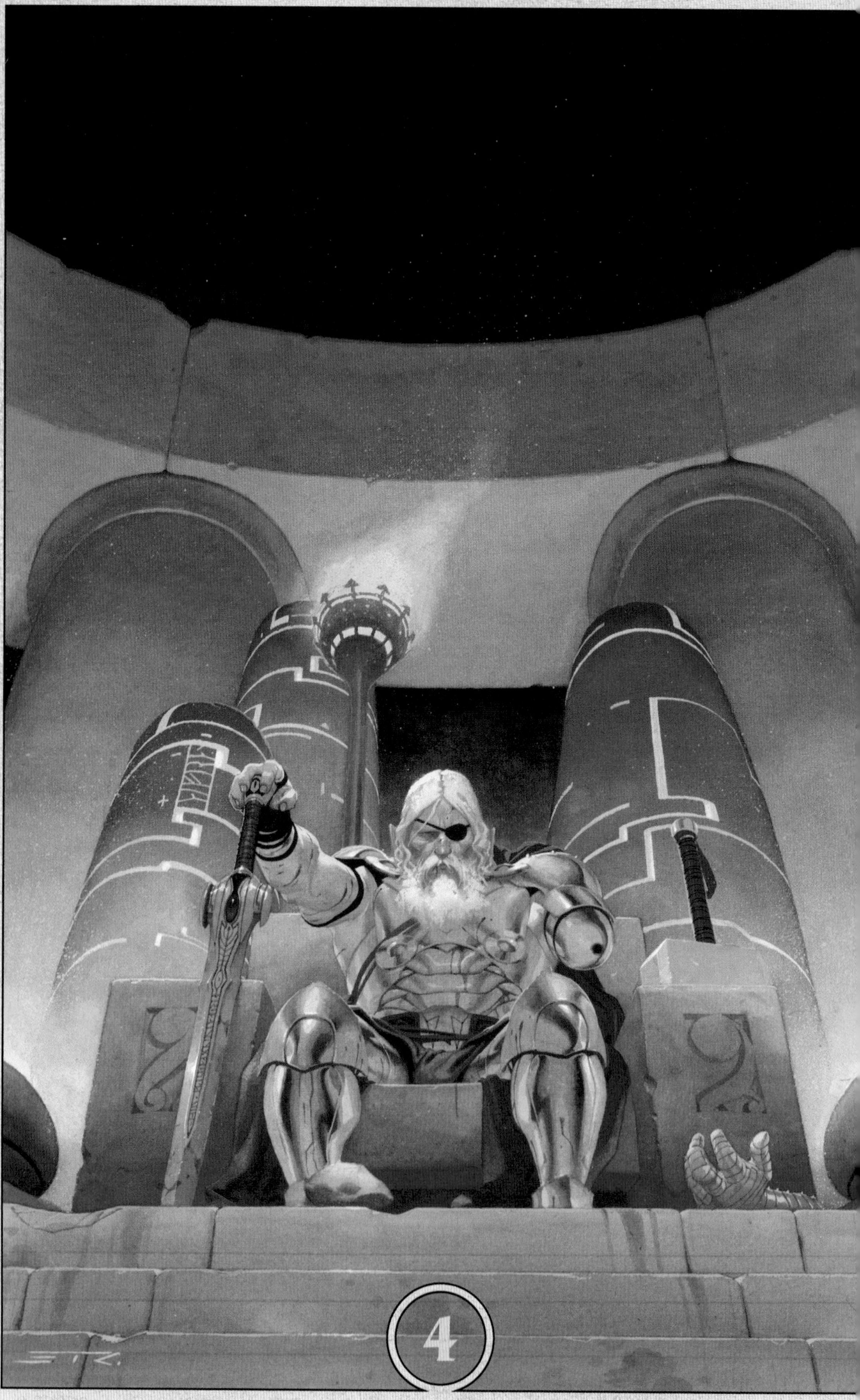
4

THE LAST GOD IN ASGARD

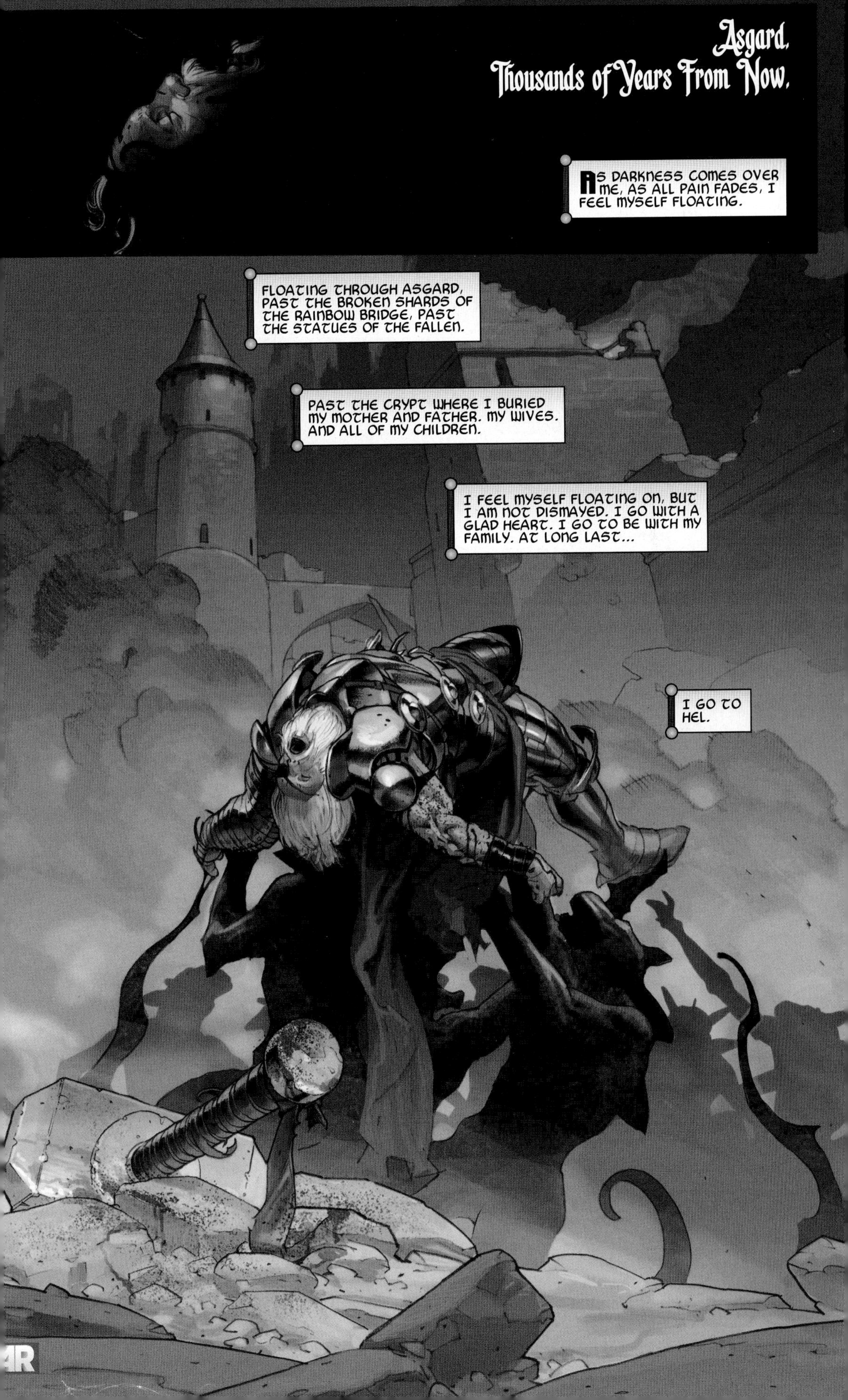

Asgard, Thousands of Years From Now.
As darkness comes over me, as all pain fades, I feel myself floating.
Floating through Asgard, past the broken shards of the rainbow bridge, past the statues of the fallen.
Past the crypt where I buried my mother and father. My wives. And all of my children.
I feel myself floating on, but I am not dismayed. I go with a glad heart. I go to be with my family. At long last...
I go to Hel.

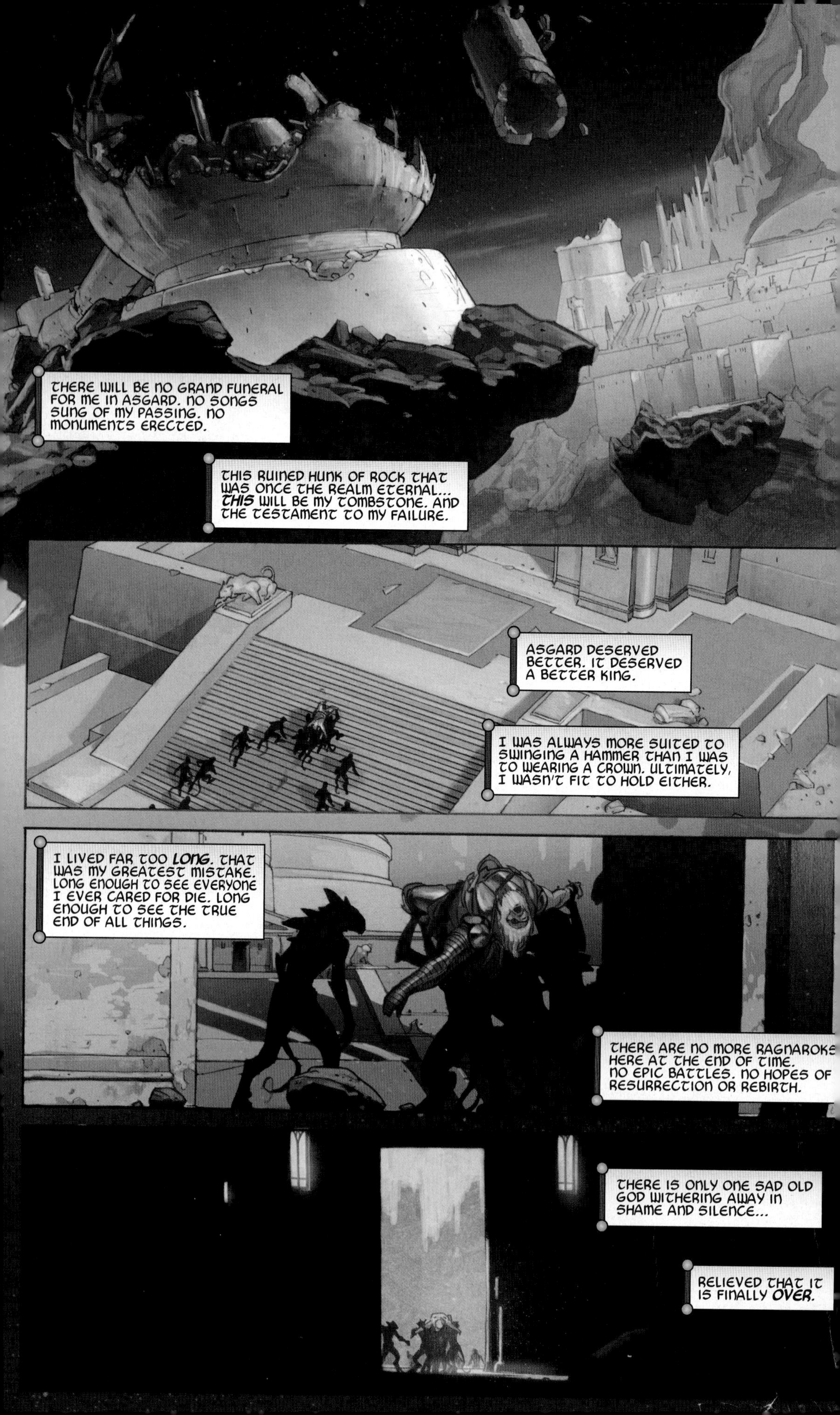
THERE WILL BE NO GRAND FUNERAL FOR ME IN ASGARD. NO SONGS SUNG OF MY PASSING. NO MONUMENTS ERECTED.
THIS RUINED HUNK OF ROCK THAT WAS ONCE THE REALM ETERNAL... *THIS* WILL BE MY TOMBSTONE. AND THE TESTAMENT TO MY FAILURE.
ASGARD DESERVED BETTER. IT DESERVED A BETTER KING.
I WAS ALWAYS MORE SUITED TO SWINGING A HAMMER THAN I WAS TO WEARING A CROWN. ULTIMATELY, I WASN'T FIT TO HOLD EITHER.
I LIVED FAR TOO *LONG*. THAT WAS MY GREATEST MISTAKE. LONG ENOUGH TO SEE EVERYONE I EVER CARED FOR DIE. LONG ENOUGH TO SEE THE TRUE END OF ALL THINGS.
THERE ARE NO MORE RAGNAROKS HERE AT THE END OF TIME. NO EPIC BATTLES. NO HOPES OF RESURRECTION OR REBIRTH.
THERE IS ONLY ONE SAD OLD GOD WITHERING AWAY IN SHAME AND SILENCE...
RELIEVED THAT IT IS FINALLY *OVER*.

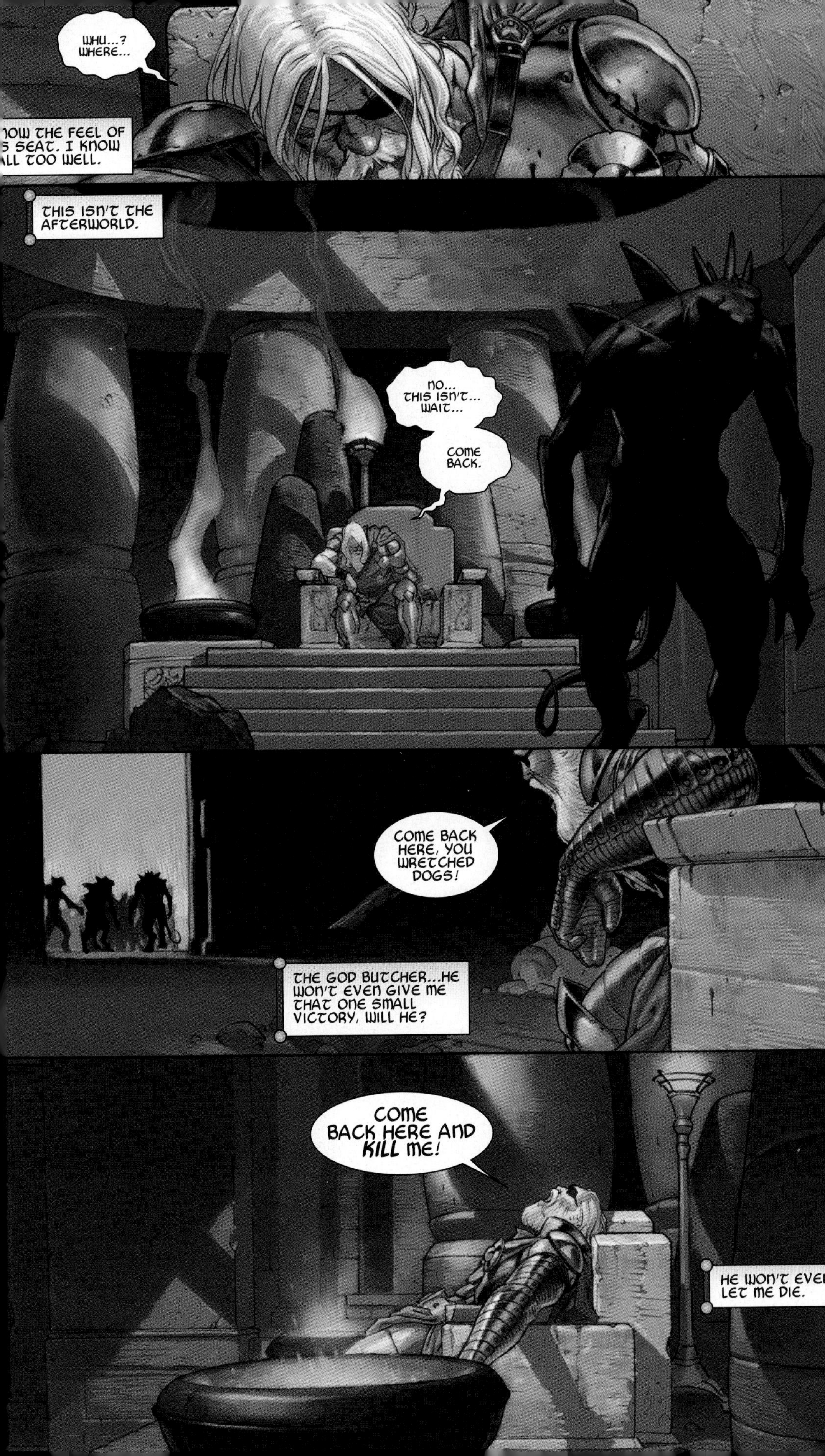
WHU...? WHERE...
...NOW THE FEEL OF ...S SEAT. I KNOW ...ALL TOO WELL.
THIS ISN'T THE AFTERWORLD.
NO... THIS ISN'T... WAIT...
COME BACK.
COME BACK HERE, YOU WRETCHED DOGS!
THE GOD BUTCHER...HE WON'T EVEN GIVE ME THAT ONE SMALL VICTORY, WILL HE?
COME BACK HERE AND KILL ME!
HE WON'T EVEN LET ME DIE.

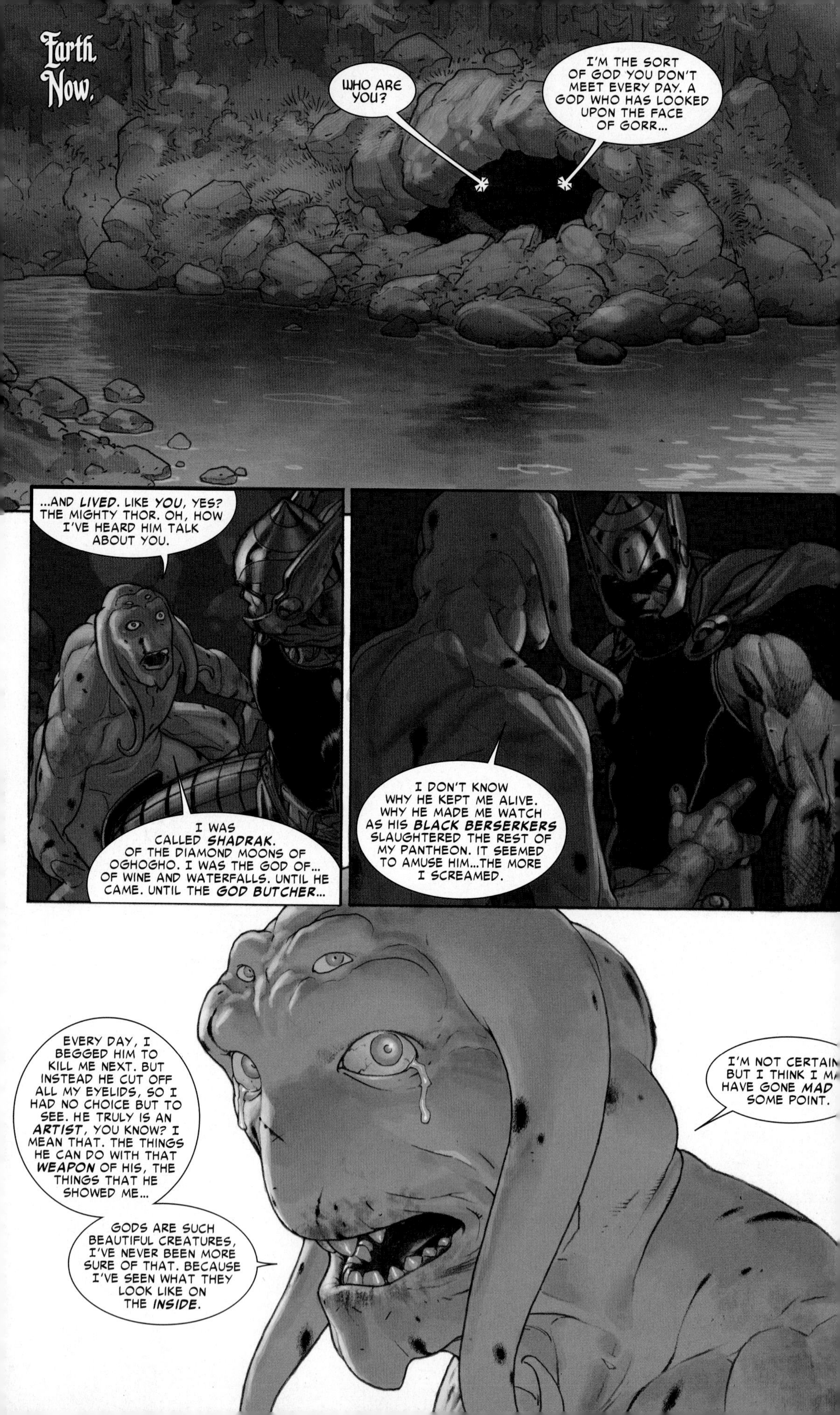
Earth. Now.
WHO ARE YOU?
I'M THE SORT OF GOD YOU DON'T MEET EVERY DAY. A GOD WHO HAS LOOKED UPON THE FACE OF GORR...
...AND LIVED. LIKE YOU, YES? THE MIGHTY THOR. OH, HOW I'VE HEARD HIM TALK ABOUT YOU.
I WAS CALLED SHADRAK. OF THE DIAMOND MOONS OF OGHOGHO. I WAS THE GOD OF... OF WINE AND WATERFALLS. UNTIL HE CAME. UNTIL THE GOD BUTCHER...
I DON'T KNOW WHY HE KEPT ME ALIVE. WHY HE MADE ME WATCH AS HIS BLACK BERSERKERS SLAUGHTERED THE REST OF MY PANTHEON. IT SEEMED TO AMUSE HIM...THE MORE I SCREAMED.
EVERY DAY, I BEGGED HIM TO KILL ME NEXT. BUT INSTEAD HE CUT OFF ALL MY EYELIDS, SO I HAD NO CHOICE BUT TO SEE. HE TRULY IS AN ARTIST, YOU KNOW? I MEAN THAT. THE THINGS HE CAN DO WITH THAT WEAPON OF HIS, THE THINGS THAT HE SHOWED ME...
GODS ARE SUCH BEAUTIFUL CREATURES, I'VE NEVER BEEN MORE SURE OF THAT. BECAUSE I'VE SEEN WHAT THEY LOOK LIKE ON THE INSIDE.
I'M NOT CERTAIN BUT I THINK I MAY HAVE GONE MAD SOME POINT.

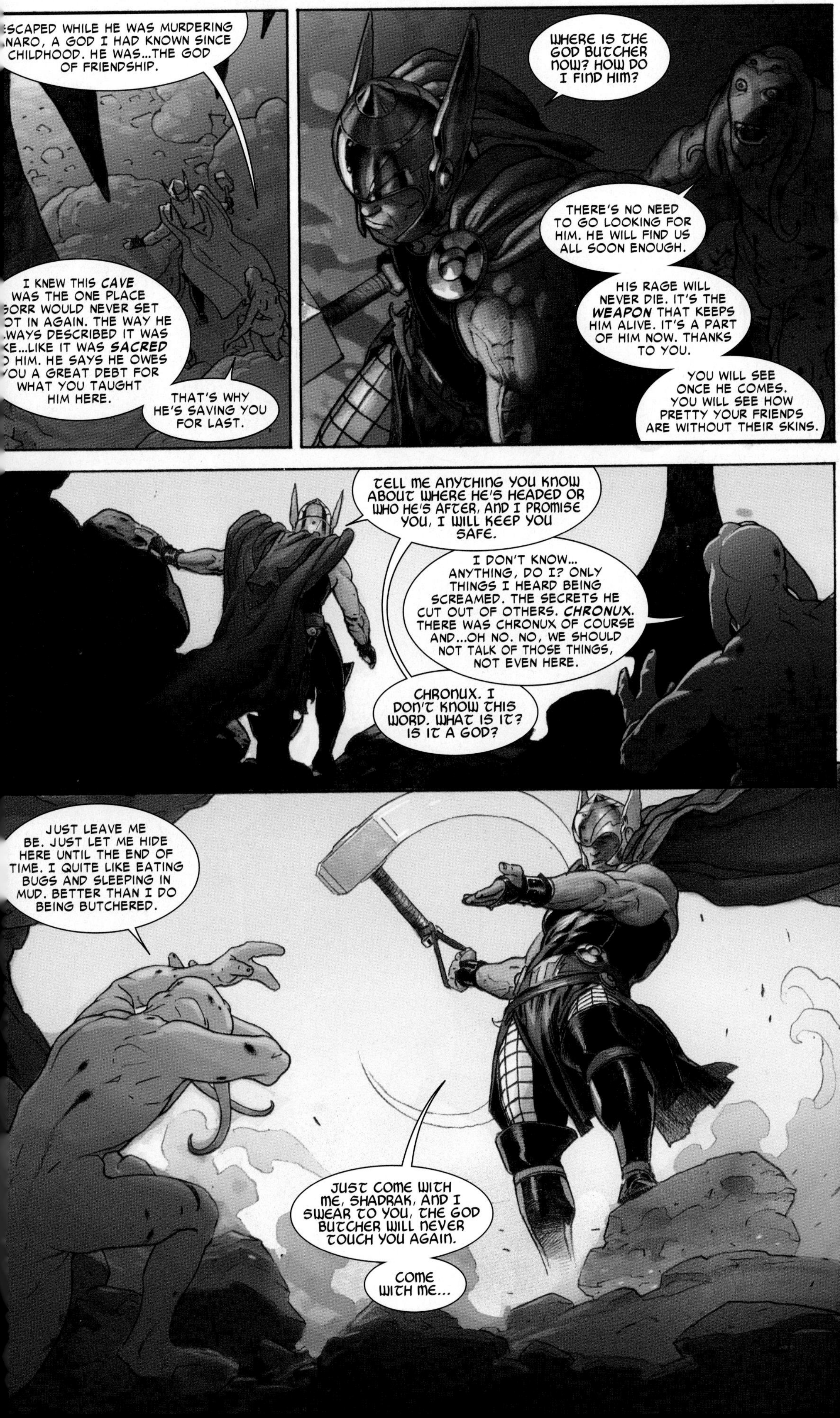
ESCAPED WHILE HE WAS MURDERING NARO, A GOD I HAD KNOWN SINCE CHILDHOOD. HE WAS...THE GOD OF FRIENDSHIP.
I KNEW THIS CAVE WAS THE ONE PLACE GORR WOULD NEVER SET OT IN AGAIN. THE WAY HE LWAYS DESCRIBED IT WAS KE...LIKE IT WAS SACRED D HIM. HE SAYS HE OWES YOU A GREAT DEBT FOR WHAT YOU TAUGHT HIM HERE.
THAT'S WHY HE'S SAVING YOU FOR LAST.
WHERE IS THE GOD BUTCHER NOW? HOW DO I FIND HIM?
THERE'S NO NEED TO GO LOOKING FOR HIM. HE WILL FIND US ALL SOON ENOUGH.
HIS RAGE WILL NEVER DIE. IT'S THE WEAPON THAT KEEPS HIM ALIVE. IT'S A PART OF HIM NOW. THANKS TO YOU.
YOU WILL SEE ONCE HE COMES. YOU WILL SEE HOW PRETTY YOUR FRIENDS ARE WITHOUT THEIR SKINS.
TELL ME ANYTHING YOU KNOW ABOUT WHERE HE'S HEADED OR WHO HE'S AFTER, AND I PROMISE YOU, I WILL KEEP YOU SAFE.
I DON'T KNOW... ANYTHING, DO I? ONLY THINGS I HEARD BEING SCREAMED. THE SECRETS HE CUT OUT OF OTHERS. CHRONUX. THERE WAS CHRONUX OF COURSE AND...OH NO. NO, WE SHOULD NOT TALK OF THOSE THINGS, NOT EVEN HERE.
CHRONUX. I DON'T KNOW THIS WORD. WHAT IS IT? IS IT A GOD?
JUST LEAVE ME BE. JUST LET ME HIDE HERE UNTIL THE END OF TIME. I QUITE LIKE EATING BUGS AND SLEEPING IN MUD. BETTER THAN I DO BEING BUTCHERED.
JUST COME WITH ME, SHADRAK, AND I SWEAR TO YOU, THE GOD BUTCHER WILL NEVER TOUCH YOU AGAIN.
COME WITH ME...

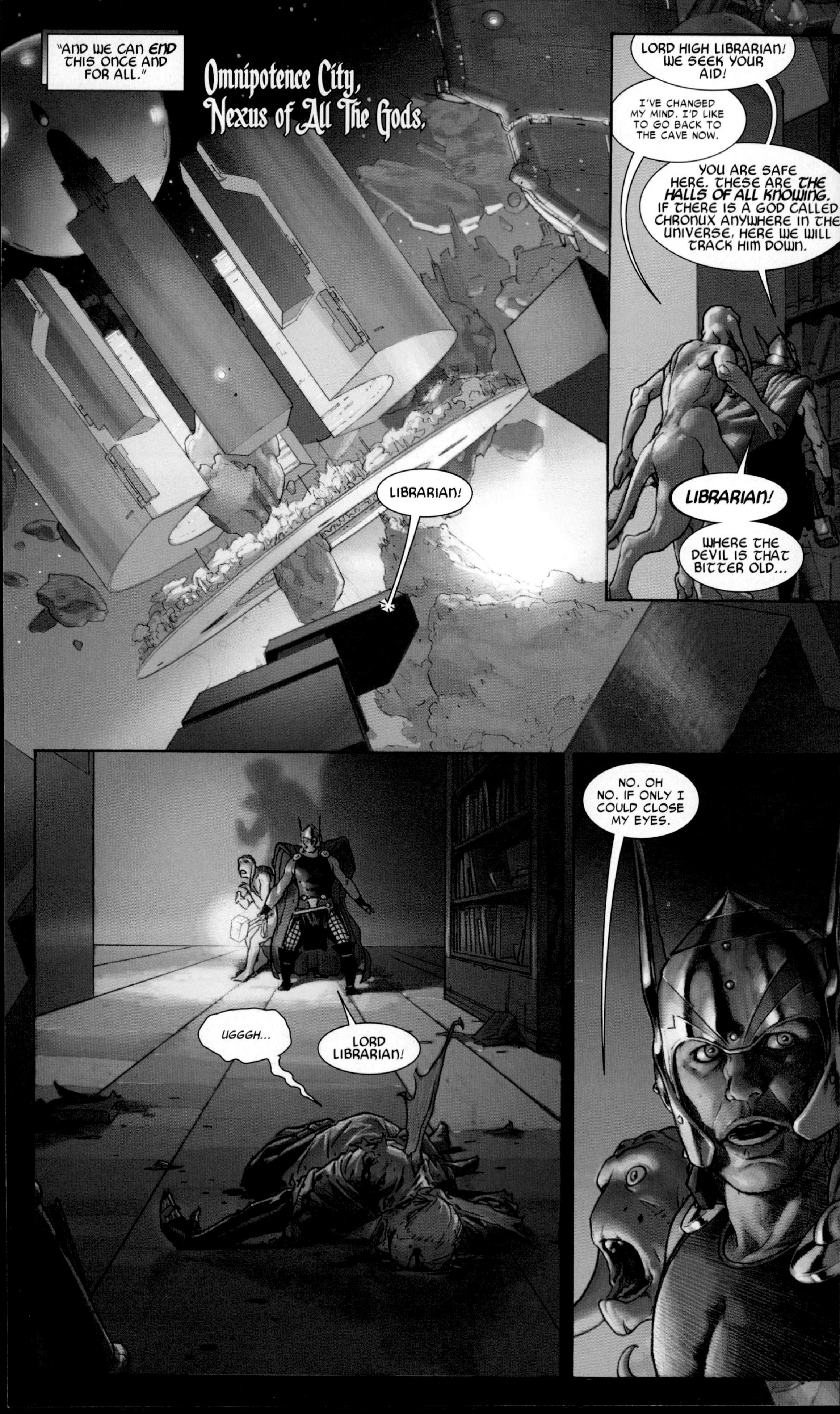
"AND WE CAN END THIS ONCE AND FOR ALL."
Omnipotence City, Nexus of All The Gods,
LIBRARIAN!
LORD HIGH LIBRARIAN! WE SEEK YOUR AID!
I'VE CHANGED MY MIND. I'D LIKE TO GO BACK TO THE CAVE NOW.
YOU ARE SAFE HERE. THESE ARE THE HALLS OF ALL KNOWING. IF THERE IS A GOD CALLED CHRONUX ANYWHERE IN THE UNIVERSE, HERE WE WILL TRACK HIM DOWN.
LIBRARIAN!
WHERE THE DEVIL IS THAT BITTER OLD...
UGGGH...
LORD LIBRARIAN!
NO. OH NO. IF ONLY I COULD CLOSE MY EYES.

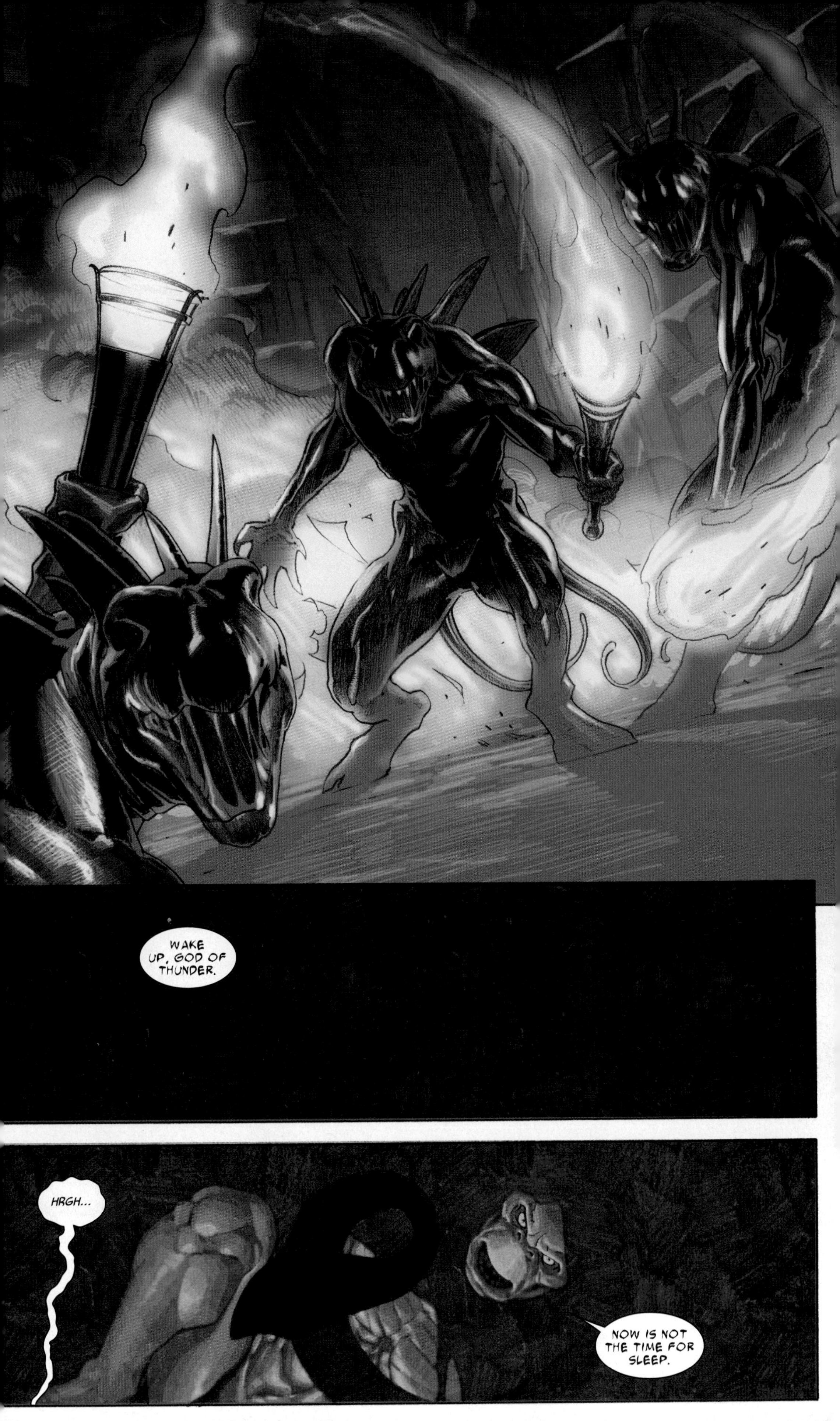
WAKE UP, GOD OF THUNDER.
HRGH...
NOW IS NOT THE TIME FOR SLEEP.

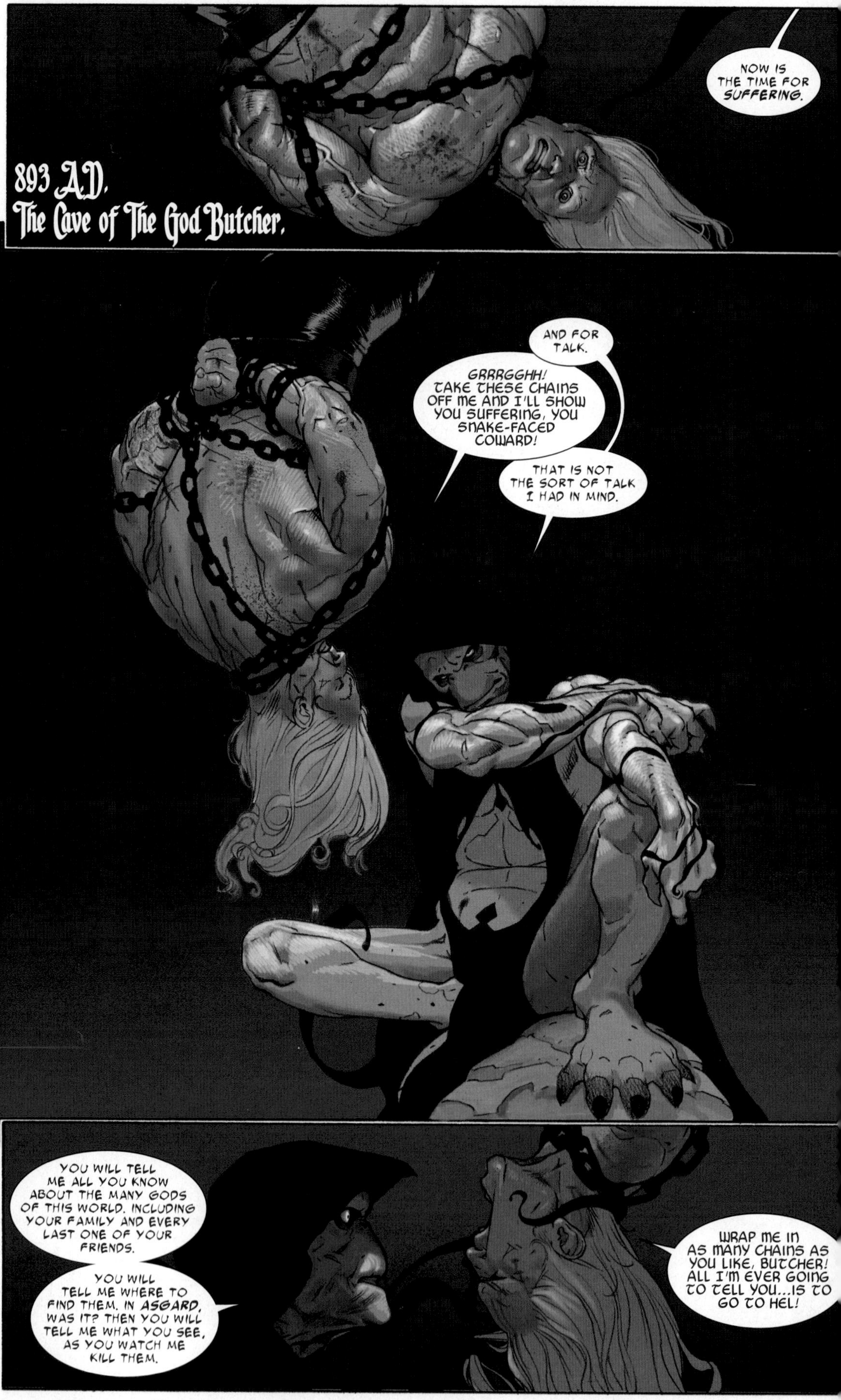
893 A.D.
The Cave of The God Butcher.
NOW IS THE TIME FOR SUFFERING.
AND FOR TALK.
GRRRGGHH! TAKE THESE CHAINS OFF ME AND I'LL SHOW YOU SUFFERING, YOU SNAKE-FACED COWARD!
THAT IS NOT THE SORT OF TALK I HAD IN MIND.
YOU WILL TELL ME ALL YOU KNOW ABOUT THE MANY GODS OF THIS WORLD. INCLUDING YOUR FAMILY AND EVERY LAST ONE OF YOUR FRIENDS.
YOU WILL TELL ME WHERE TO FIND THEM. IN ASGARD, WAS IT? THEN YOU WILL TELL ME WHAT YOU SEE, AS YOU WATCH ME KILL THEM.
WRAP ME IN AS MANY CHAINS AS YOU LIKE, BUTCHER! ALL I'M EVER GOING TO TELL YOU...IS TO GO TO HEL!

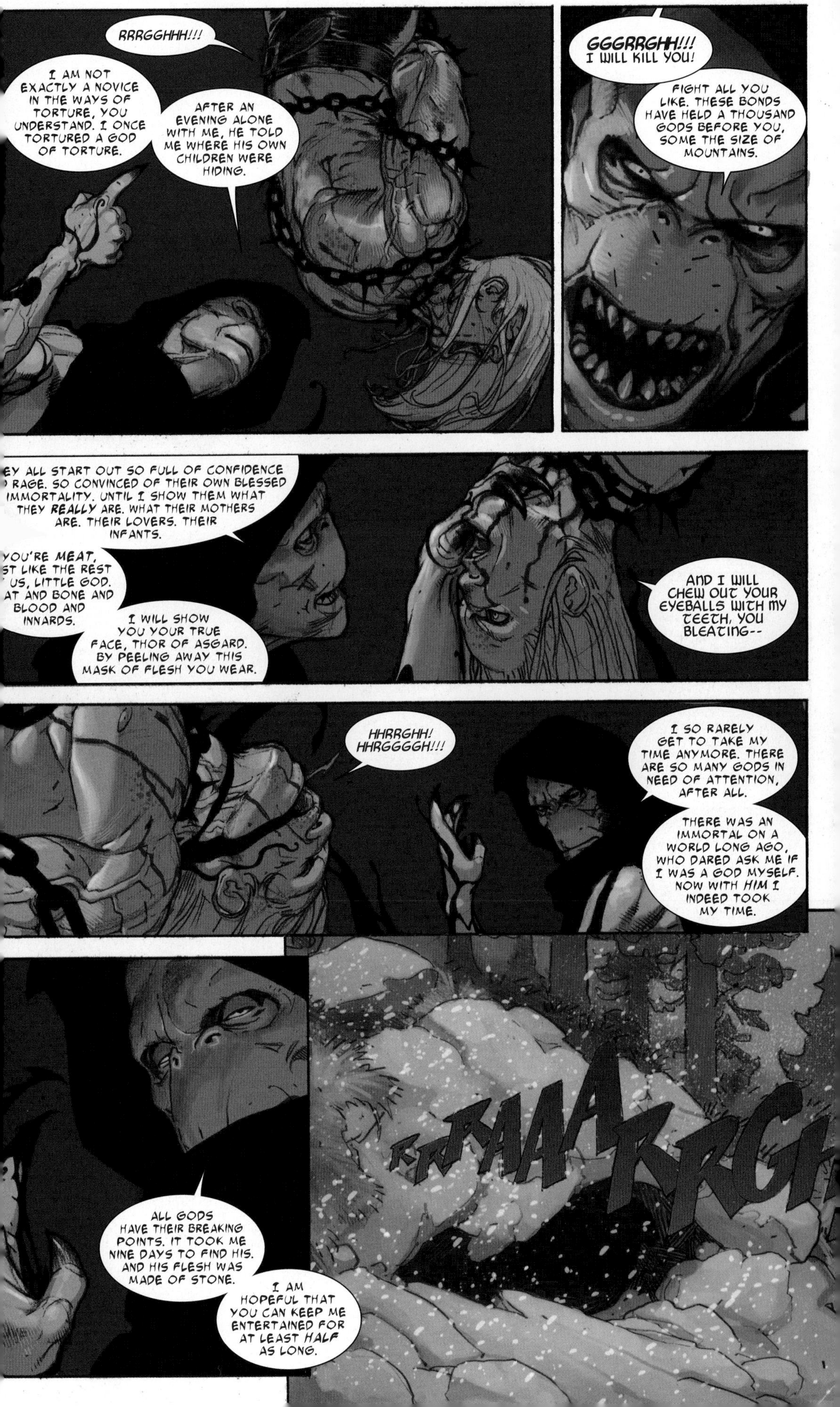
RRRGGHHH!!!
I AM NOT EXACTLY A NOVICE IN THE WAYS OF TORTURE, YOU UNDERSTAND. I ONCE TORTURED A GOD OF TORTURE.
AFTER AN EVENING ALONE WITH ME, HE TOLD ME WHERE HIS OWN CHILDREN WERE HIDING.
GGGRRGHH!!! I WILL KILL YOU!
FIGHT ALL YOU LIKE. THESE BONDS HAVE HELD A THOUSAND GODS BEFORE YOU, SOME THE SIZE OF MOUNTAINS.
EY ALL START OUT SO FULL OF CONFIDENCE RAGE. SO CONVINCED OF THEIR OWN BLESSED IMMORTALITY. UNTIL I SHOW THEM WHAT THEY REALLY ARE. WHAT THEIR MOTHERS ARE. THEIR LOVERS. THEIR INFANTS.
YOU'RE MEAT, ST LIKE THE REST US, LITTLE GOD. AT AND BONE AND BLOOD AND INNARDS.
I WILL SHOW YOU YOUR TRUE FACE, THOR OF ASGARD. BY PEELING AWAY THIS MASK OF FLESH YOU WEAR.
AND I WILL CHEW OUT YOUR EYEBALLS WITH MY TEETH, YOU BLEATING--
HHRRGHH! HHRGGGGH!!!
I SO RARELY GET TO TAKE MY TIME ANYMORE. THERE ARE SO MANY GODS IN NEED OF ATTENTION, AFTER ALL.
THERE WAS AN IMMORTAL ON A WORLD LONG AGO, WHO DARED ASK ME IF I WAS A GOD MYSELF. NOW WITH HIM I INDEED TOOK MY TIME.
ALL GODS HAVE THEIR BREAKING POINTS. IT TOOK ME NINE DAYS TO FIND HIS. AND HIS FLESH WAS MADE OF STONE.
I AM HOPEFUL THAT YOU CAN KEEP ME ENTERTAINED FOR AT LEAST HALF AS LONG.
RRRAAARRGH

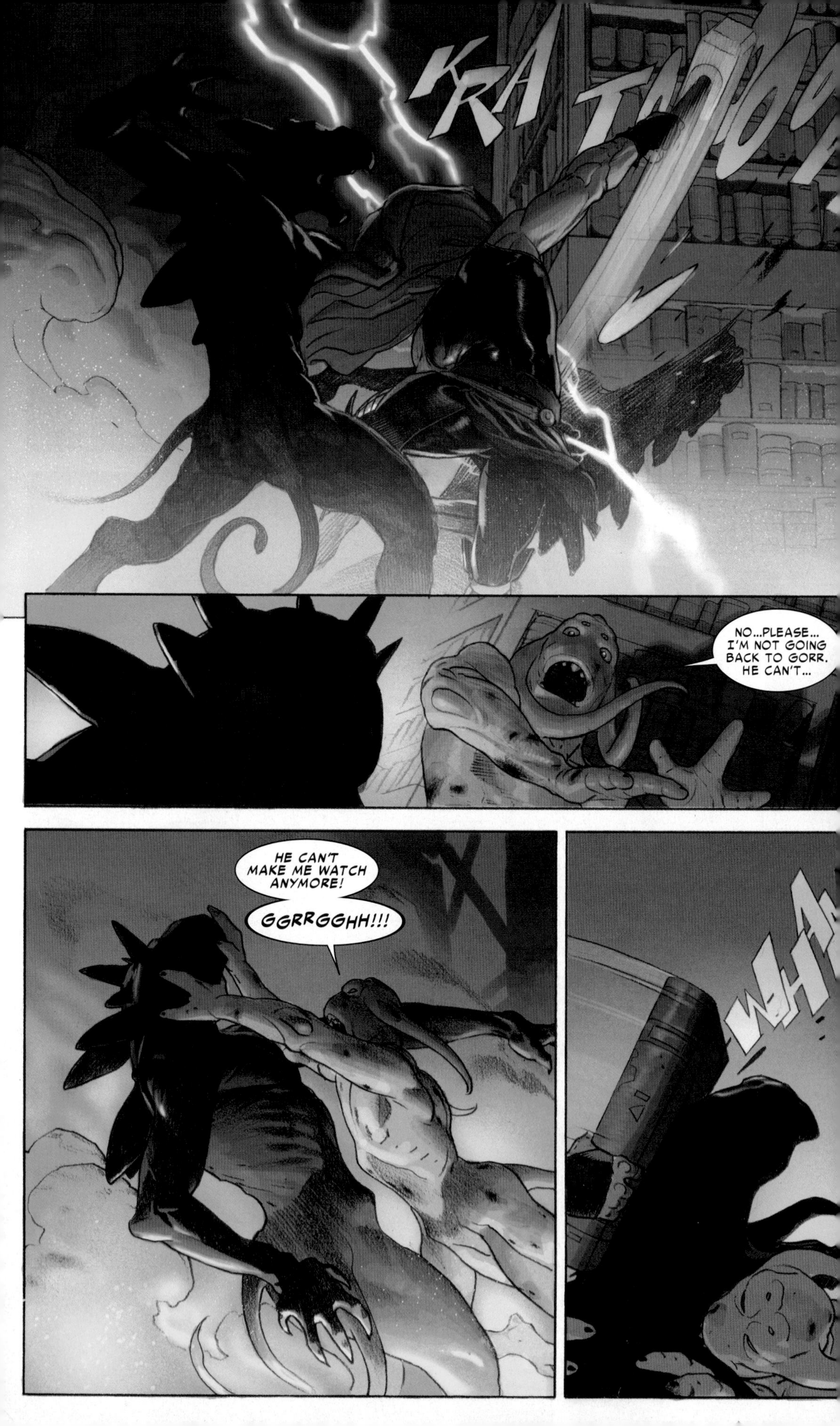
KRA TADOOM
NO...PLEASE... I'M NOT GOING BACK TO GORR. HE CAN'T...
HE CAN'T MAKE ME WATCH ANYMORE!
GGRRGGHH!!!
WHA

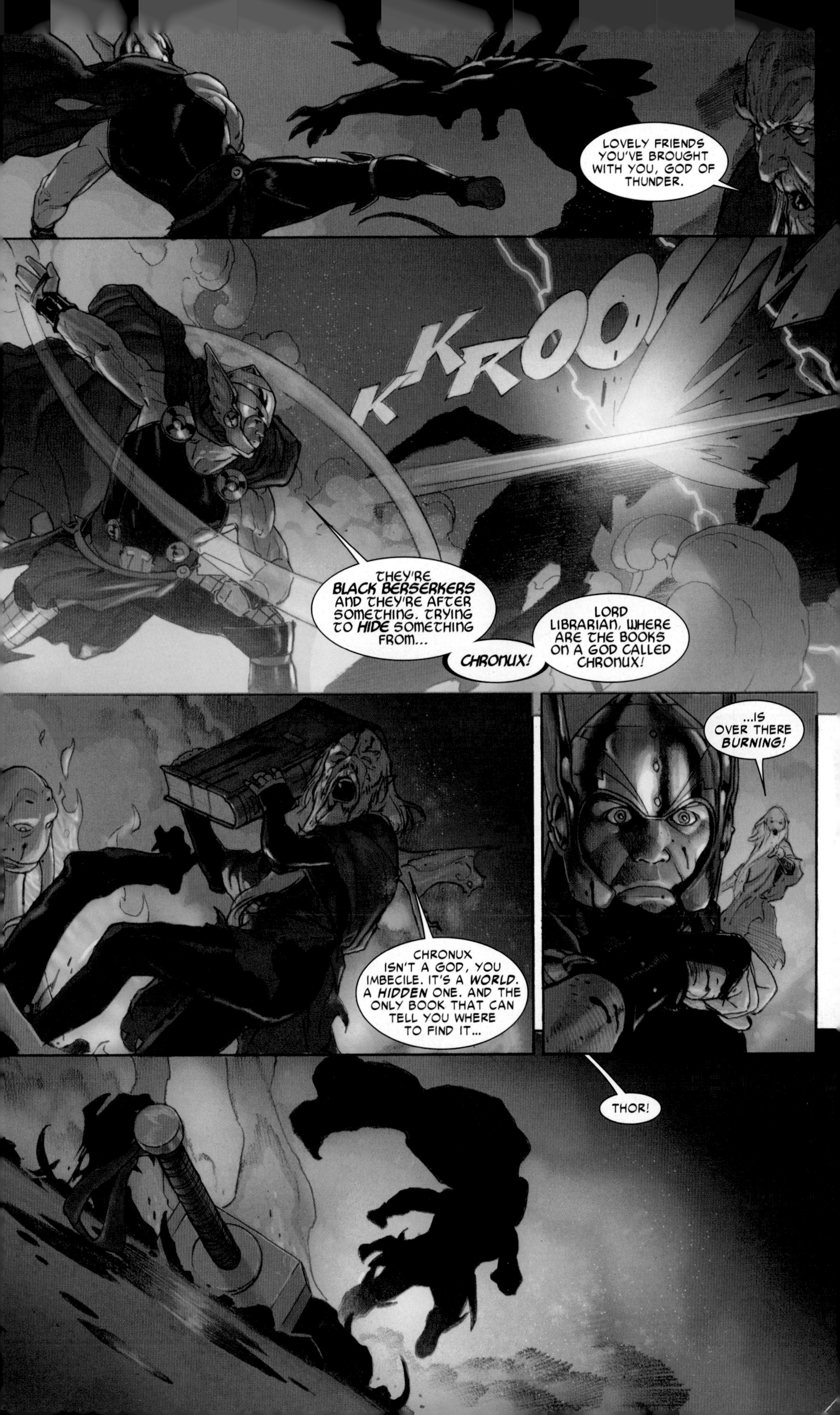
LOVELY FRIENDS YOU'VE BROUGHT WITH YOU, GOD OF THUNDER.
KKKROOOM
THEY'RE BLACK BERSERKERS AND THEY'RE AFTER SOMETHING. TRYING TO HIDE SOMETHING FROM...
CHRONUX!
LORD LIBRARIAN, WHERE ARE THE BOOKS ON A GOD CALLED CHRONUX!
CHRONUX ISN'T A GOD, YOU IMBECILE. IT'S A WORLD. A HIDDEN ONE. AND THE ONLY BOOK THAT CAN TELL YOU WHERE TO FIND IT...
...IS OVER THERE BURNING!
THOR!

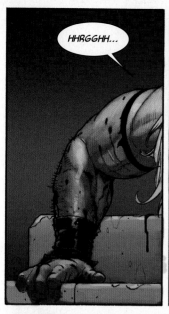

HHRGGHH...

I WILL NOT SIT... ON THAT BLASTED THRONE...A SECOND LONGER.

IF I CANNOT WALK TO MY DEATH LIKE A GOD OF THE VIKINGS...

I WILL *CRAWL* TO IT...LIKE A WOUNDED DOG.

COME, MJOLNIR, OLD FRIEND.

SHOW ME THERE'S STILL SOME MAGIC LEFT IN THESE DEAD HALLS.

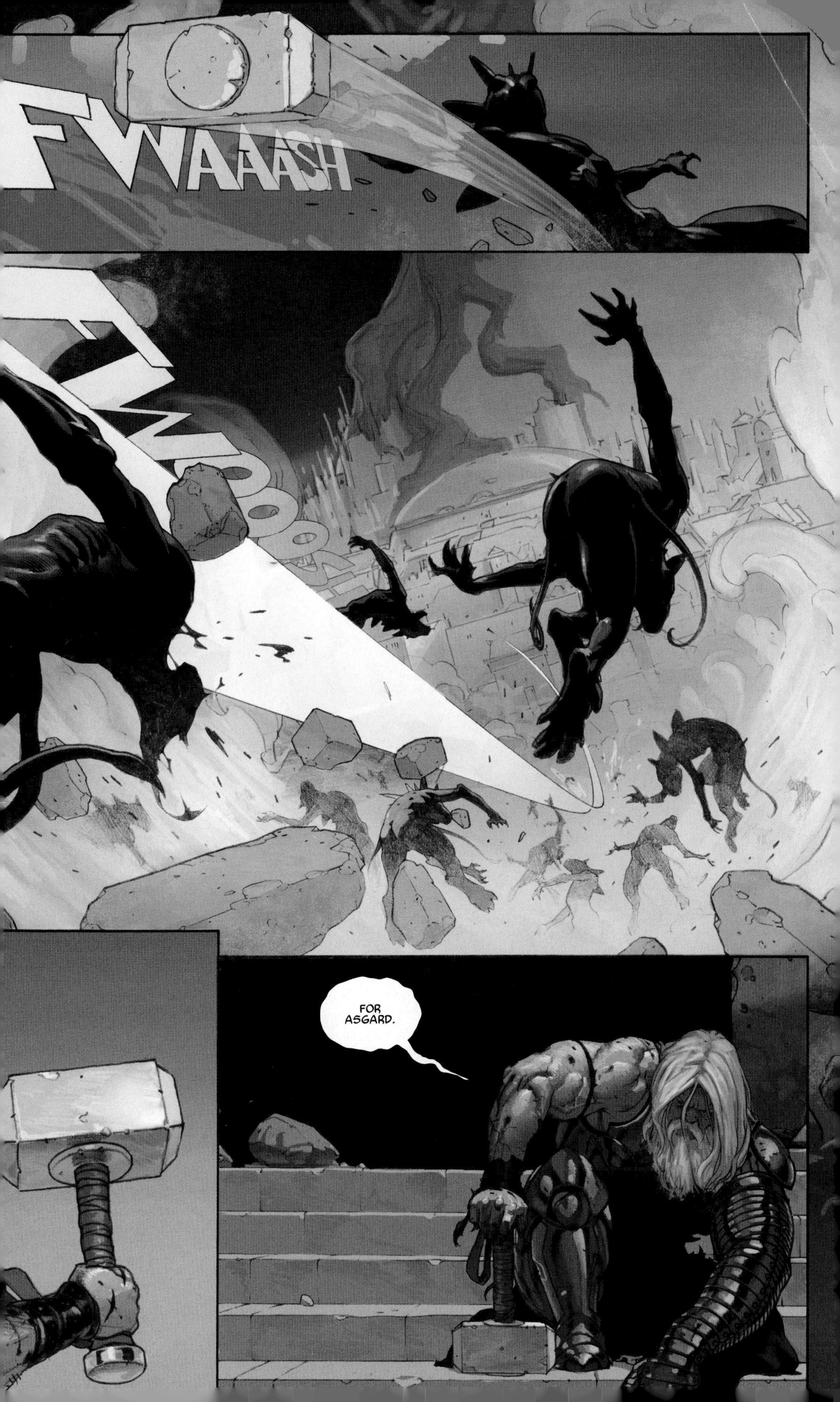
FWAAASH
FOR ASGARD.

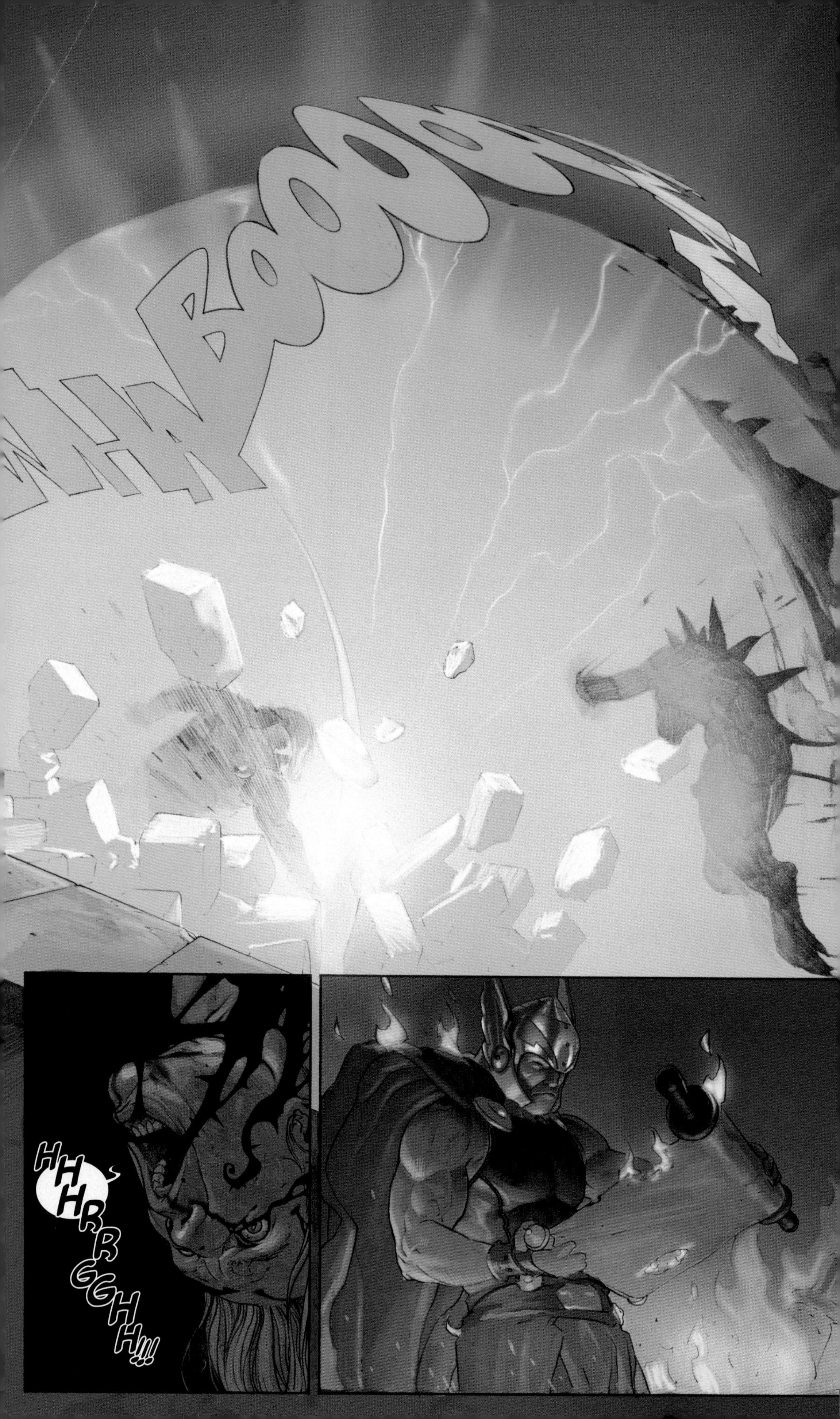
WHABOOOOM
HHHRRRGGHH!!!

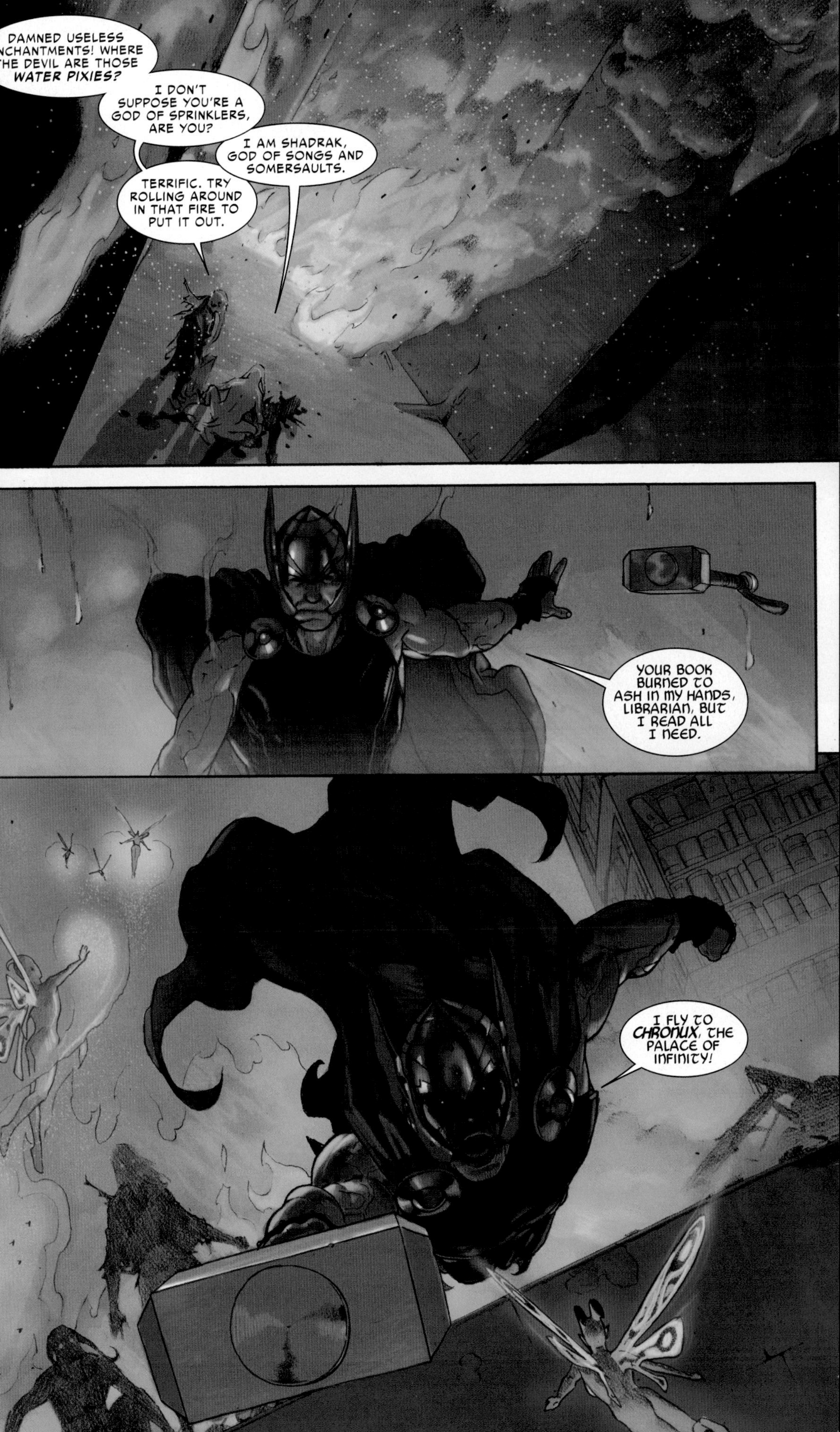
DAMNED USELESS ENCHANTMENTS! WHERE THE DEVIL ARE THOSE WATER PIXIES?
I DON'T SUPPOSE YOU'RE A GOD OF SPRINKLERS, ARE YOU?
I AM SHADRAK, GOD OF SONGS AND SOMERSAULTS.
TERRIFIC. TRY ROLLING AROUND IN THAT FIRE TO PUT IT OUT.
YOUR BOOK BURNED TO ASH IN MY HANDS, LIBRARIAN, BUT I READ ALL I NEED.
I FLY TO CHRONUX, THE PALACE OF INFINITY!

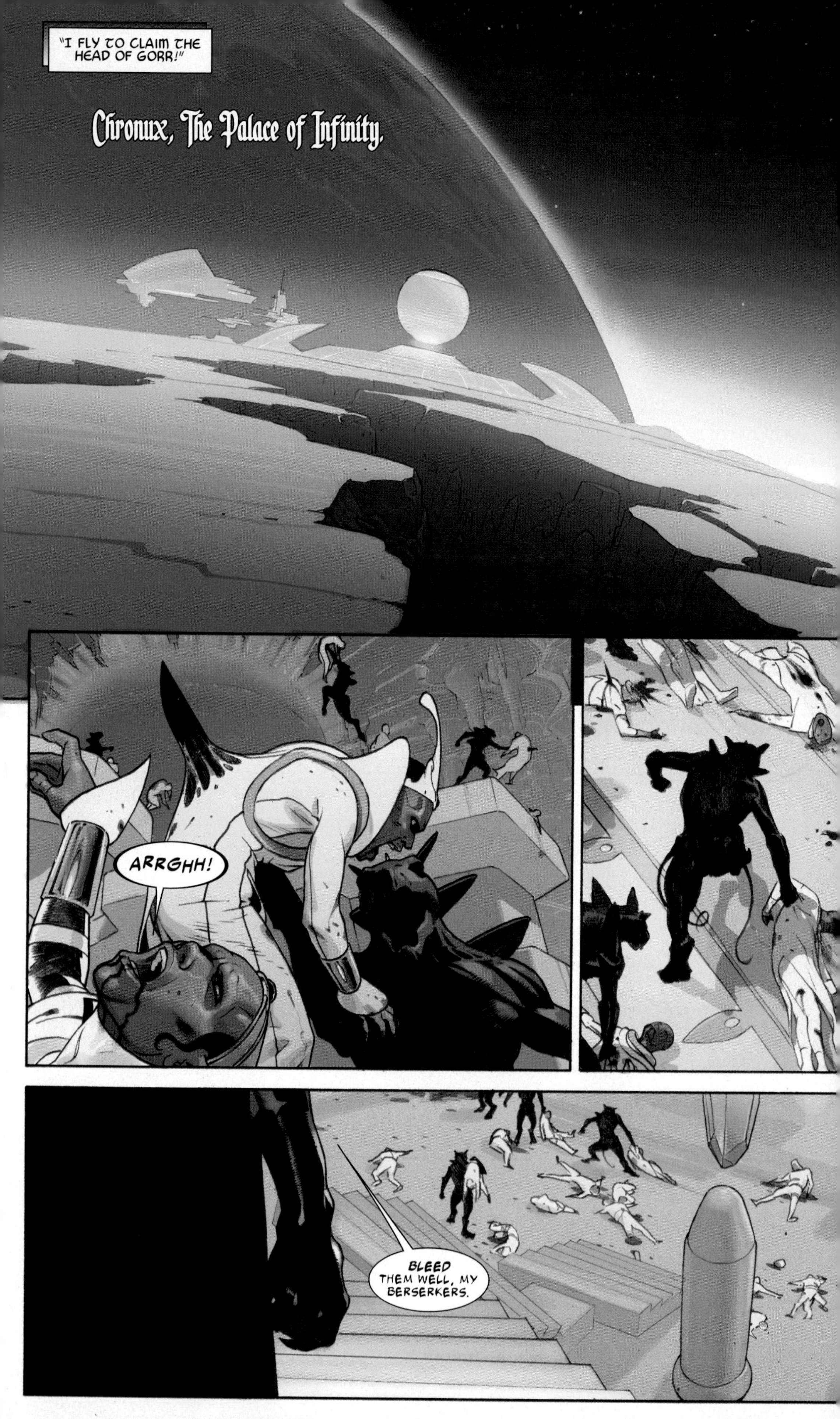
"I FLY TO CLAIM THE HEAD OF GORR!"
Chronux, The Palace of Infinity.
ARRGHH!
BLEED THEM WELL, MY BERSERKERS.

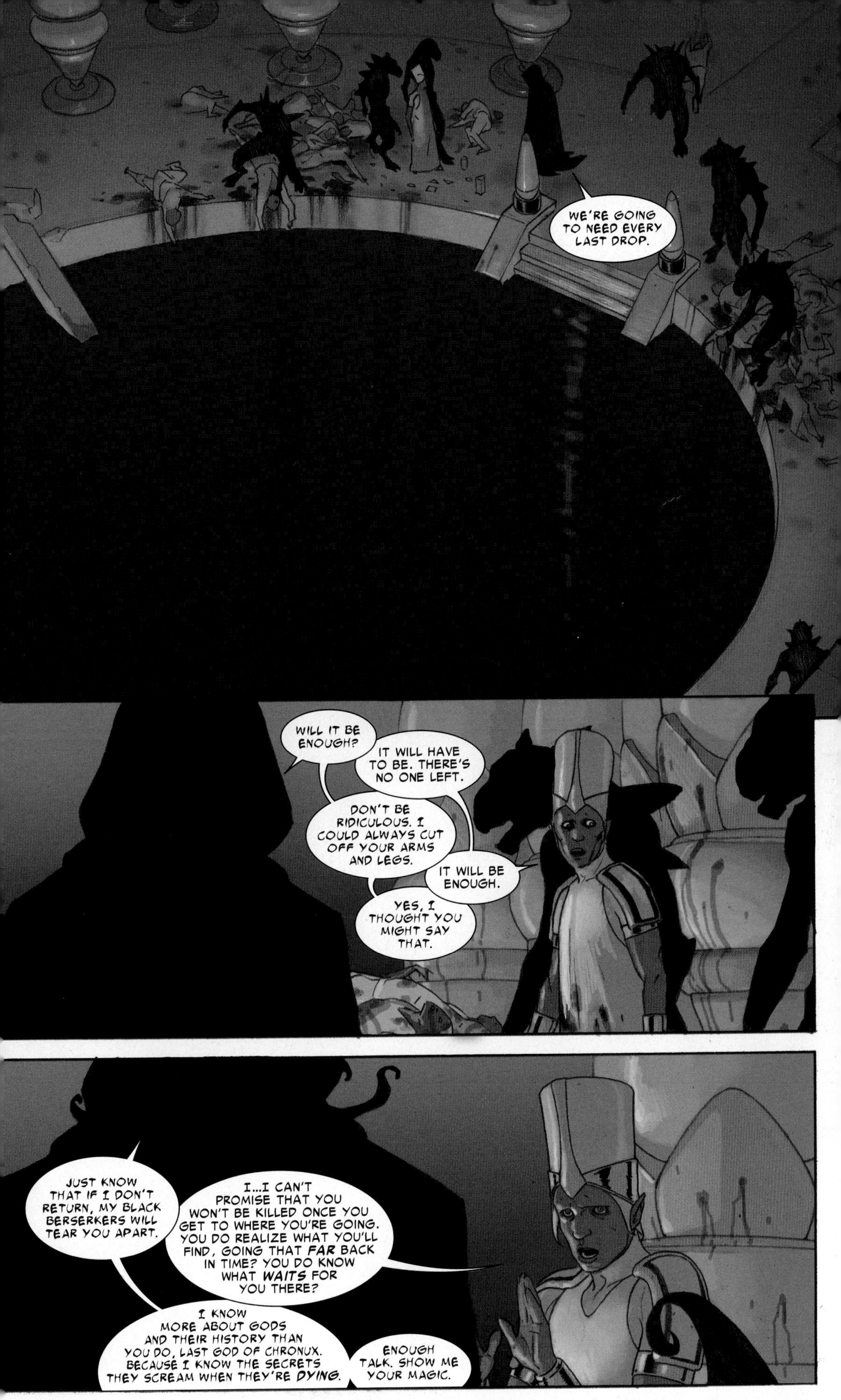
WE'RE GOING TO NEED EVERY LAST DROP.
WILL IT BE ENOUGH?
IT WILL HAVE TO BE. THERE'S NO ONE LEFT.
DON'T BE RIDICULOUS. I COULD ALWAYS CUT OFF YOUR ARMS AND LEGS.
IT WILL BE ENOUGH.
YES, I THOUGHT YOU MIGHT SAY THAT.
JUST KNOW THAT IF I DON'T RETURN, MY BLACK BERSERKERS WILL TEAR YOU APART.
I...I CAN'T PROMISE THAT YOU WON'T BE KILLED ONCE YOU GET TO WHERE YOU'RE GOING. YOU DO REALIZE WHAT YOU'LL FIND, GOING THAT FAR BACK IN TIME? YOU DO KNOW WHAT WAITS FOR YOU THERE?
I KNOW MORE ABOUT GODS AND THEIR HISTORY THAN YOU DO, LAST GOD OF CHRONUX. BECAUSE I KNOW THE SECRETS THEY SCREAM WHEN THEY'RE DYING.
ENOUGH TALK. SHOW ME YOUR MAGIC.

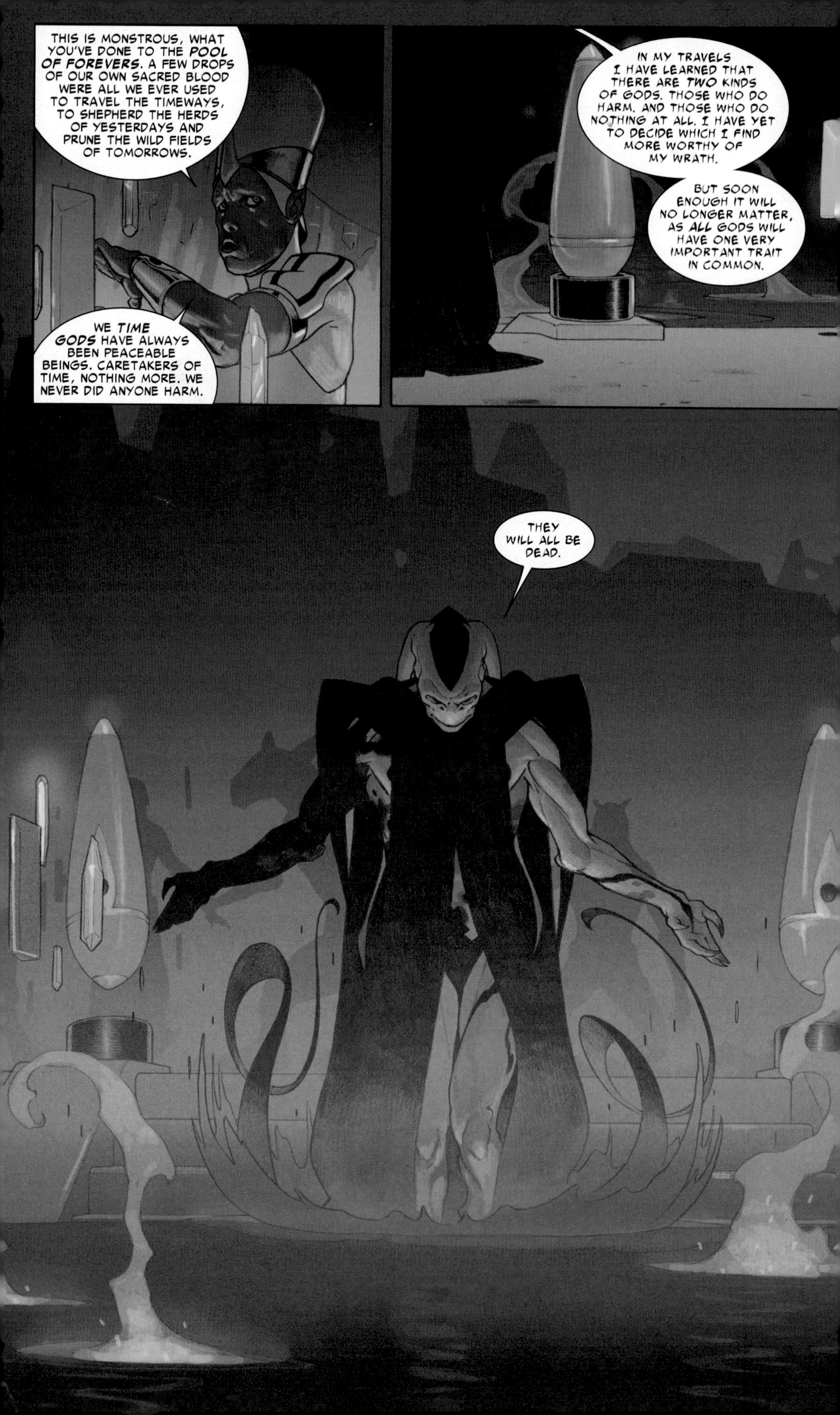
THIS IS MONSTROUS, WHAT YOU'VE DONE TO THE POOL OF FOREVERS. A FEW DROPS OF OUR OWN SACRED BLOOD WERE ALL WE EVER USED TO TRAVEL THE TIMEWAYS, TO SHEPHERD THE HERDS OF YESTERDAYS AND PRUNE THE WILD FIELDS OF TOMORROWS.
WE TIME GODS HAVE ALWAYS BEEN PEACEABLE BEINGS. CARETAKERS OF TIME, NOTHING MORE. WE NEVER DID ANYONE HARM.
IN MY TRAVELS I HAVE LEARNED THAT THERE ARE TWO KINDS OF GODS. THOSE WHO DO HARM. AND THOSE WHO DO NOTHING AT ALL. I HAVE YET TO DECIDE WHICH I FIND MORE WORTHY OF MY WRATH.
BUT SOON ENOUGH IT WILL NO LONGER MATTER, AS ALL GODS WILL HAVE ONE VERY IMPORTANT TRAIT IN COMMON.
THEY WILL ALL BE DEAD.

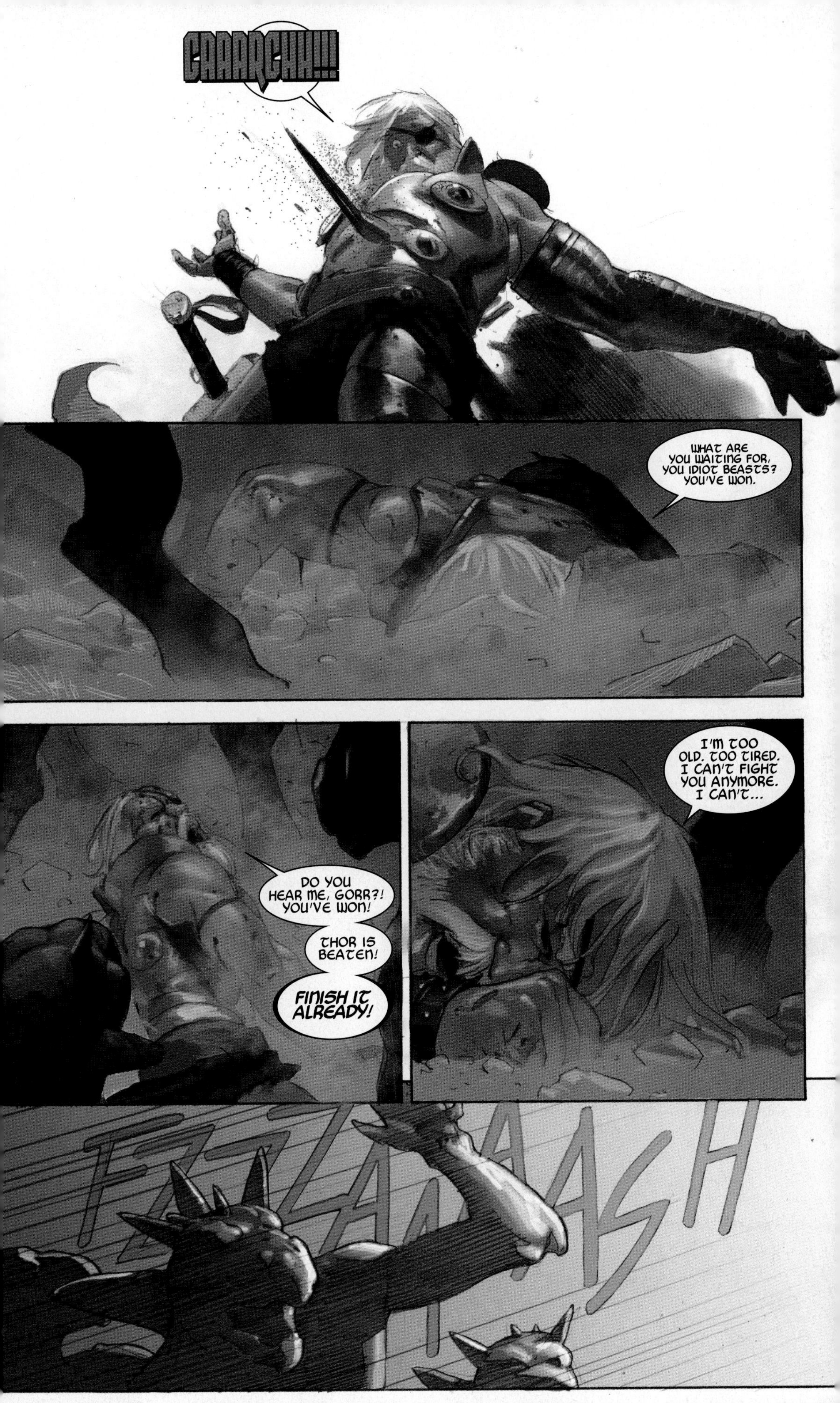

GAAARGHH!!!!
WHAT ARE YOU WAITING FOR, YOU IDIOT BEASTS? YOU'VE WON.
DO YOU HEAR ME, GORR?! YOU'VE WON!
THOR IS BEATEN!
FINISH IT ALREADY!
I'M TOO OLD. TOO TIRED. I CAN'T FIGHT YOU ANYMORE. I CAN'T...
FZZZAAAASH

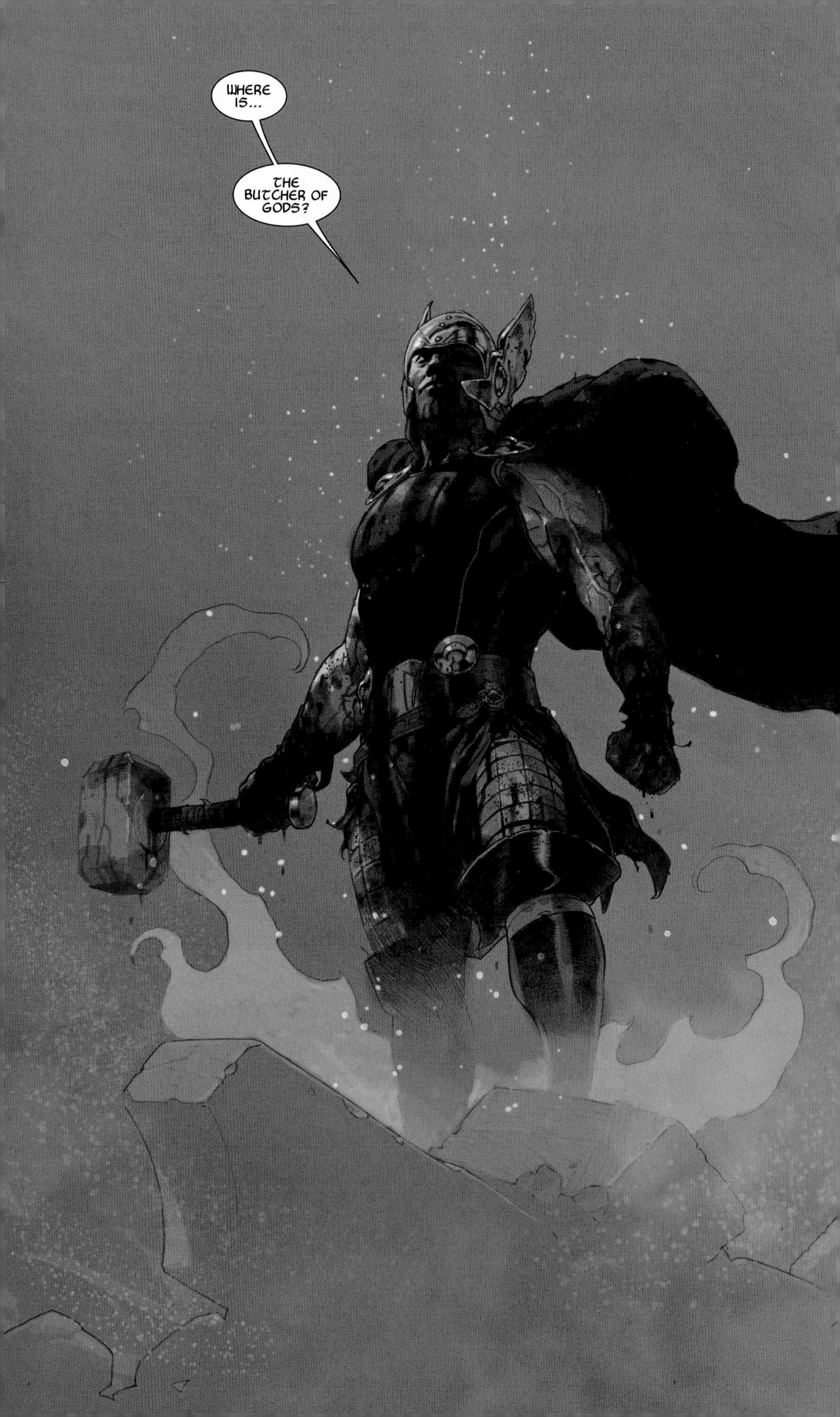
WHERE IS...
THE BUTCHER OF GODS?

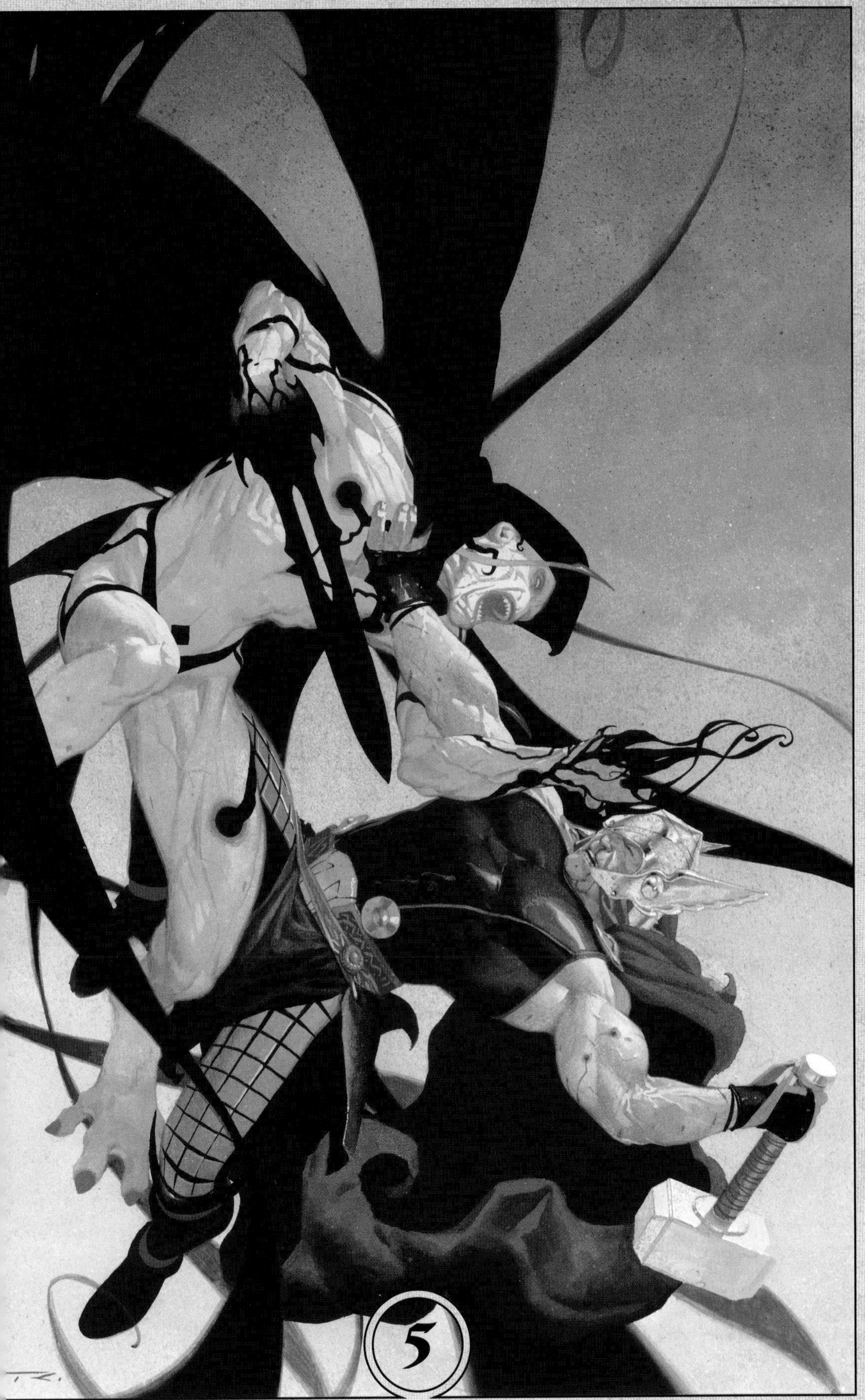
5

DREAM OF A GODLESS AGE

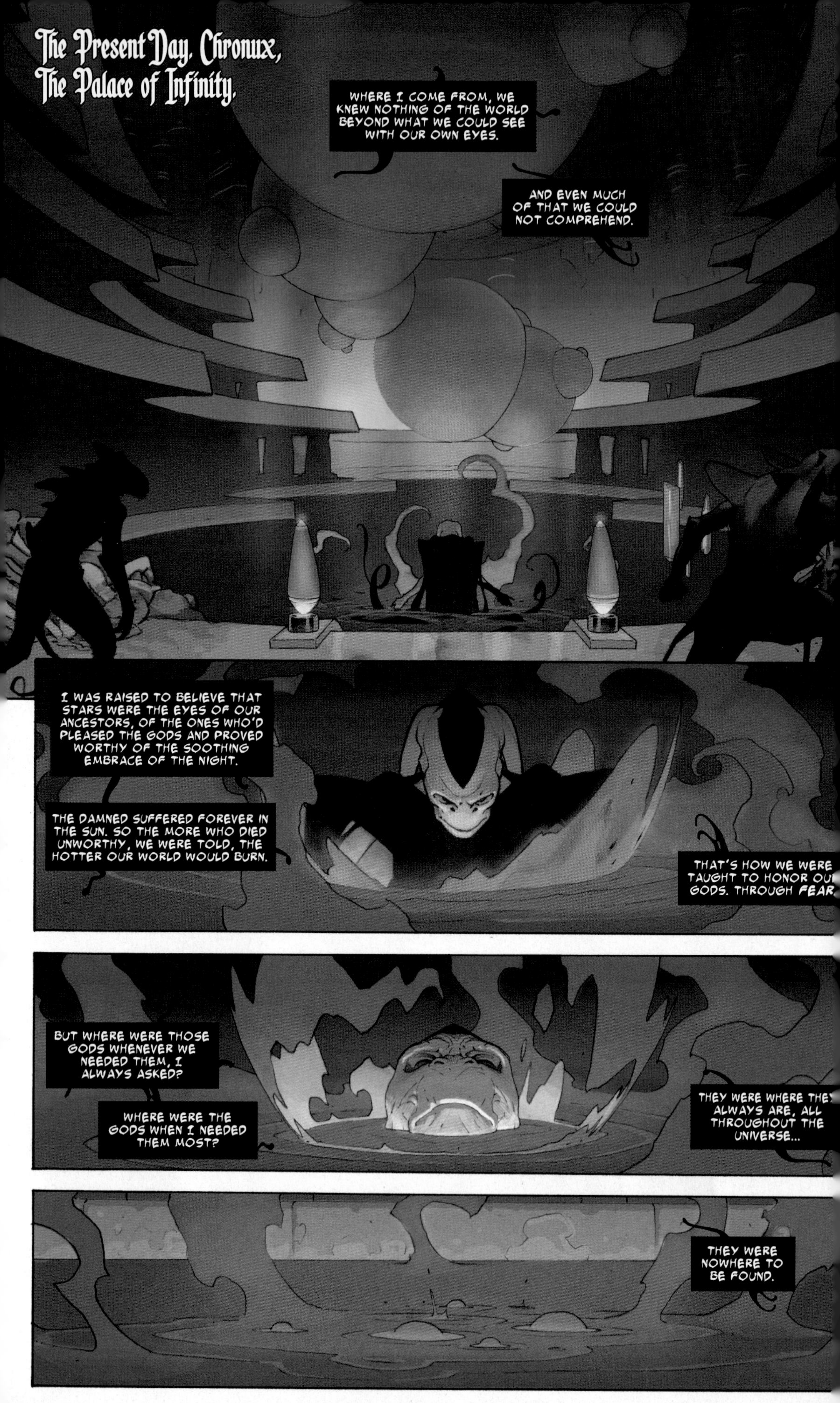

The Present Day, Chronux, The Palace of Infinity.
WHERE I COME FROM, WE KNEW NOTHING OF THE WORLD BEYOND WHAT WE COULD SEE WITH OUR OWN EYES.
AND EVEN MUCH OF THAT WE COULD NOT COMPREHEND.
I WAS RAISED TO BELIEVE THAT STARS WERE THE EYES OF OUR ANCESTORS, OF THE ONES WHO'D PLEASED THE GODS AND PROVED WORTHY OF THE SOOTHING EMBRACE OF THE NIGHT.
THE DAMNED SUFFERED FOREVER IN THE SUN. SO THE MORE WHO DIED UNWORTHY, WE WERE TOLD, THE HOTTER OUR WORLD WOULD BURN.
THAT'S HOW WE WERE TAUGHT TO HONOR OU GODS. THROUGH FEAR
BUT WHERE WERE THOSE GODS WHENEVER WE NEEDED THEM, I ALWAYS ASKED?
WHERE WERE THE GODS WHEN I NEEDED THEM MOST?
THEY WERE WHERE THE ALWAYS ARE, ALL THROUGHOUT THE UNIVERSE...
THEY WERE NOWHERE TO BE FOUND.

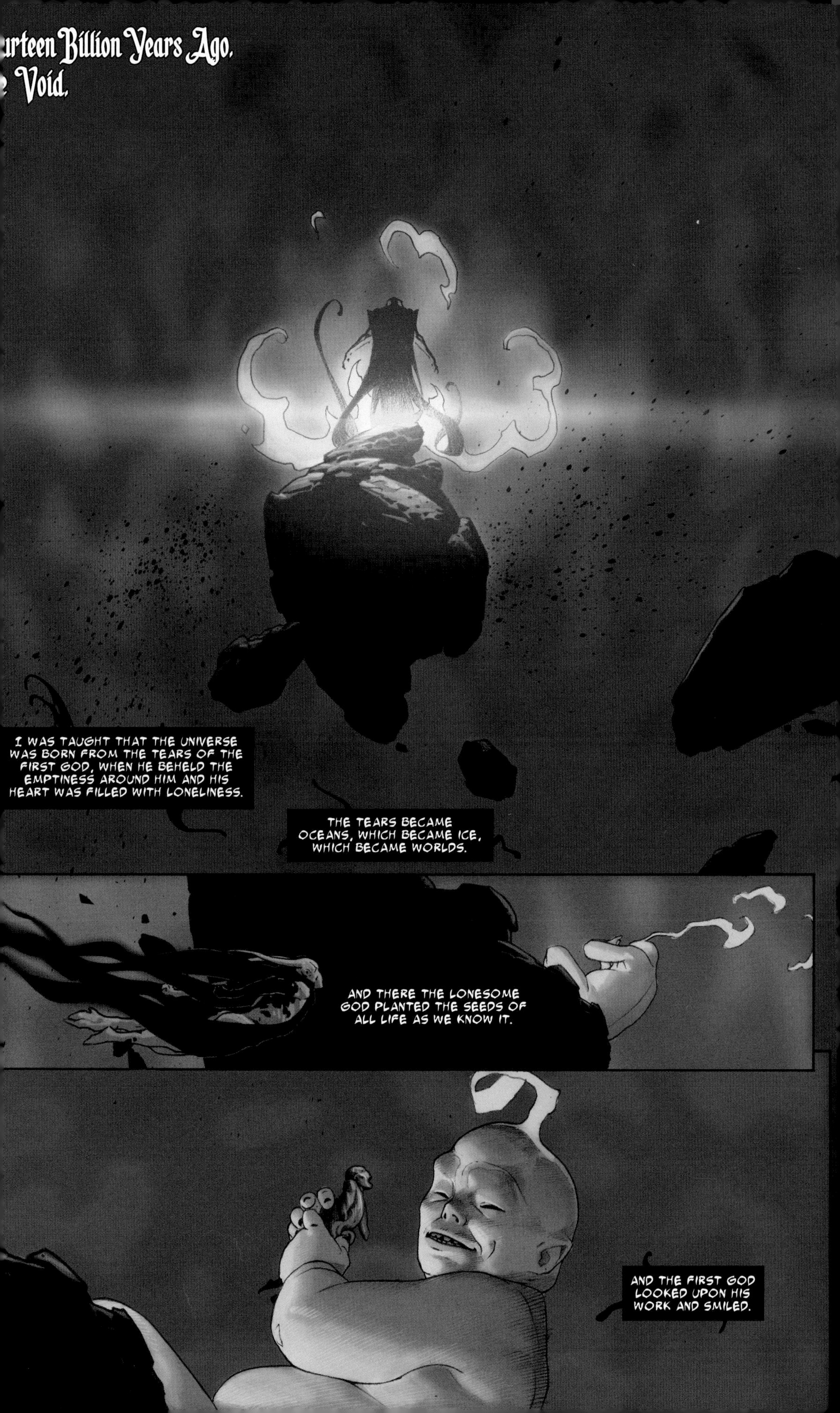

urteen Billion Years Ago.
Void.
I WAS TAUGHT THAT THE UNIVERSE WAS BORN FROM THE TEARS OF THE FIRST GOD, WHEN HE BEHELD THE EMPTINESS AROUND HIM AND HIS HEART WAS FILLED WITH LONELINESS.
THE TEARS BECAME OCEANS, WHICH BECAME ICE, WHICH BECAME WORLDS.
AND THERE THE LONESOME GOD PLANTED THE SEEDS OF ALL LIFE AS WE KNOW IT.
AND THE FIRST GOD LOOKED UPON HIS WORK AND SMILED.

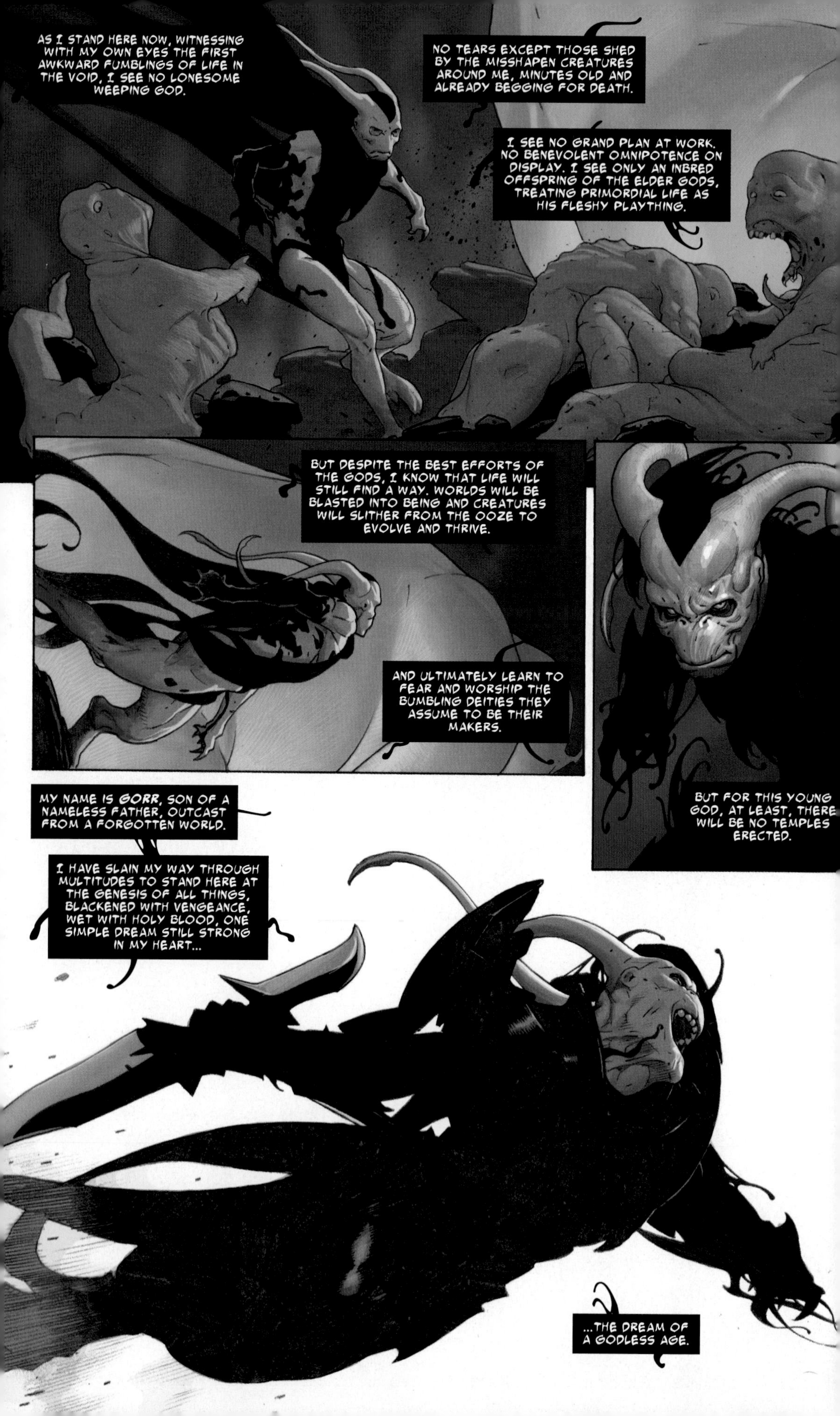
AS I STAND HERE NOW, WITNESSING WITH MY OWN EYES THE FIRST AWKWARD FUMBLINGS OF LIFE IN THE VOID, I SEE NO LONESOME WEEPING GOD.
NO TEARS EXCEPT THOSE SHED BY THE MISSHAPEN CREATURES AROUND ME, MINUTES OLD AND ALREADY BEGGING FOR DEATH.
I SEE NO GRAND PLAN AT WORK. NO BENEVOLENT OMNIPOTENCE ON DISPLAY. I SEE ONLY AN INBRED OFFSPRING OF THE ELDER GODS, TREATING PRIMORDIAL LIFE AS HIS FLESHY PLAYTHING.
BUT DESPITE THE BEST EFFORTS OF THE GODS, I KNOW THAT LIFE WILL STILL FIND A WAY. WORLDS WILL BE BLASTED INTO BEING AND CREATURES WILL SLITHER FROM THE OOZE TO EVOLVE AND THRIVE.
AND ULTIMATELY LEARN TO FEAR AND WORSHIP THE BUMBLING DEITIES THEY ASSUME TO BE THEIR MAKERS.
BUT FOR THIS YOUNG GOD, AT LEAST, THERE WILL BE NO TEMPLES ERECTED.
MY NAME IS GORR, SON OF A NAMELESS FATHER, OUTCAST FROM A FORGOTTEN WORLD.
I HAVE SLAIN MY WAY THROUGH MULTITUDES TO STAND HERE AT THE GENESIS OF ALL THINGS, BLACKENED WITH VENGEANCE, WET WITH HOLY BLOOD, ONE SIMPLE DREAM STILL STRONG IN MY HEART...
...THE DREAM OF A GODLESS AGE.

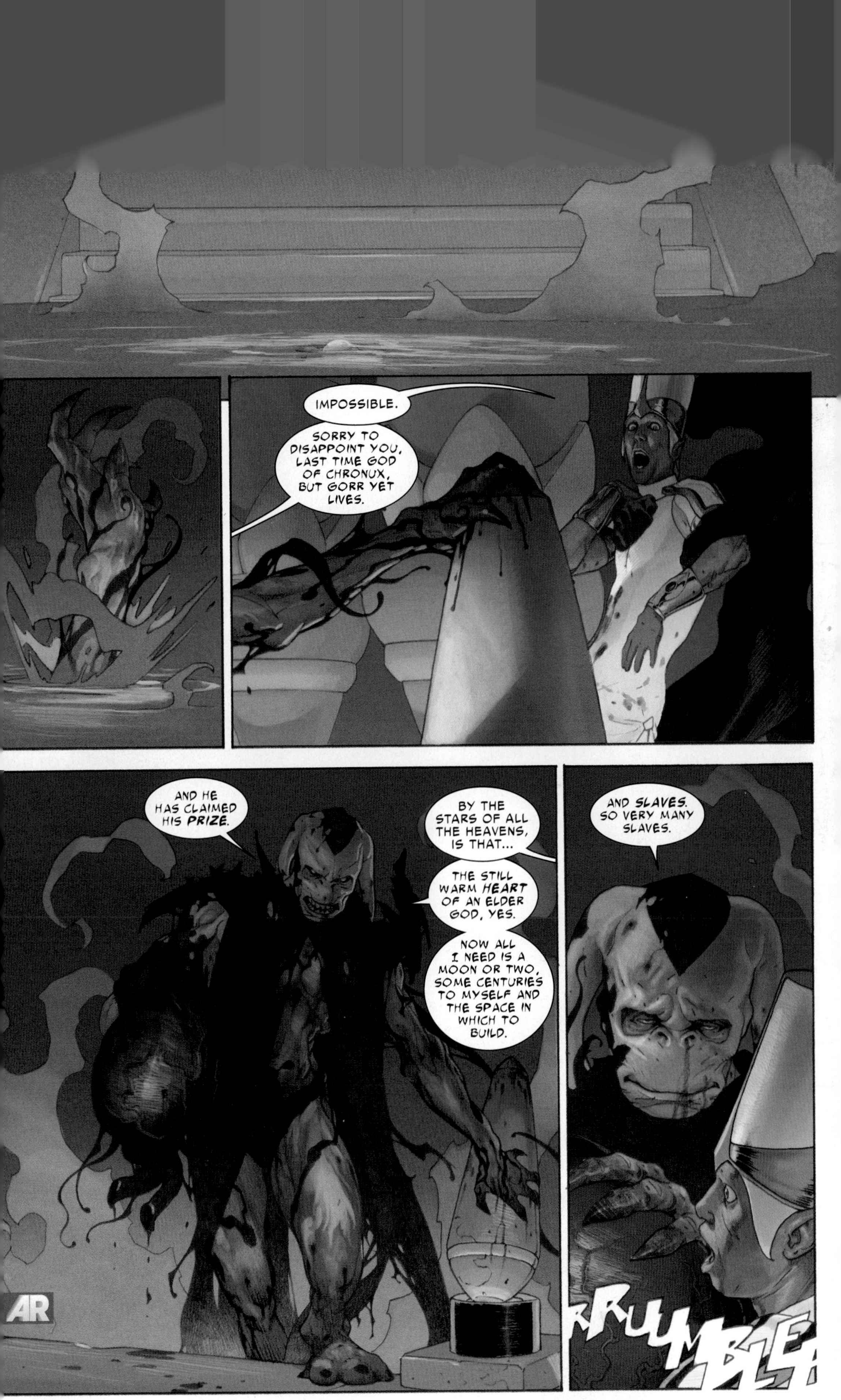
IMPOSSIBLE.
SORRY TO DISAPPOINT YOU, LAST TIME GOD OF CHRONUX, BUT GORR YET LIVES.
AND HE HAS CLAIMED HIS PRIZE.
BY THE STARS OF ALL THE HEAVENS, IS THAT...
THE STILL WARM HEART OF AN ELDER GOD, YES.
NOW ALL I NEED IS A MOON OR TWO, SOME CENTURIES TO MYSELF AND THE SPACE IN WHICH TO BUILD.
AND SLAVES. SO VERY MANY SLAVES.
RRUUMBLE

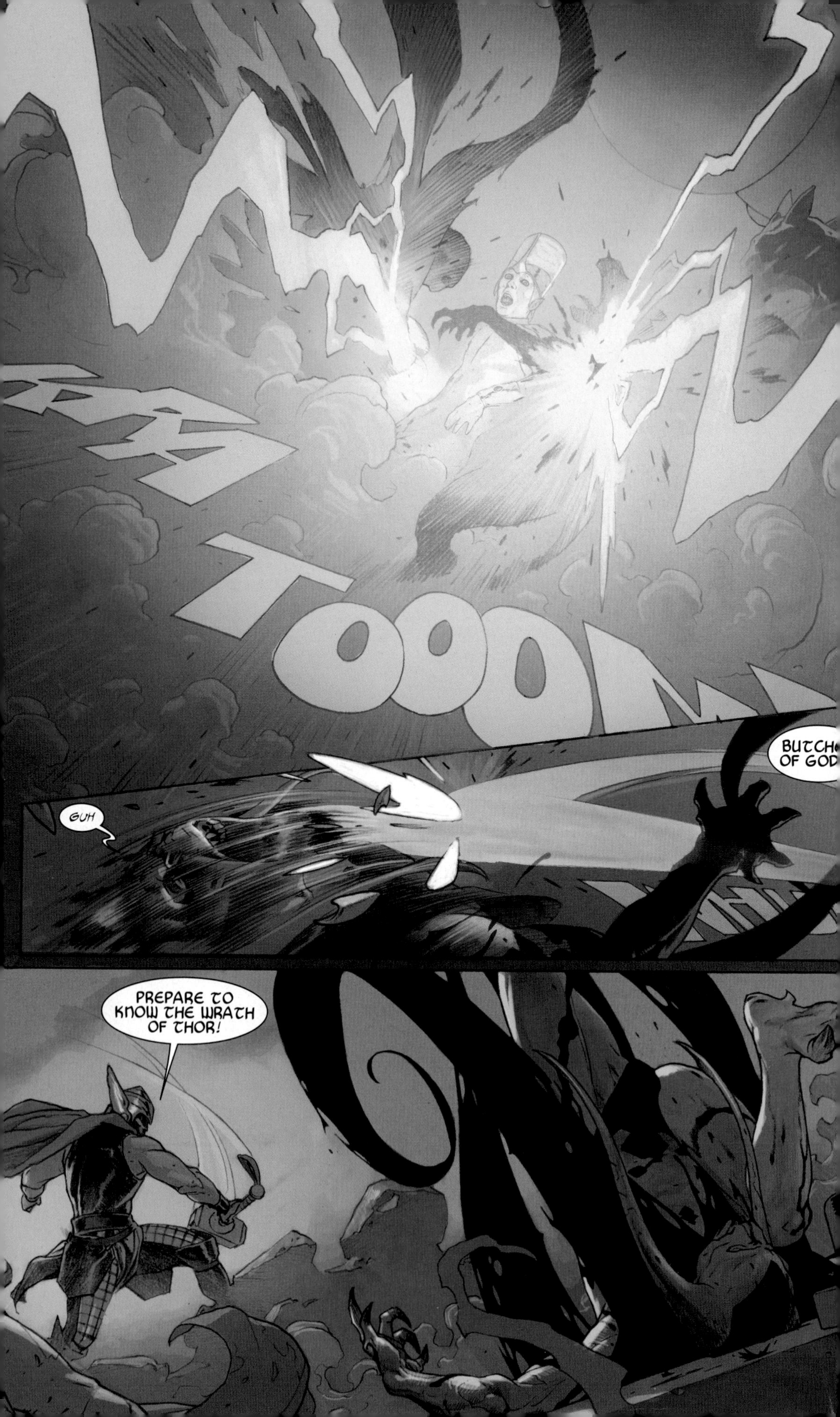
BUTCH
OF GOD
GUH
PREPARE TO KNOW THE WRATH OF THOR!

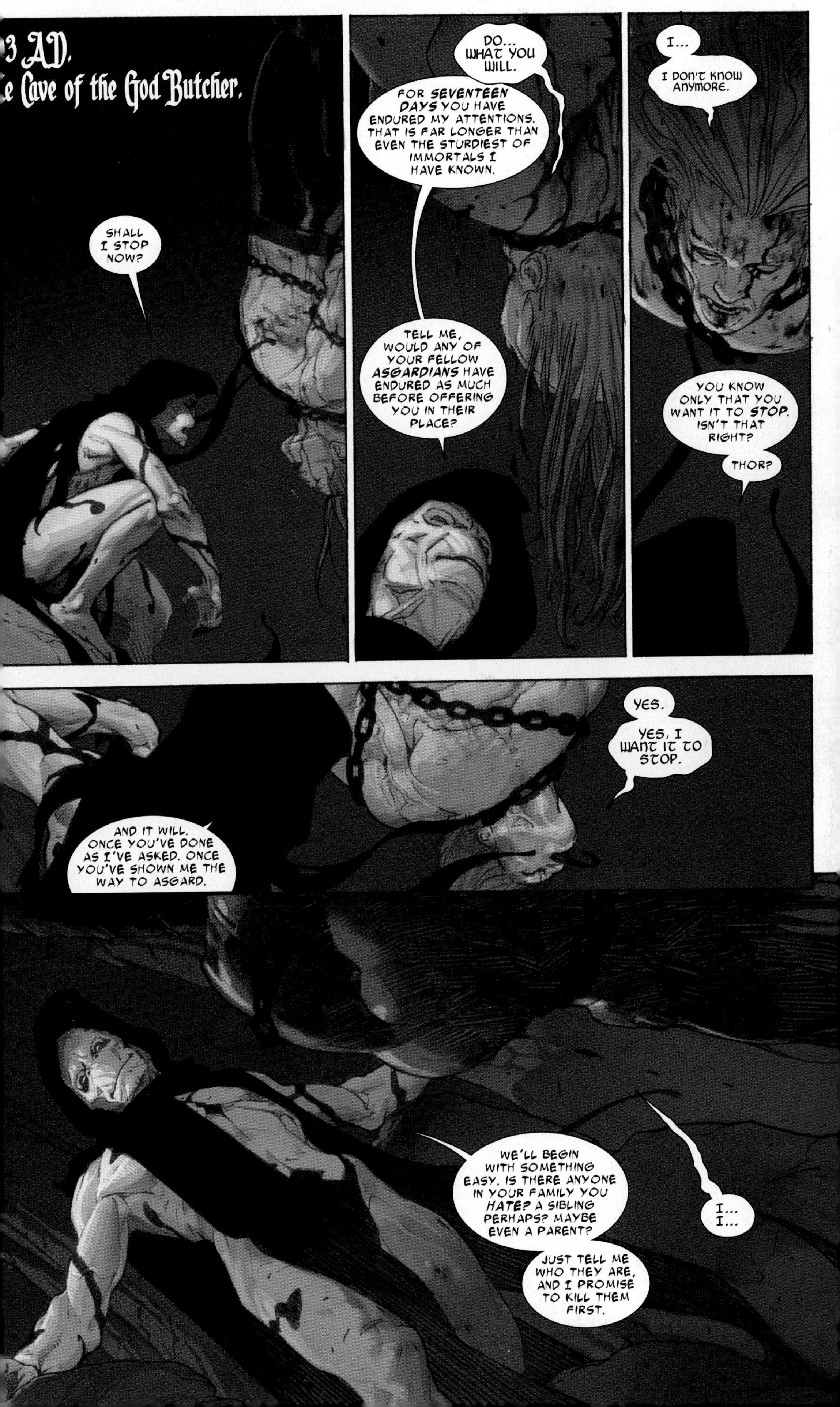
3 A.D.
e Cave of the God Butcher.
SHALL I STOP NOW?
DO... WHAT YOU WILL.
FOR SEVENTEEN DAYS YOU HAVE ENDURED MY ATTENTIONS. THAT IS FAR LONGER THAN EVEN THE STURDIEST OF IMMORTALS I HAVE KNOWN.
TELL ME, WOULD ANY OF YOUR FELLOW ASGARDIANS HAVE ENDURED AS MUCH BEFORE OFFERING YOU IN THEIR PLACE?
I...
I DON'T KNOW ANYMORE.
YOU KNOW ONLY THAT YOU WANT IT TO STOP. ISN'T THAT RIGHT?
THOR?
YES.
YES, I WANT IT TO STOP.
AND IT WILL. ONCE YOU'VE DONE AS I'VE ASKED. ONCE YOU'VE SHOWN ME THE WAY TO ASGARD.
WE'LL BEGIN WITH SOMETHING EASY. IS THERE ANYONE IN YOUR FAMILY YOU HATE? A SIBLING PERHAPS? MAYBE EVEN A PARENT?
JUST TELL ME WHO THEY ARE, AND I PROMISE TO KILL THEM FIRST.
I... I...

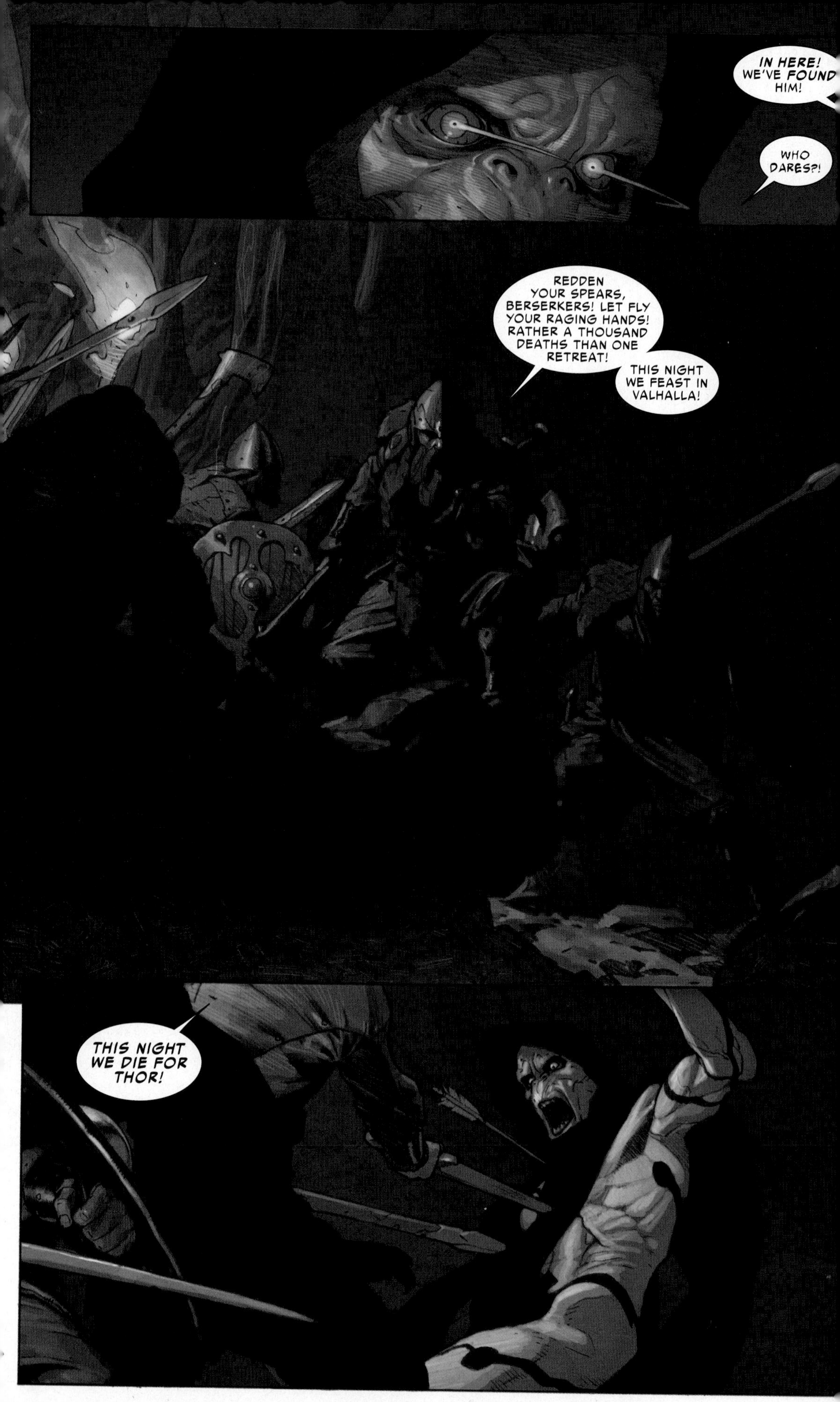
IN HERE! WE'VE FOUND HIM!
WHO DARES?!
REDDEN YOUR SPEARS, BERSERKERS! LET FLY YOUR RAGING HANDS! RATHER A THOUSAND DEATHS THAN ONE RETREAT!
THIS NIGHT WE FEAST IN VALHALLA!
THIS NIGHT WE DIE FOR THOR!

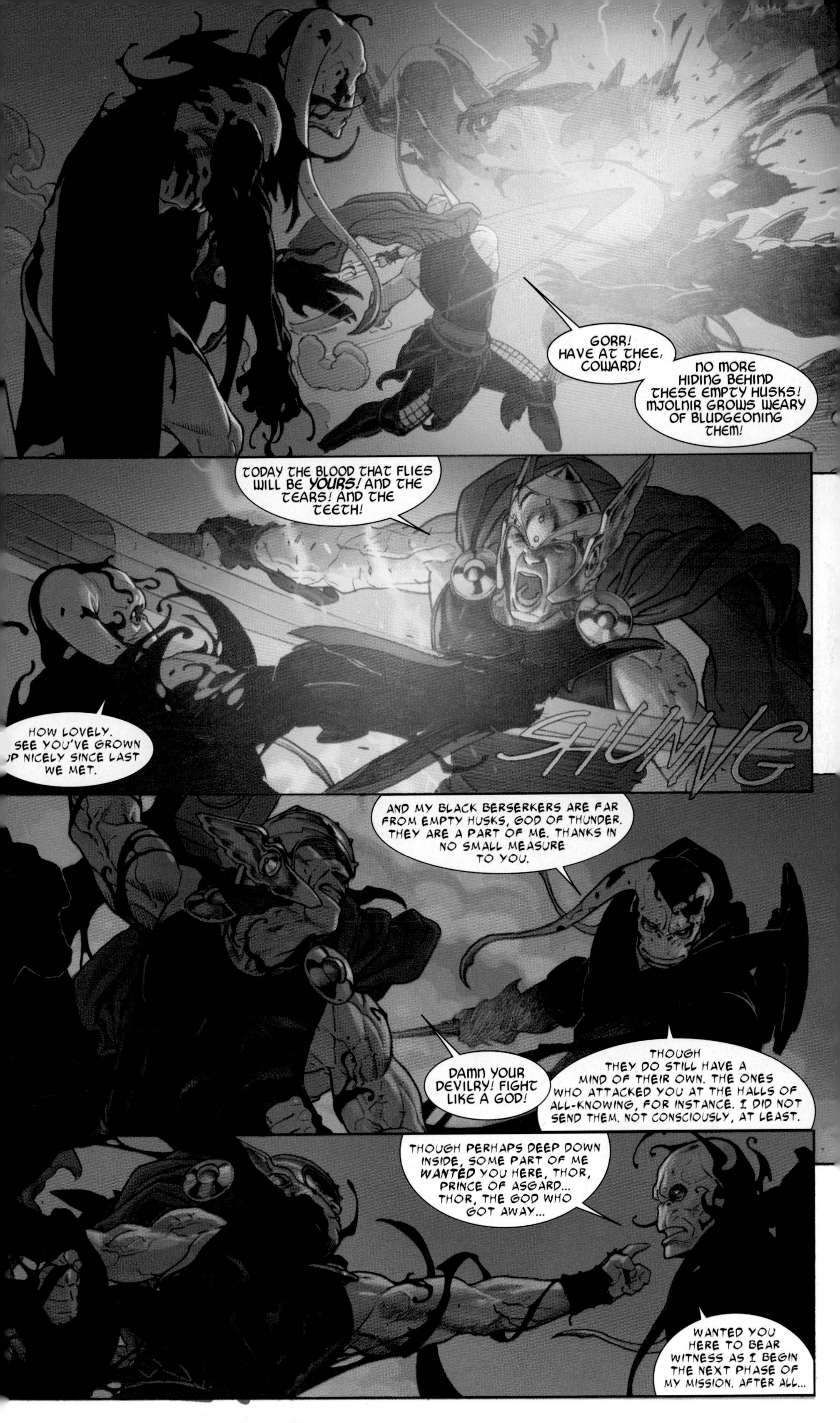
GORR! HAVE AT THEE, COWARD!
NO MORE HIDING BEHIND THESE EMPTY HUSKS! MJOLNIR GROWS WEARY OF BLUDGEONING THEM!
TODAY THE BLOOD THAT FLIES WILL BE YOURS! AND THE TEARS! AND THE TEETH!
HOW LOVELY. SEE YOU'VE GROWN UP NICELY SINCE LAST WE MET.
SHUNNG
AND MY BLACK BERSERKERS ARE FAR FROM EMPTY HUSKS, GOD OF THUNDER. THEY ARE A PART OF ME. THANKS IN NO SMALL MEASURE TO YOU.
DAMN YOUR DEVILRY! FIGHT LIKE A GOD!
THOUGH THEY DO STILL HAVE A MIND OF THEIR OWN. THE ONES WHO ATTACKED YOU AT THE HALLS OF ALL-KNOWING, FOR INSTANCE. I DID NOT SEND THEM. NOT CONSCIOUSLY, AT LEAST.
THOUGH PERHAPS DEEP DOWN INSIDE, SOME PART OF ME WANTED YOU HERE, THOR, PRINCE OF ASGARD... THOR, THE GOD WHO GOT AWAY...
WANTED YOU HERE TO BEAR WITNESS AS I BEGIN THE NEXT PHASE OF MY MISSION. AFTER ALL...

"NONE OF THIS WOULD HAVE BEEN POSSIBLE WITHOUT YOU."

STOP THIS! I AM NOT HERE TO HURT YOU, MEN OF EARTH! I COME INSTEAD TO LIBERATE YOU AND YOUR KIND FROM THE YOKE OF DIVINE SERVITUDE!

DON'T WORRY, LORD THOR, WE'LL HAVE YOU FREE OF THESE CHAINS OR DIE TRY--

AND WE COME TO LIBERATE THAT HIDEOUS HEAD OF YOURS FROM ITS SHOULDERS! CUT HIM DOWN!

LISTEN TO ME, YOU FOOLS! DO NOT THROW YOUR LIVES AWAY ON SOMETHING AS USELESS AS A GOD!

GAAHHHK!!!

HE ISN'T WORTH YOUR DEVOTION! NONE OF THEM ARE! JUST LISTEN TO ME! LISTEN AND LET ME TELL YOU OF MY DREAM! A DREAM OF A--

FOR THE LOVE OF ODIN, SOMEONE GET A SPEAR IN THAT THROAT AND STOP THIS WRETCH'S MEWLING!

VERY WELL. DIE FOR YOUR GOD IF YOU WISH. SEE IF HE EVEN TAKES NOTICE.

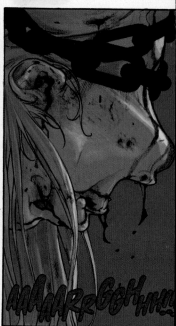

MMRRGGHHH!

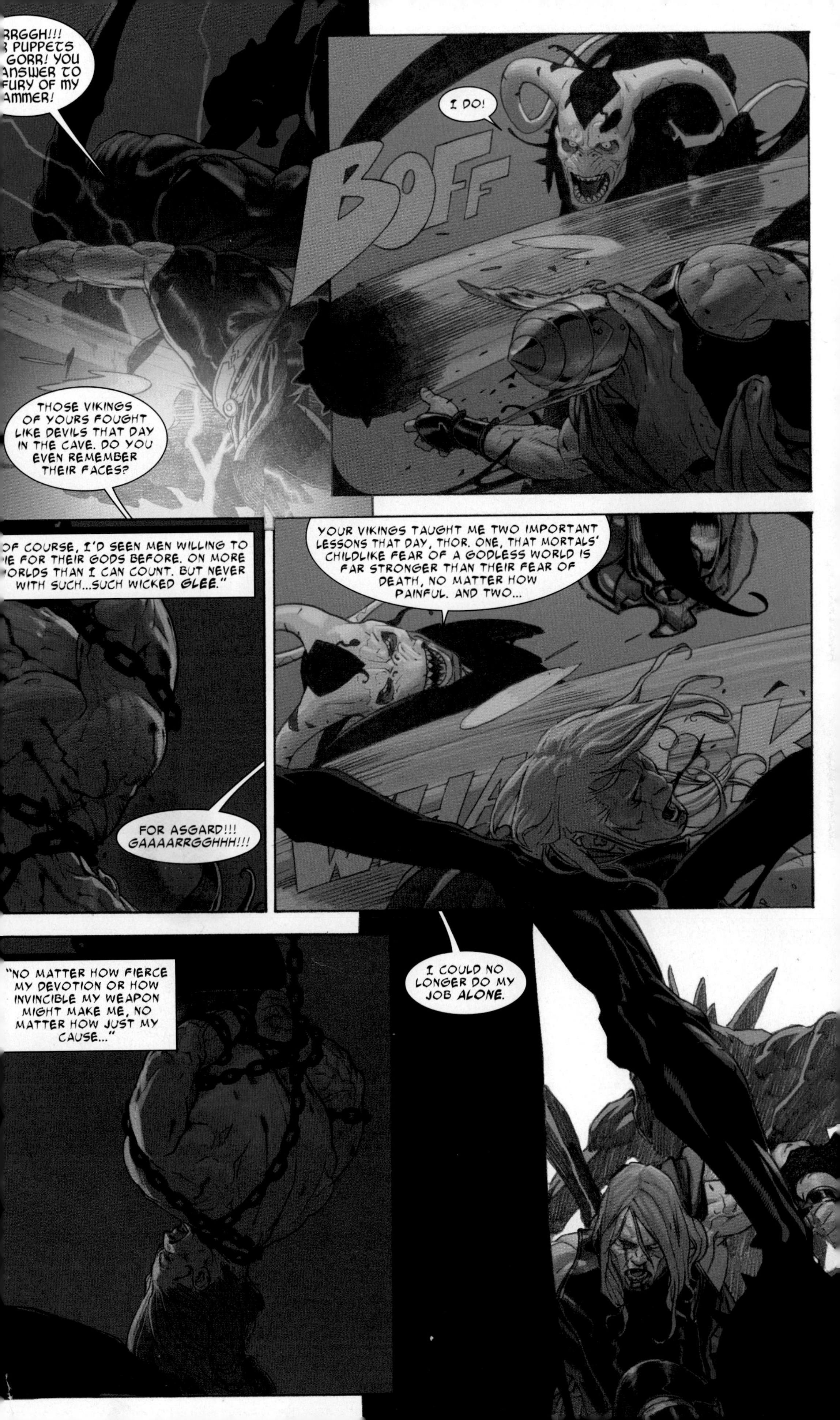
RRGGH!!! R PUPPETS GORR! YOU ANSWER TO FURY OF MY AMMER!
I DO!
BOFF
THOSE VIKINGS OF YOURS FOUGHT LIKE DEVILS THAT DAY IN THE CAVE. DO YOU EVEN REMEMBER THEIR FACES?
OF COURSE, I'D SEEN MEN WILLING TO IE FOR THEIR GODS BEFORE. ON MORE ORLDS THAN I CAN COUNT. BUT NEVER WITH SUCH...SUCH WICKED GLEE."
YOUR VIKINGS TAUGHT ME TWO IMPORTANT LESSONS THAT DAY, THOR. ONE, THAT MORTALS' CHILDLIKE FEAR OF A GODLESS WORLD IS FAR STRONGER THAN THEIR FEAR OF DEATH, NO MATTER HOW PAINFUL. AND TWO...
FOR ASGARD!!! GAAAARRGGHHH!!!
"NO MATTER HOW FIERCE MY DEVOTION OR HOW INVINCIBLE MY WEAPON MIGHT MAKE ME, NO MATTER HOW JUST MY CAUSE..."
I COULD NO LONGER DO MY JOB ALONE.

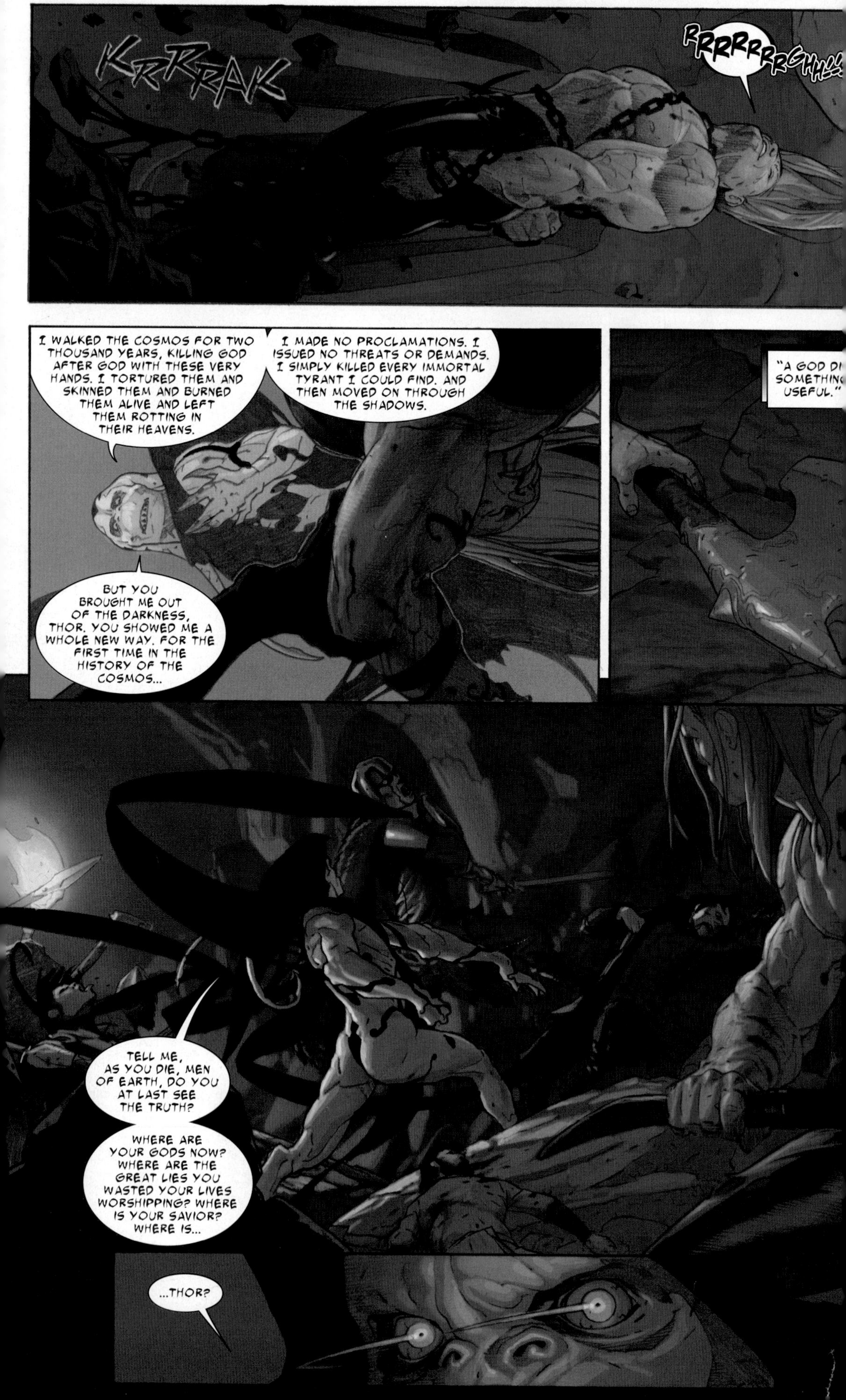
KRRRAK
RRRRRRRGHH!!
I WALKED THE COSMOS FOR TWO THOUSAND YEARS, KILLING GOD AFTER GOD WITH THESE VERY HANDS. I TORTURED THEM AND SKINNED THEM AND BURNED THEM ALIVE AND LEFT THEM ROTTING IN THEIR HEAVENS.
I MADE NO PROCLAMATIONS. I ISSUED NO THREATS OR DEMANDS. I SIMPLY KILLED EVERY IMMORTAL TYRANT I COULD FIND. AND THEN MOVED ON THROUGH THE SHADOWS.
BUT YOU BROUGHT ME OUT OF THE DARKNESS, THOR. YOU SHOWED ME A WHOLE NEW WAY. FOR THE FIRST TIME IN THE HISTORY OF THE COSMOS...
"A GOD DI
SOMETHIN
USEFUL."
TELL ME, AS YOU DIE, MEN OF EARTH, DO YOU AT LAST SEE THE TRUTH?
WHERE ARE YOUR GODS NOW? WHERE ARE THE GREAT LIES YOU WASTED YOUR LIVES WORSHIPPING? WHERE IS YOUR SAVIOR? WHERE IS...
...THOR?

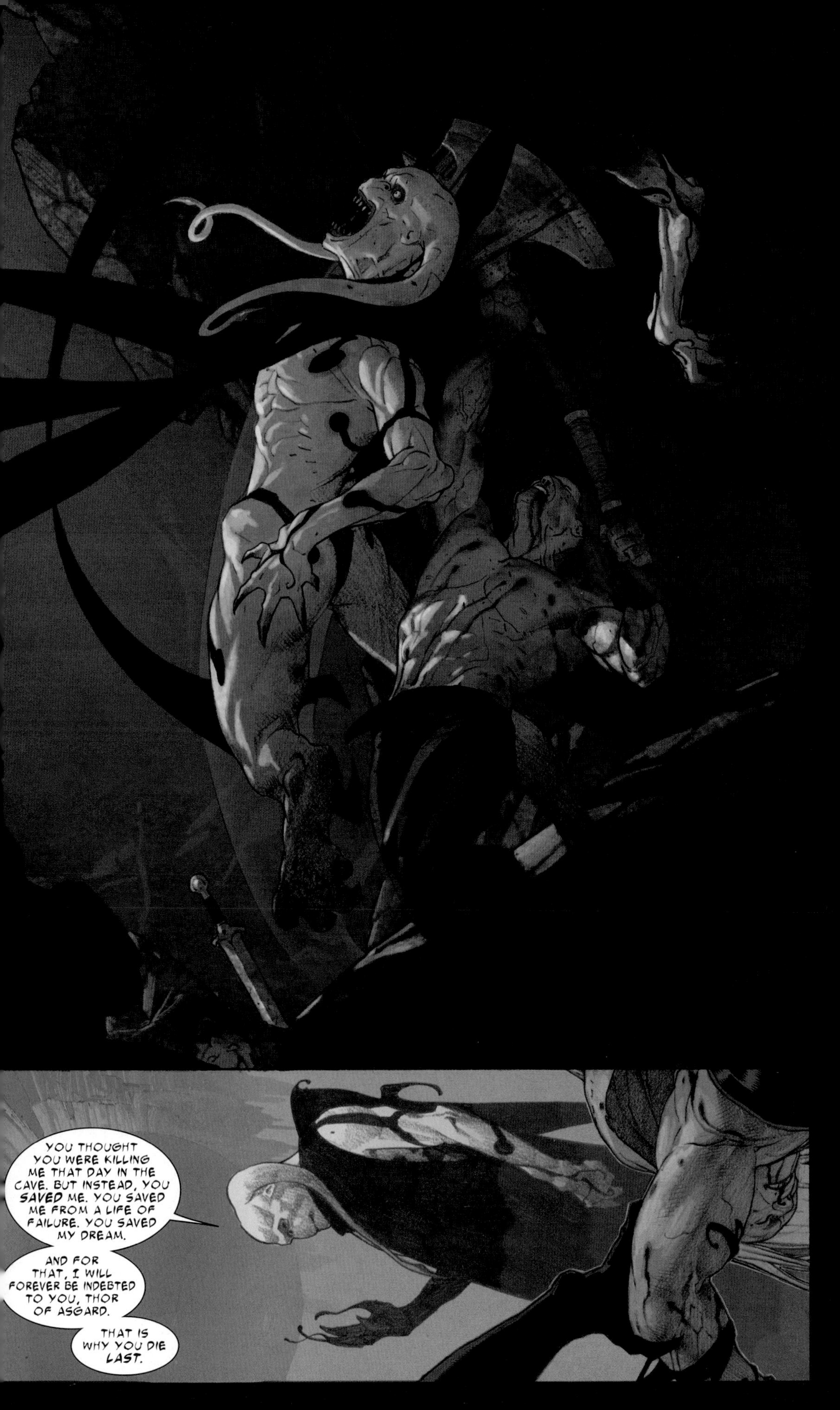
YOU THOUGHT YOU WERE KILLING ME THAT DAY IN THE CAVE. BUT INSTEAD, YOU SAVED ME. YOU SAVED ME FROM A LIFE OF FAILURE. YOU SAVED MY DREAM.
AND FOR THAT, I WILL FOREVER BE INDEBTED TO YOU, THOR OF ASGARD.
THAT IS WHY YOU DIE LAST.

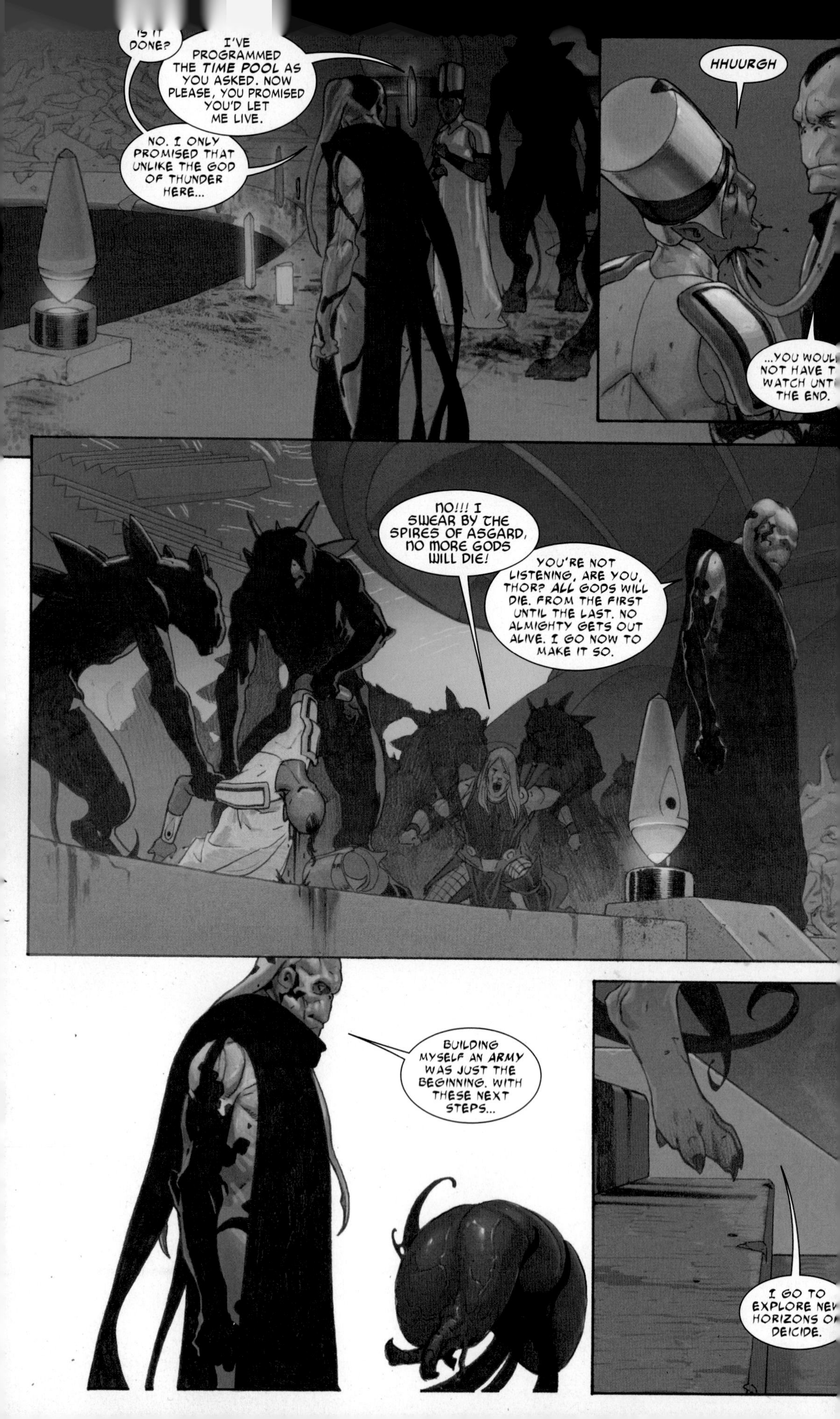
IS IT DONE?
I'VE PROGRAMMED THE TIME POOL AS YOU ASKED. NOW PLEASE, YOU PROMISED YOU'D LET ME LIVE.
NO. I ONLY PROMISED THAT UNLIKE THE GOD OF THUNDER HERE...
HHUURGH
...YOU WOUL NOT HAVE T WATCH UNT THE END.
NO!!! I SWEAR BY THE SPIRES OF ASGARD, NO MORE GODS WILL DIE!
YOU'RE NOT LISTENING, ARE YOU, THOR? ALL GODS WILL DIE. FROM THE FIRST UNTIL THE LAST. NO ALMIGHTY GETS OUT ALIVE. I GO NOW TO MAKE IT SO.
BUILDING MYSELF AN ARMY WAS JUST THE BEGINNING. WITH THESE NEXT STEPS...
I GO TO EXPLORE NEW HORIZONS OF DEICIDE.

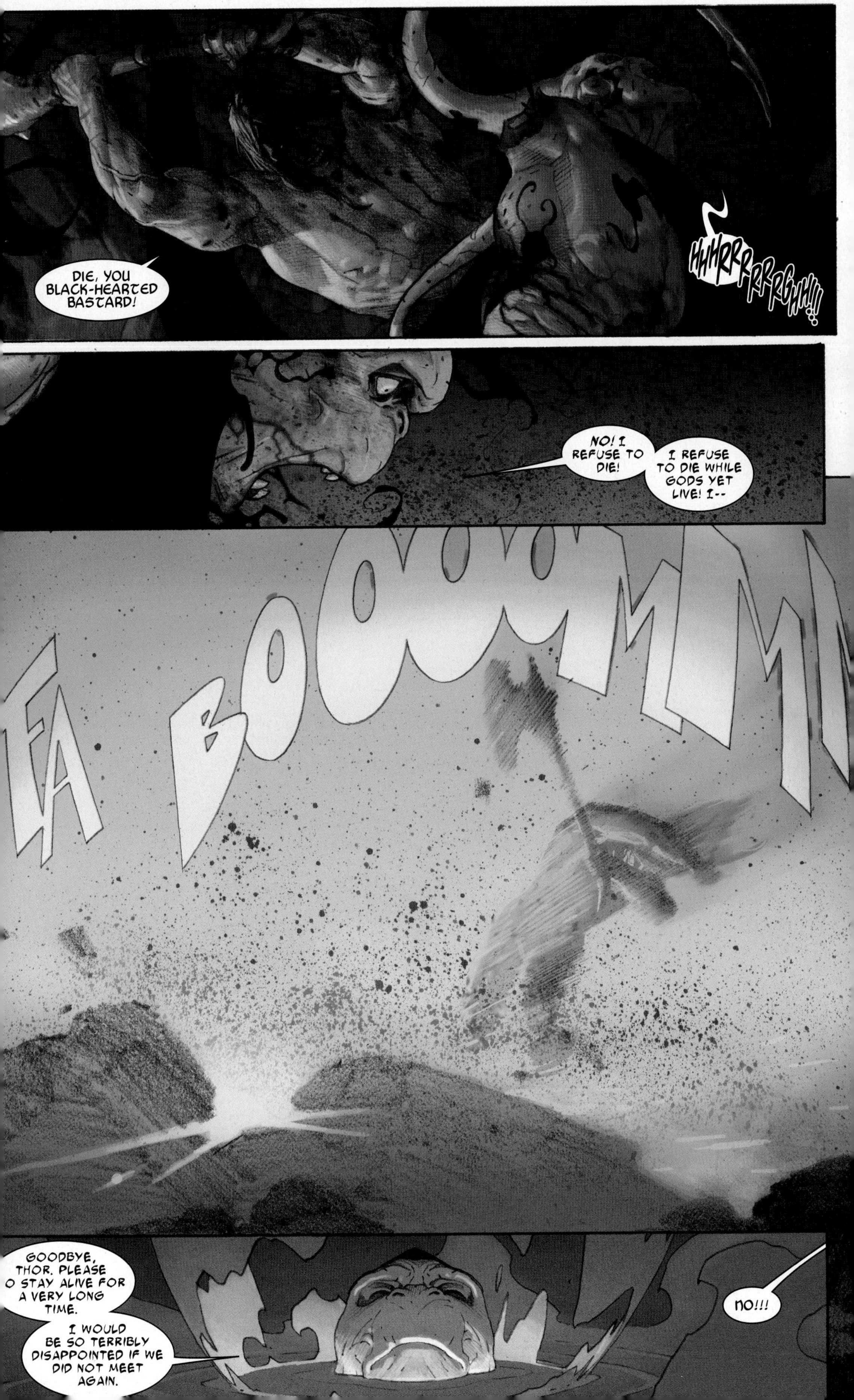
DIE, YOU BLACK-HEARTED BASTARD!
HHHRRRRRRGHH!!!
NO! I REFUSE TO DIE!
I REFUSE TO DIE WHILE GODS YET LIVE! I--
FA BOOOOMMM
GOODBYE, THOR. PLEASE DO STAY ALIVE FOR A VERY LONG TIME.
I WOULD BE SO TERRIBLY DISAPPOINTED IF WE DID NOT MEET AGAIN.
no!!!

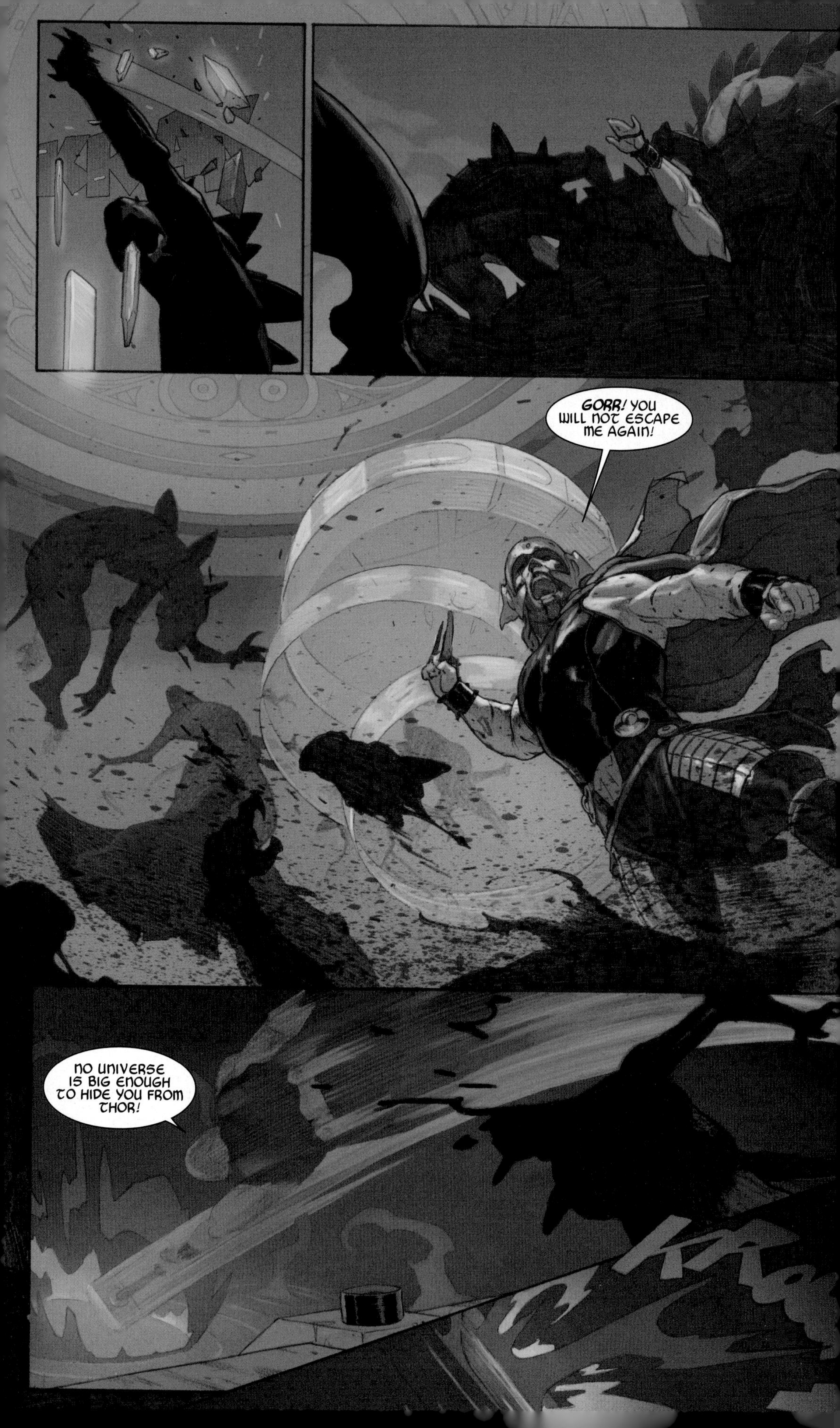
GORR! YOU WILL NOT ESCAPE ME AGAIN!
NO UNIVERSE IS BIG ENOUGH TO HIDE YOU FROM THOR!

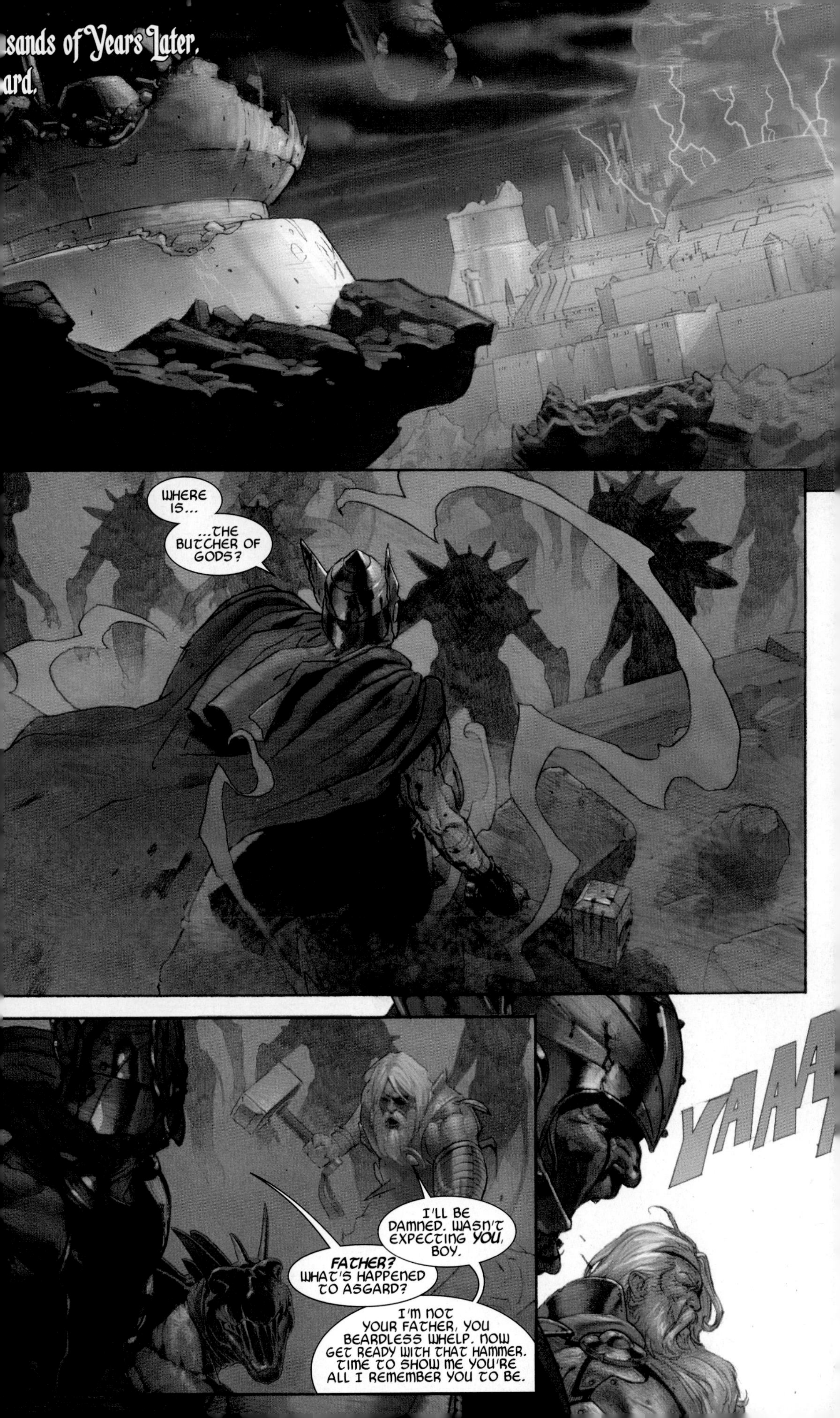
sands of Years Later,
ard.
WHERE IS...
...THE BUTCHER OF GODS?
FATHER? WHAT'S HAPPENED TO ASGARD?
I'LL BE DAMNED. WASN'T EXPECTING YOU, BOY.
I'M NOT YOUR FATHER, YOU BEARDLESS WHELP. NOW GET READY WITH THAT HAMMER. TIME TO SHOW ME YOU'RE ALL I REMEMBER YOU TO BE.

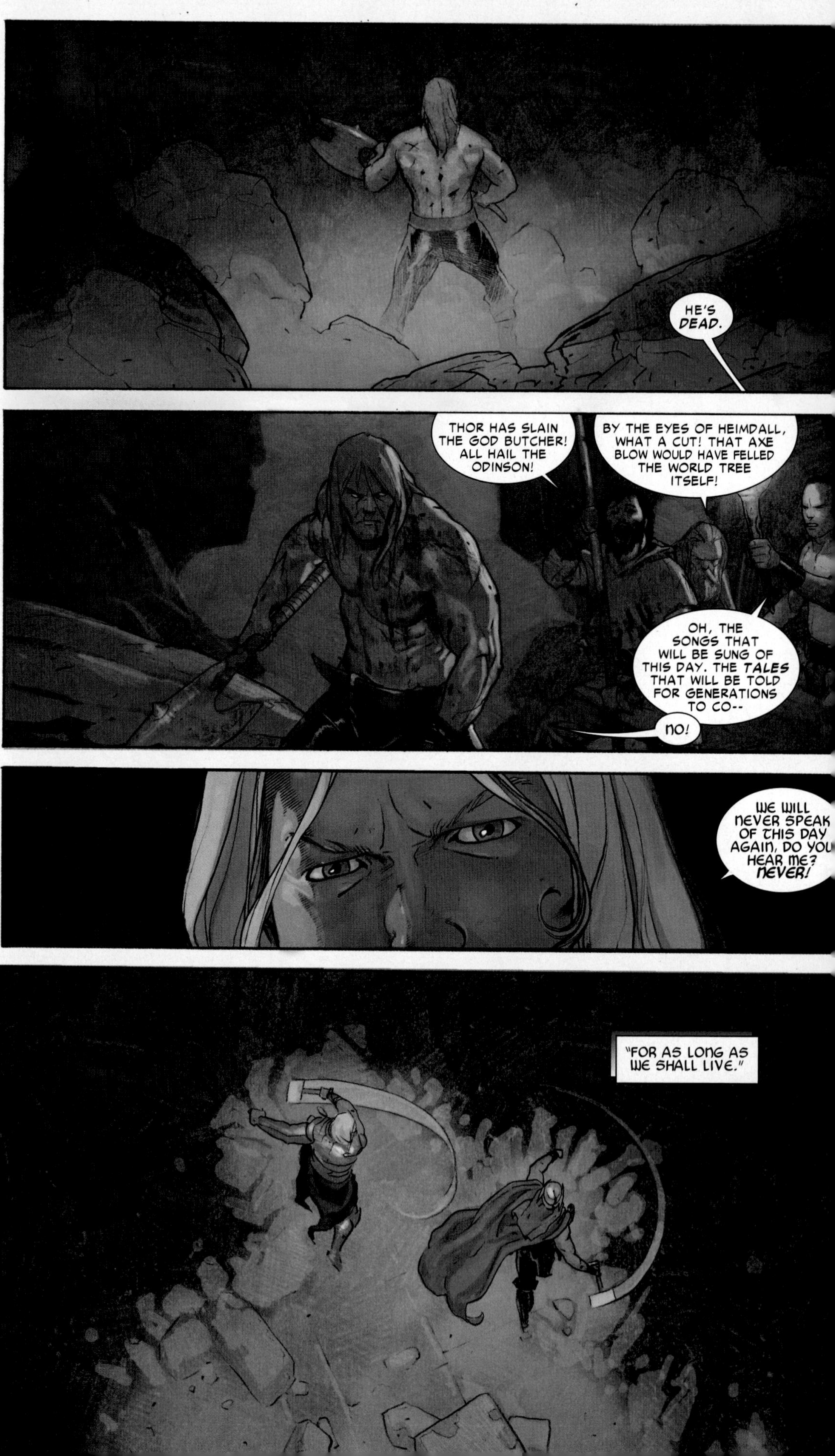
HE'S DEAD.
THOR HAS SLAIN THE GOD BUTCHER! ALL HAIL THE ODINSON!
BY THE EYES OF HEIMDALL, WHAT A CUT! THAT AXE BLOW WOULD HAVE FELLED THE WORLD TREE ITSELF!
OH, THE SONGS THAT WILL BE SUNG OF THIS DAY. THE TALES THAT WILL BE TOLD FOR GENERATIONS TO CO--
NO!
WE WILL NEVER SPEAK OF THIS DAY AGAIN, DO YOU HEAR ME? NEVER!
"FOR AS LONG AS WE SHALL LIVE."

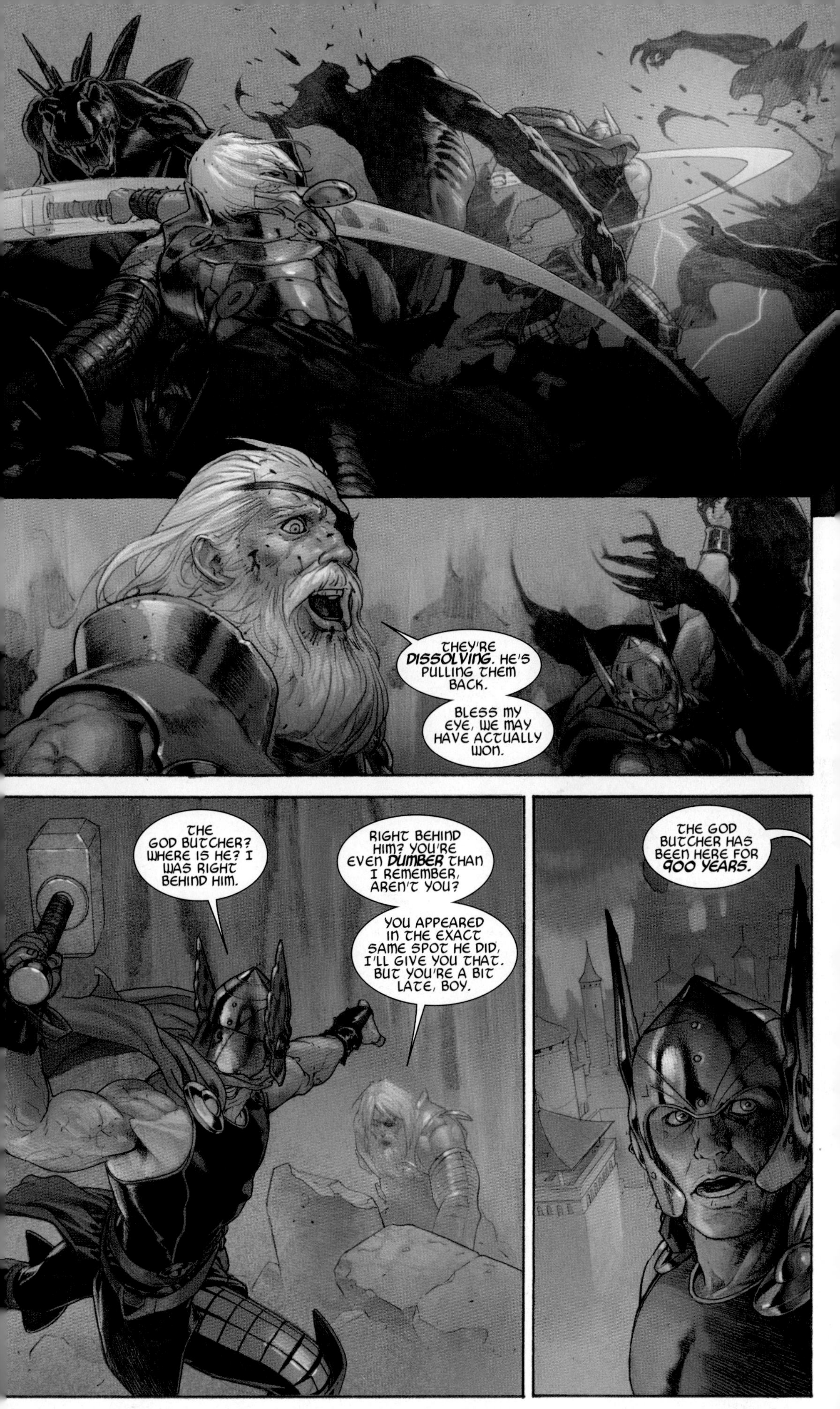
THEY'RE DISSOLVING. HE'S PULLING THEM BACK.
BLESS MY EYE, WE MAY HAVE ACTUALLY WON.
THE GOD BUTCHER? WHERE IS HE? I WAS RIGHT BEHIND HIM.
RIGHT BEHIND HIM? YOU'RE EVEN DUMBER THAN I REMEMBER, AREN'T YOU?
YOU APPEARED IN THE EXACT SAME SPOT HE DID, I'LL GIVE YOU THAT. BUT YOU'RE A BIT LATE, BOY.
THE GOD BUTCHER HAS BEEN HERE FOR 900 YEARS.

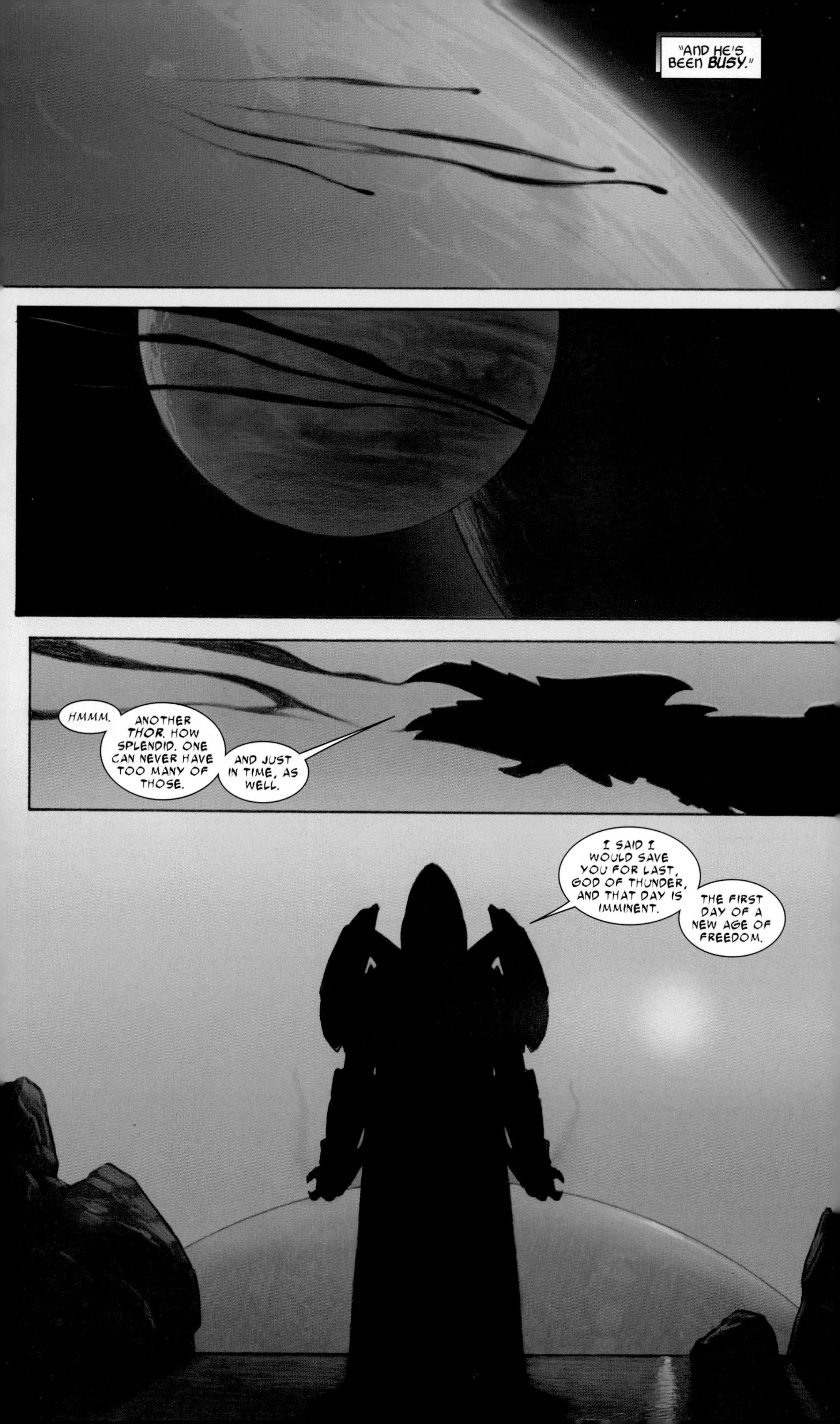
"AND HE'S BEEN BUSY."
HMMM.
ANOTHER THOR. HOW SPLENDID. ONE CAN NEVER HAVE TOO MANY OF THOSE.
AND JUST IN TIME, AS WELL.
I SAID I WOULD SAVE YOU FOR LAST, GOD OF THUNDER, AND THAT DAY IS IMMINENT.
THE FIRST DAY OF A NEW AGE OF FREEDOM.

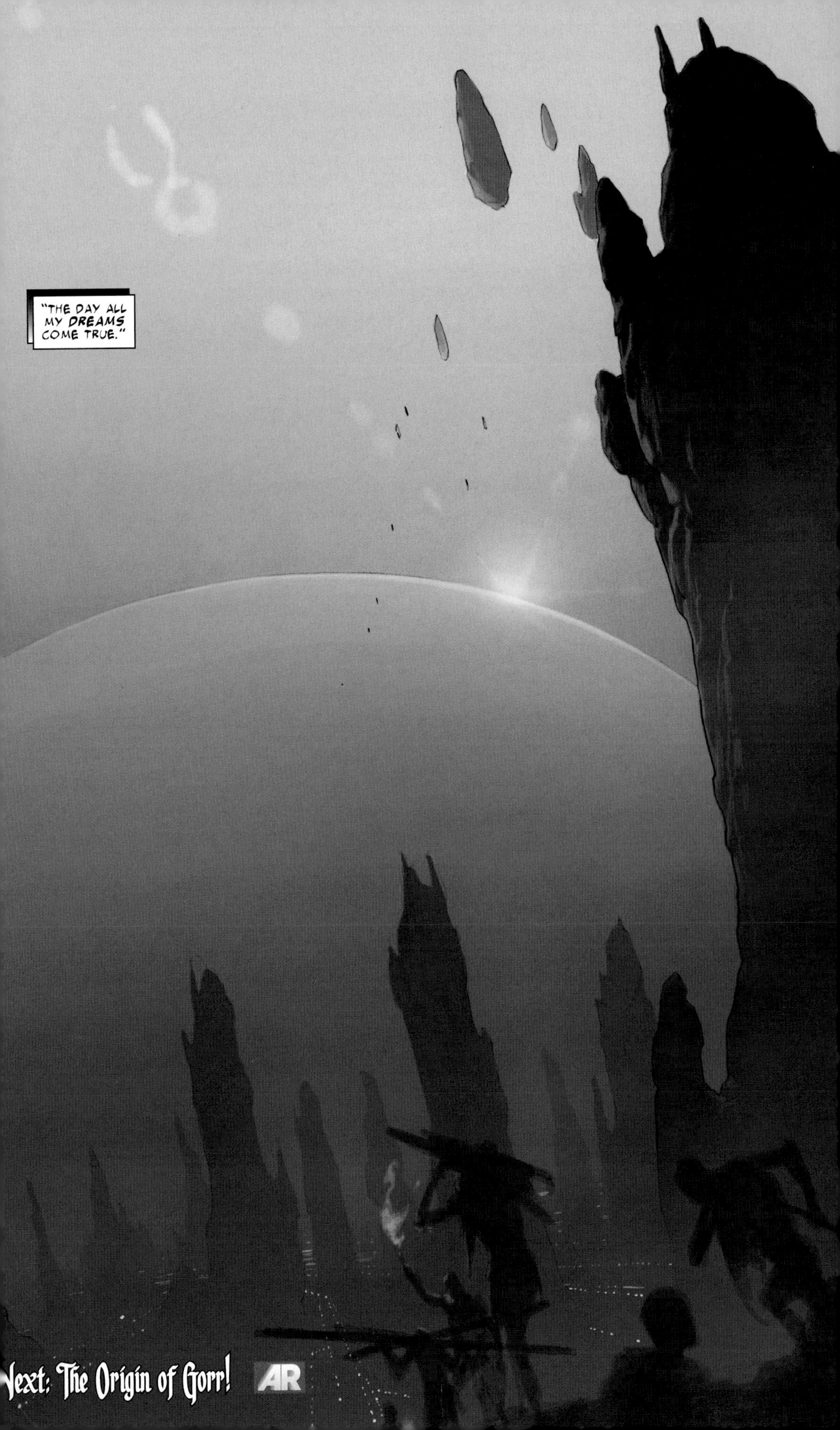
"THE DAY ALL MY DREAMS COME TRUE."
Next: The Origin of Gorr!

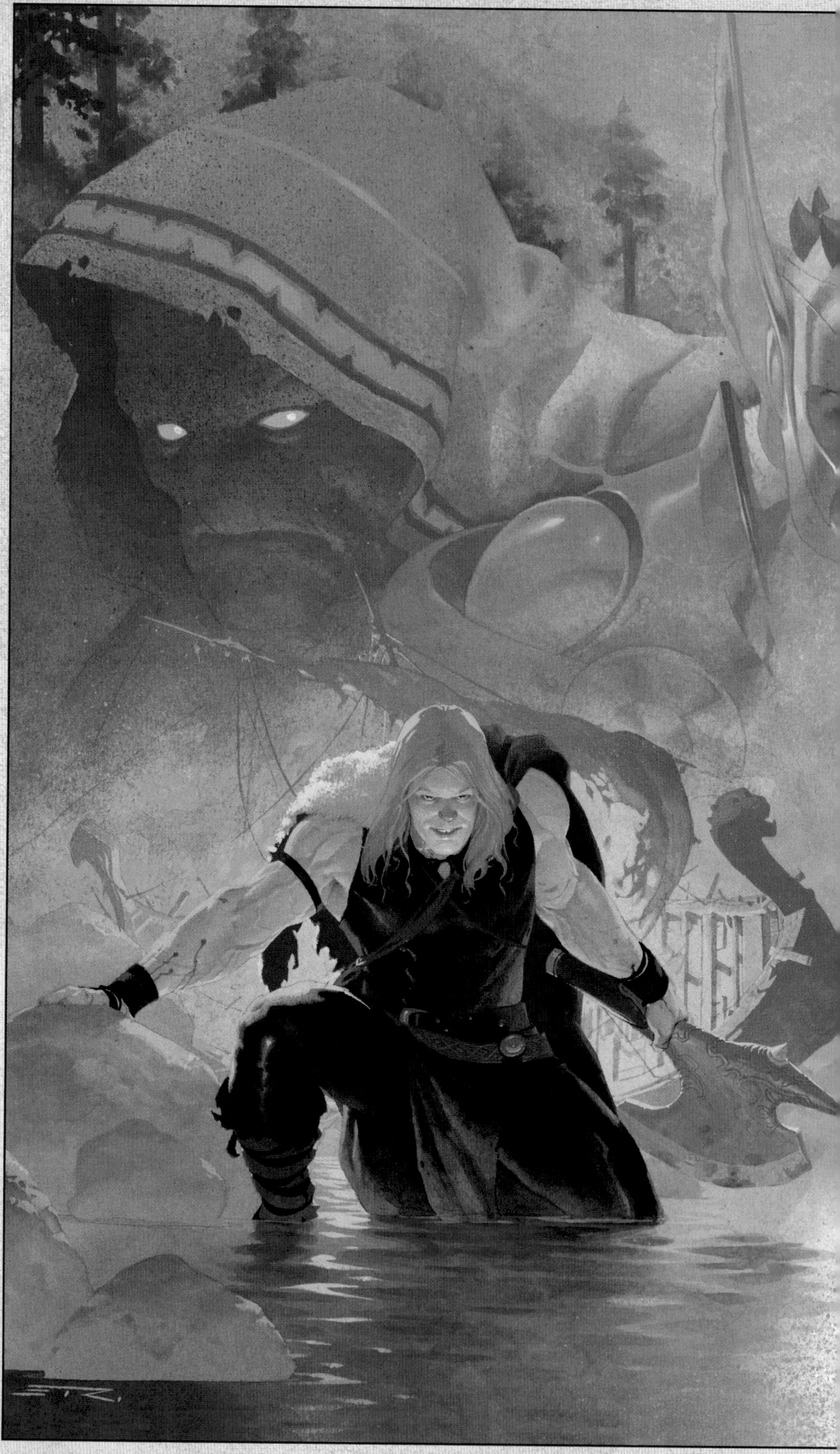

#1-2 COMBINED COVERS BY ESAD RIBIC

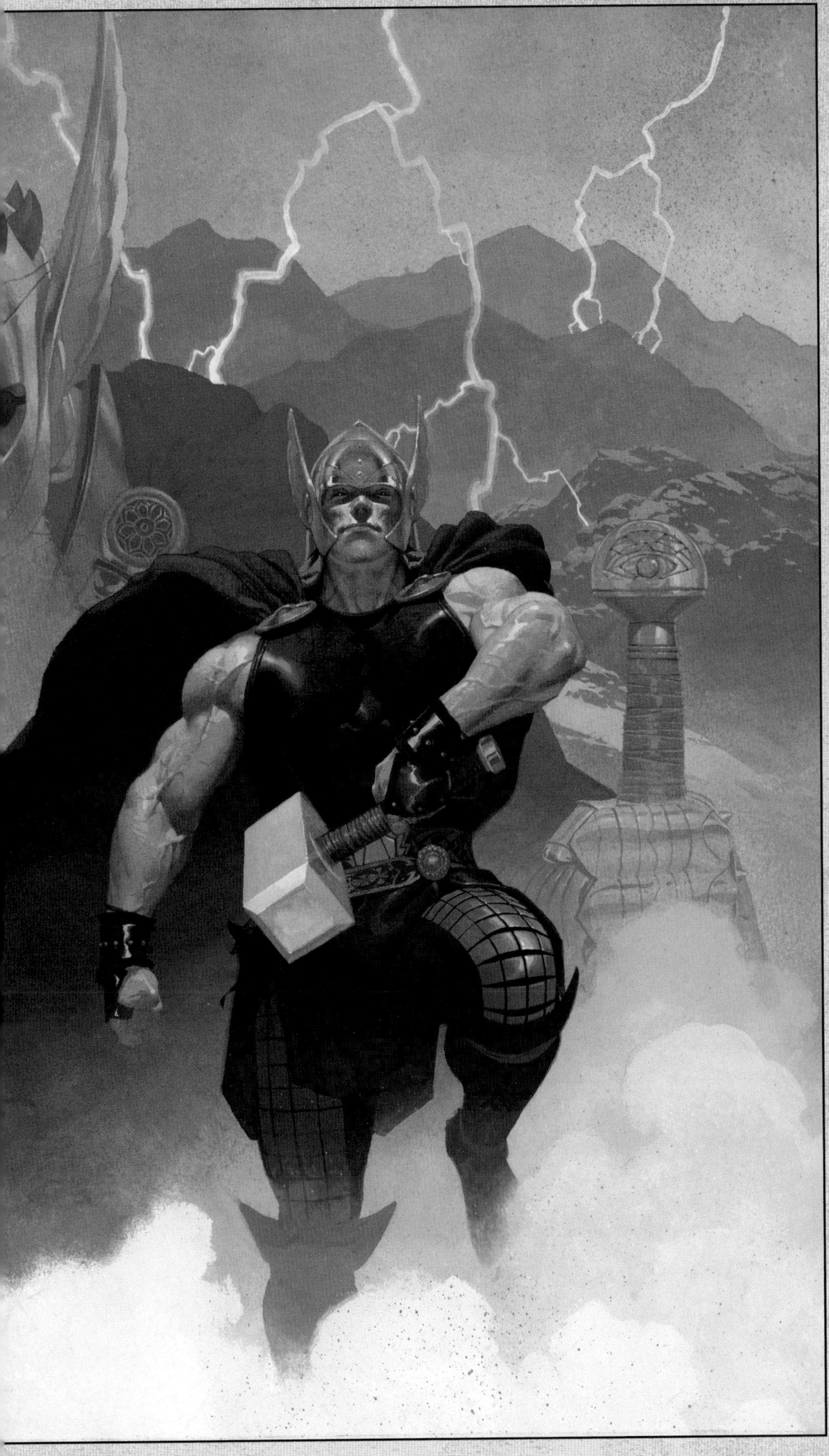

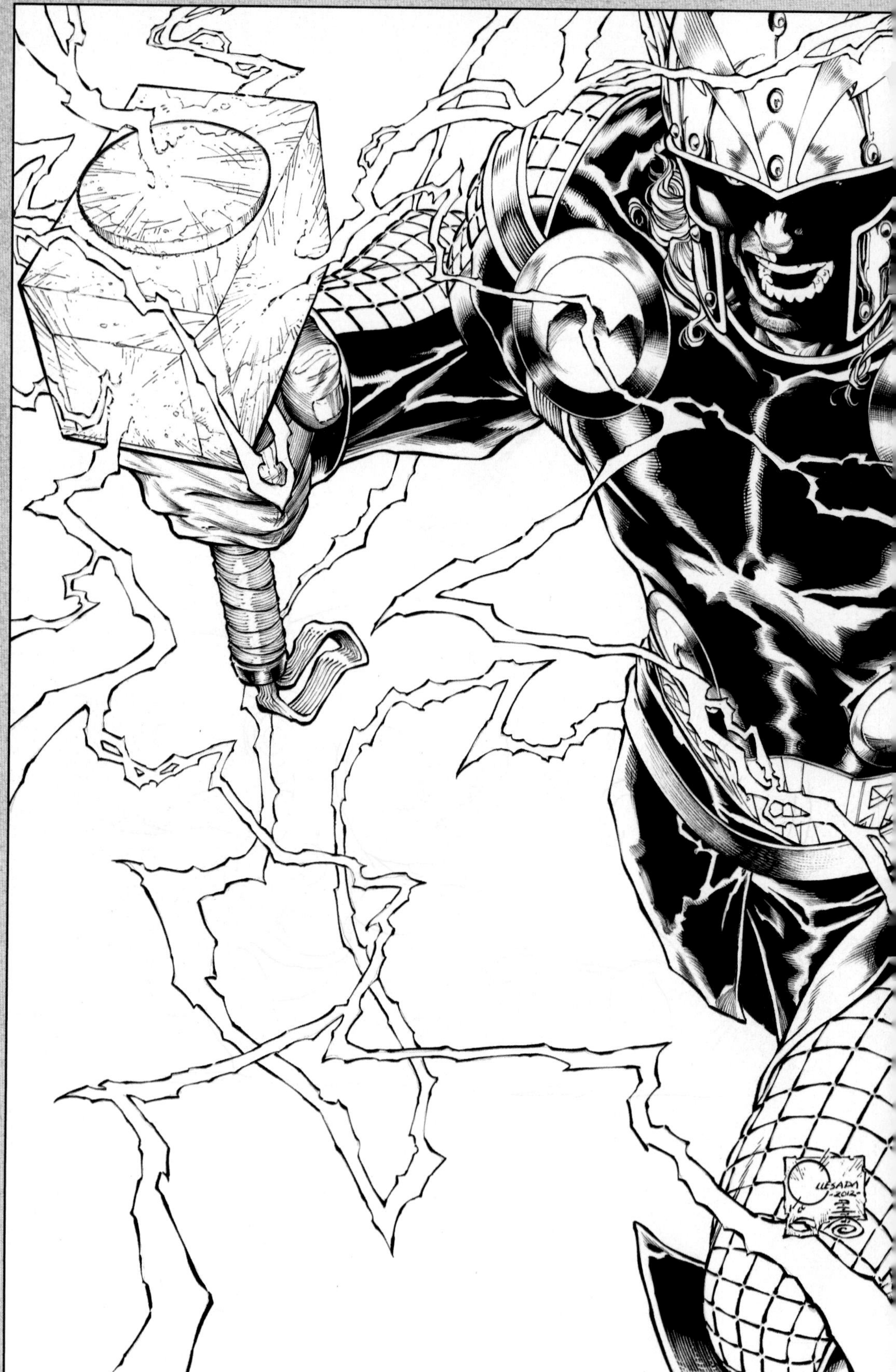

#1 SKETCH VARIANT
BY JOE QUESADA & DANNY MIKI

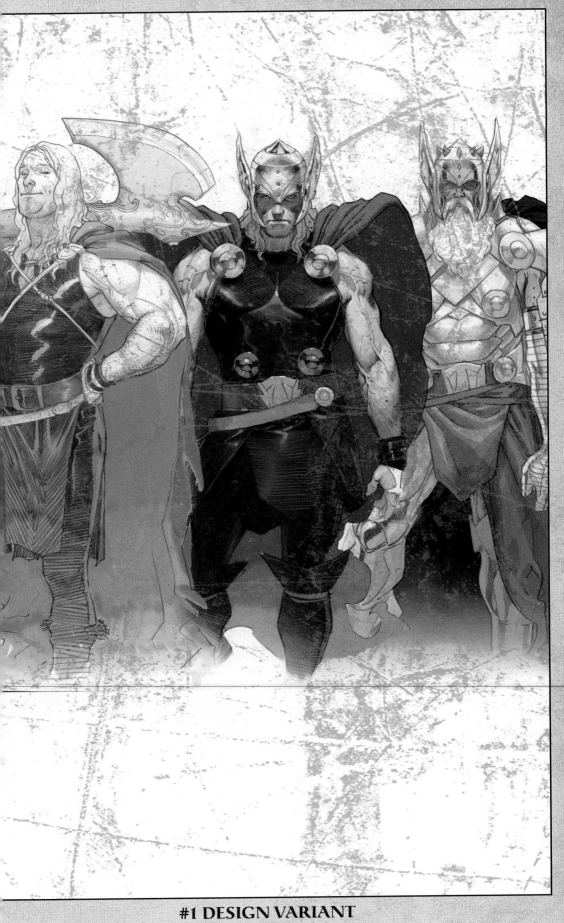

#1 DESIGN VARIANT
BY ESAD RIBIC

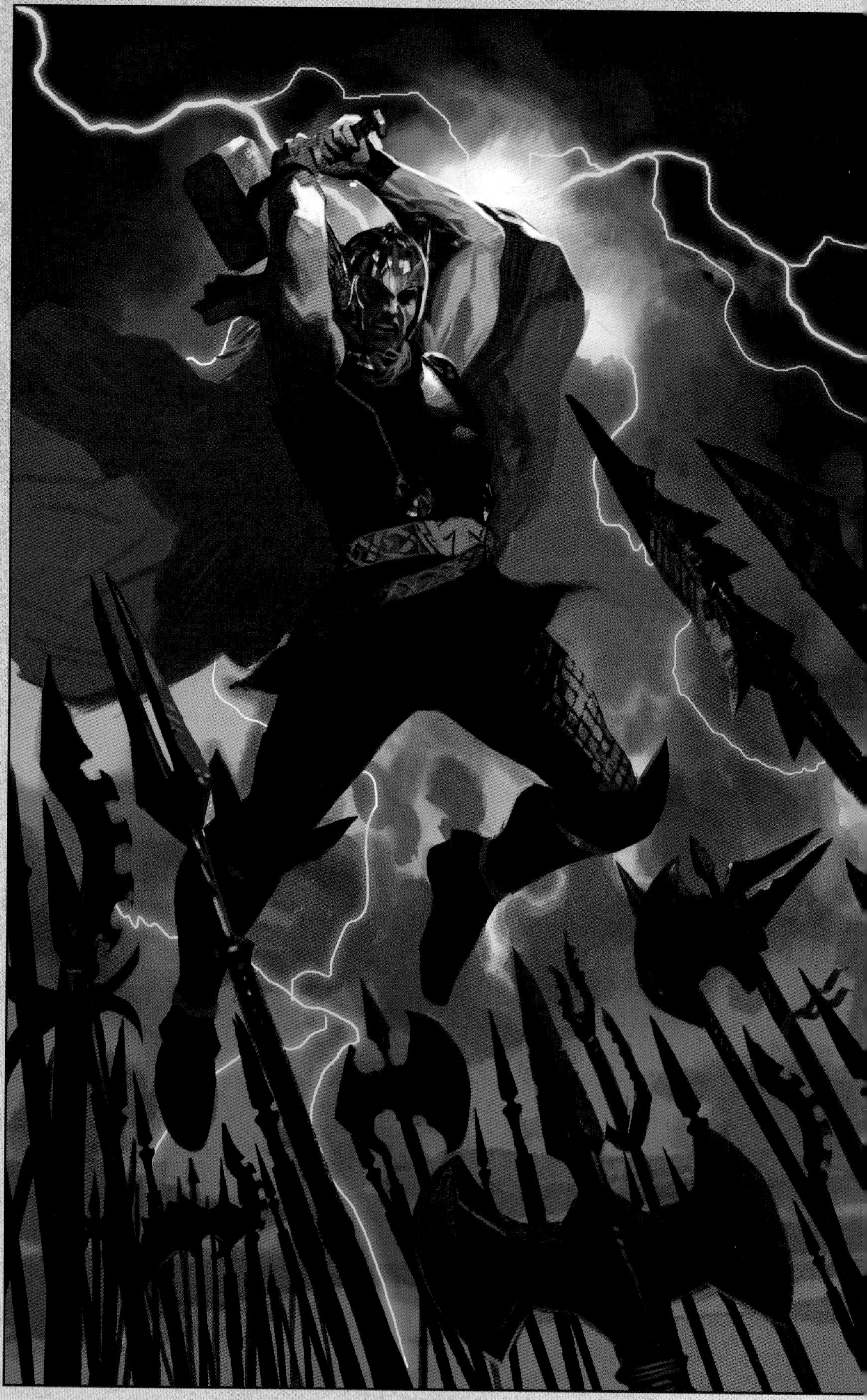

#1 VARIANT
BY DANIEL ACUÑA

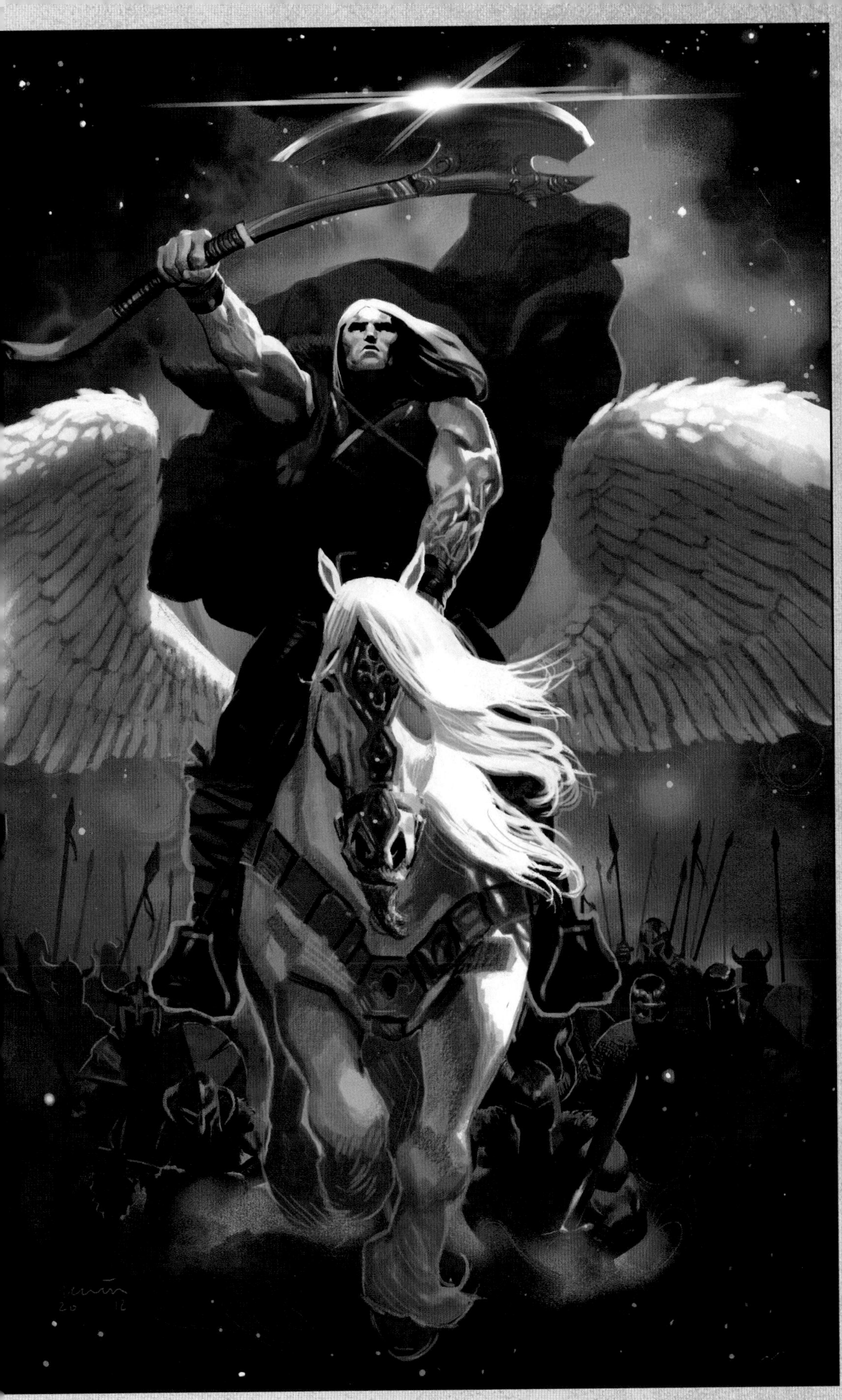

#2 VARIANT
BY DANIEL ACUÑA

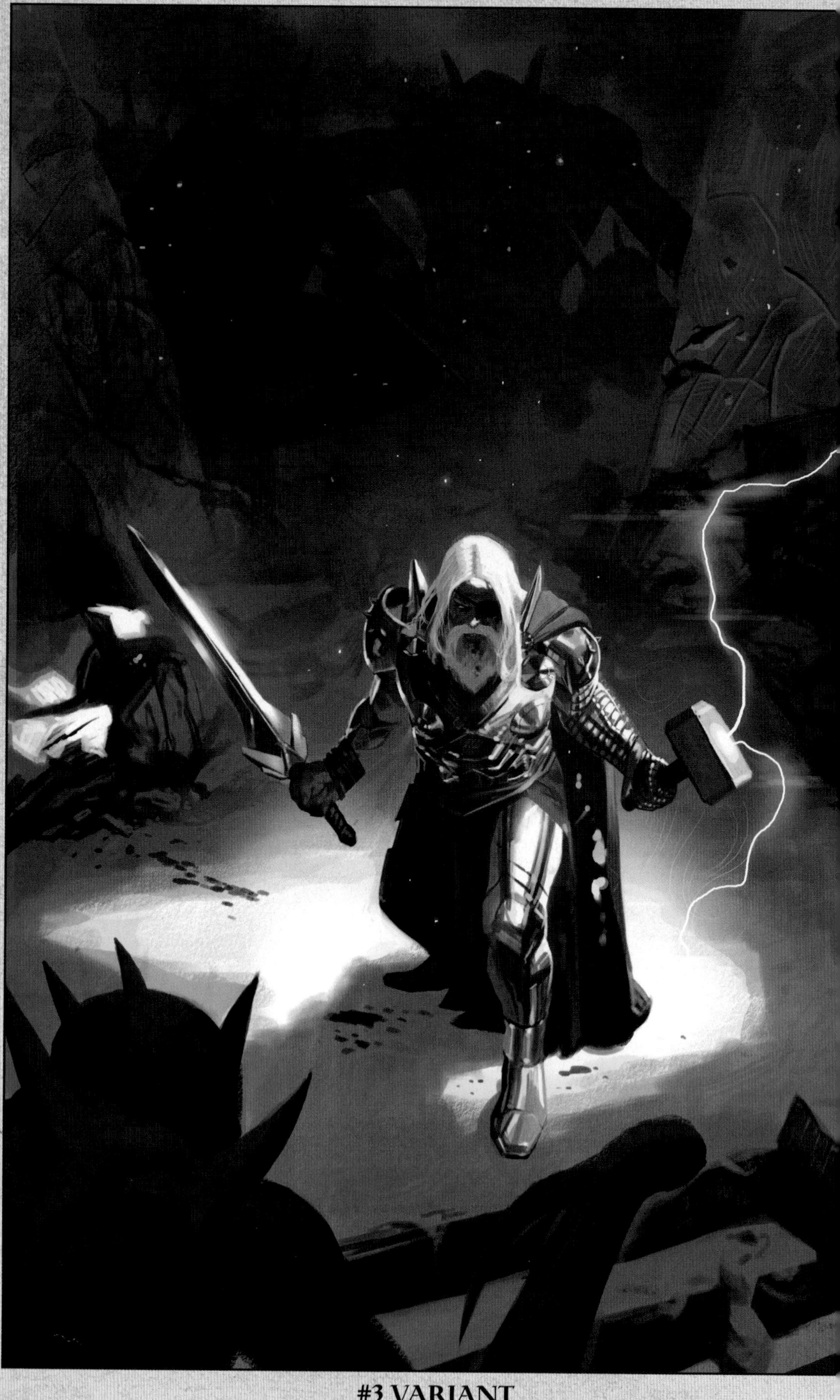

#3 VARIANT
BY DANIEL ACUÑA

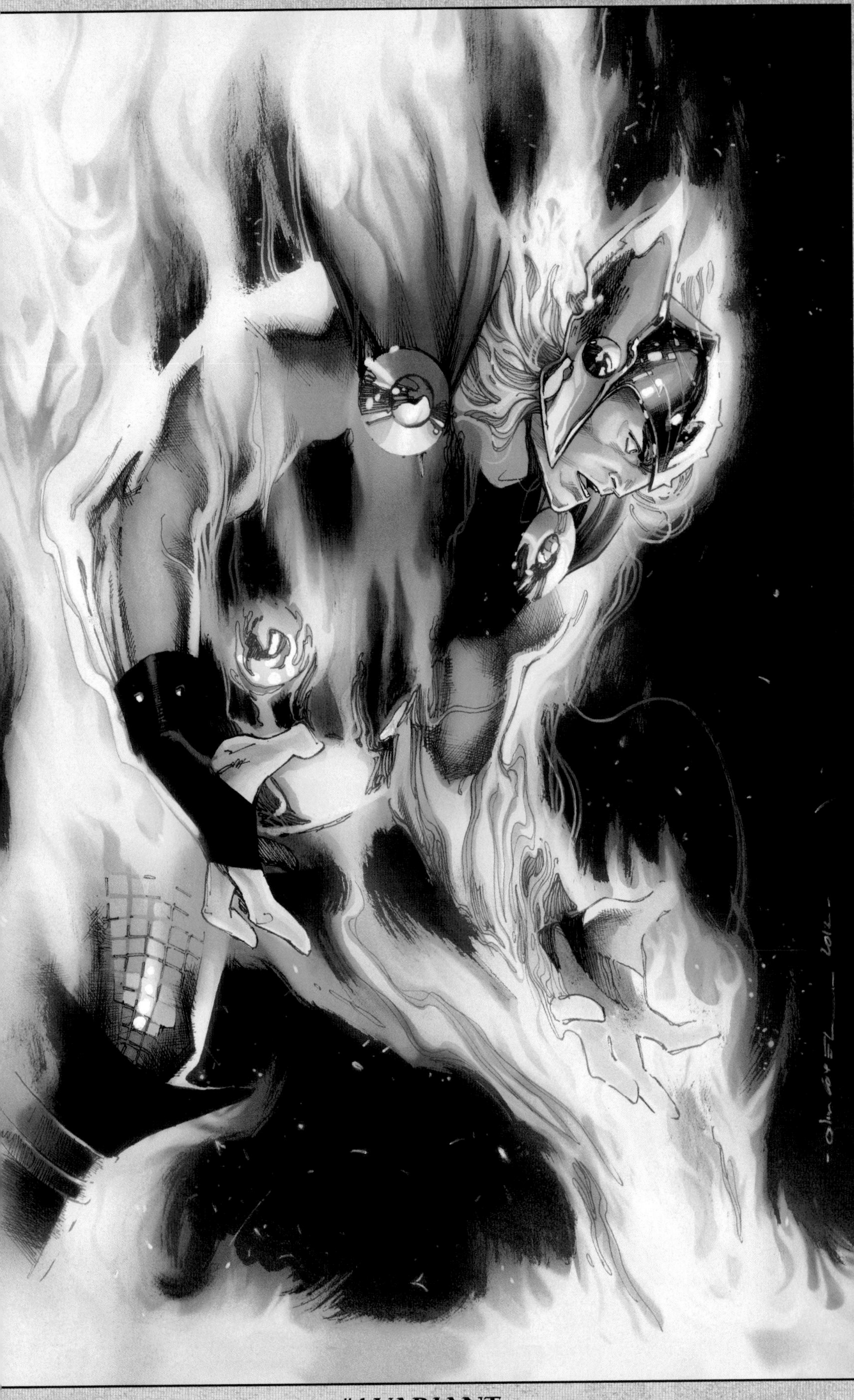

#4 VARIANT
BY OLIVIER COIPEL & LAURA MARTIN

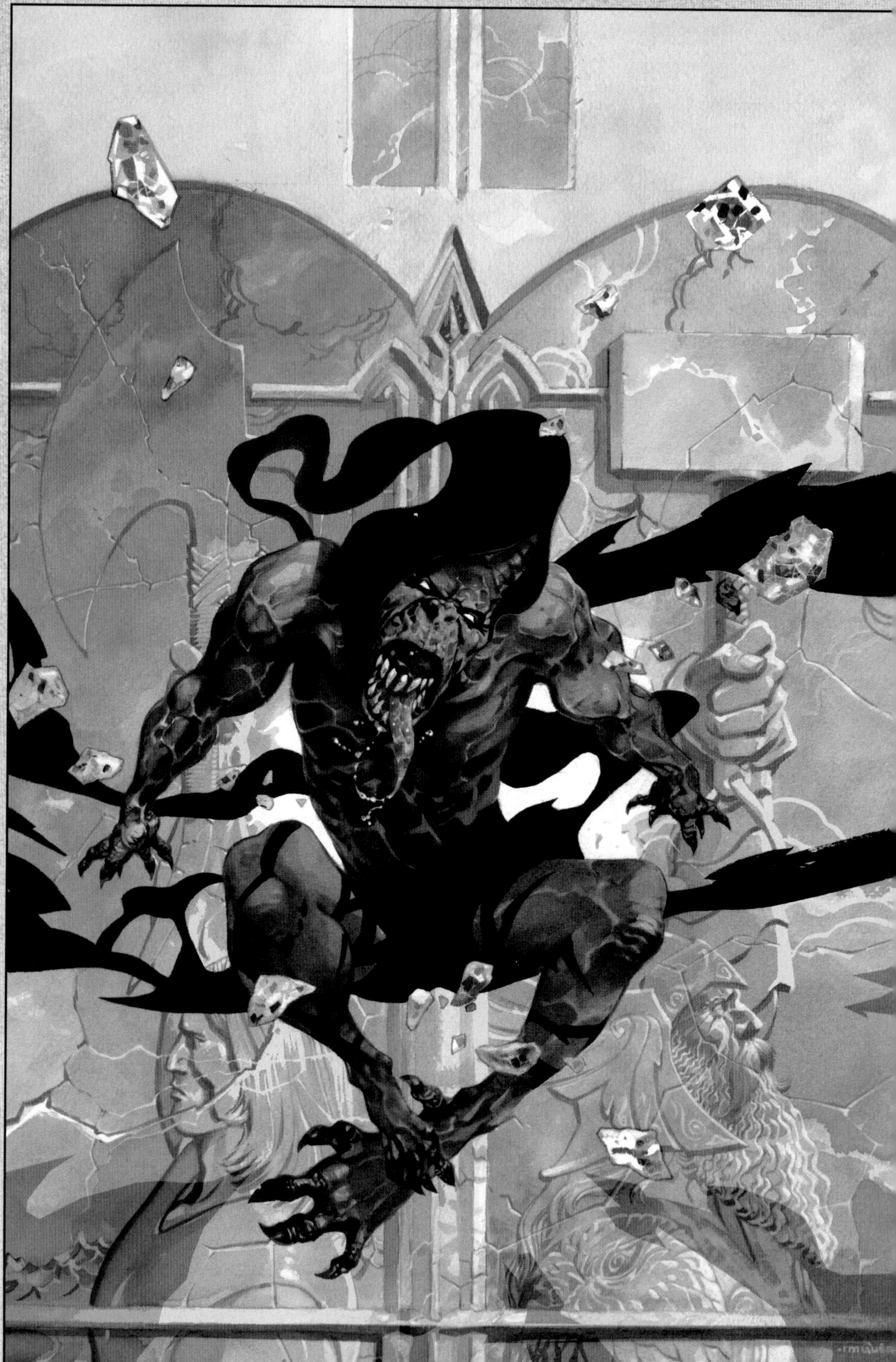

#5 VARIANT
BY R.M. GUÊRA

ESAD RIBIC SKETCHBOOK

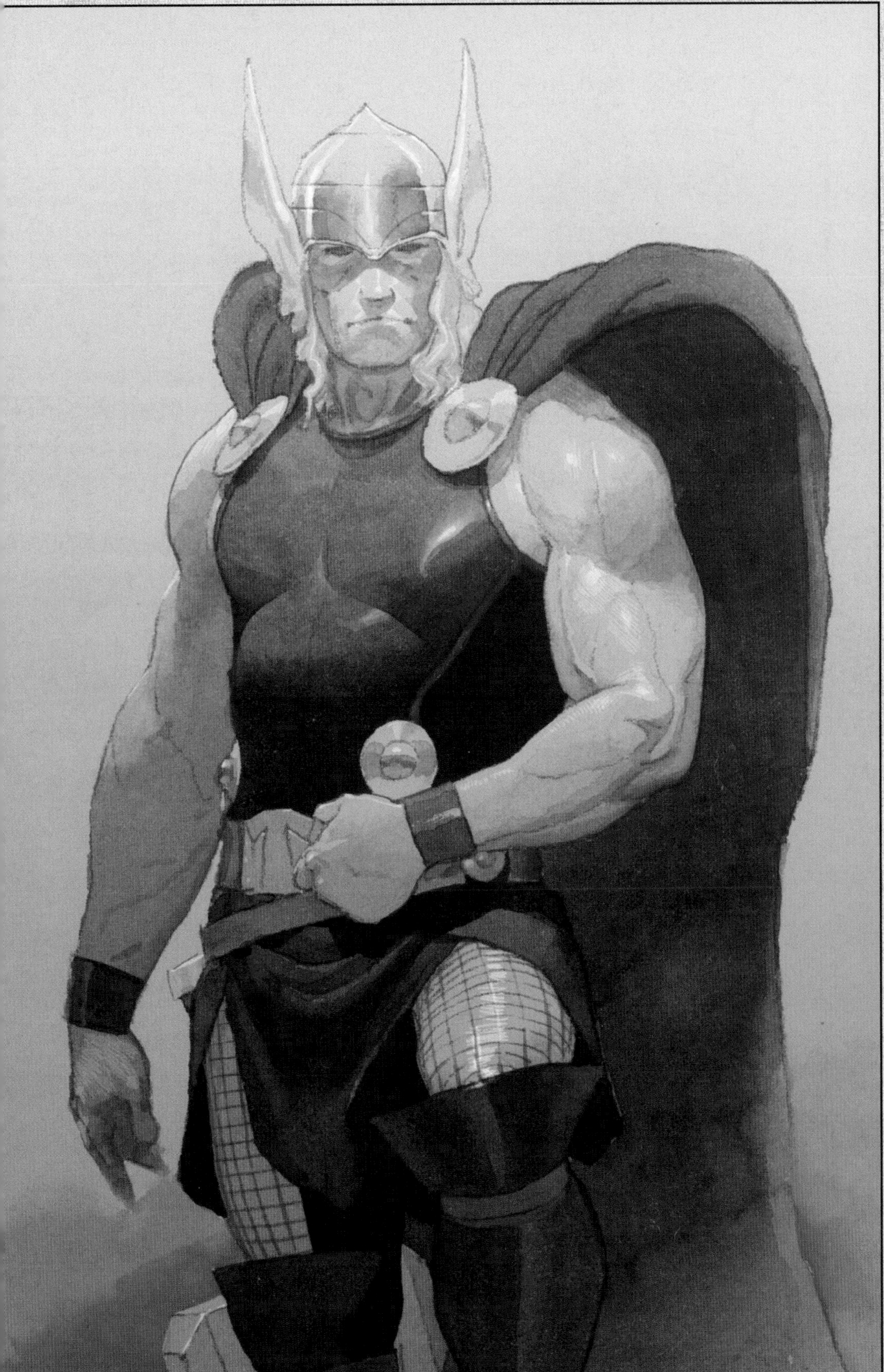

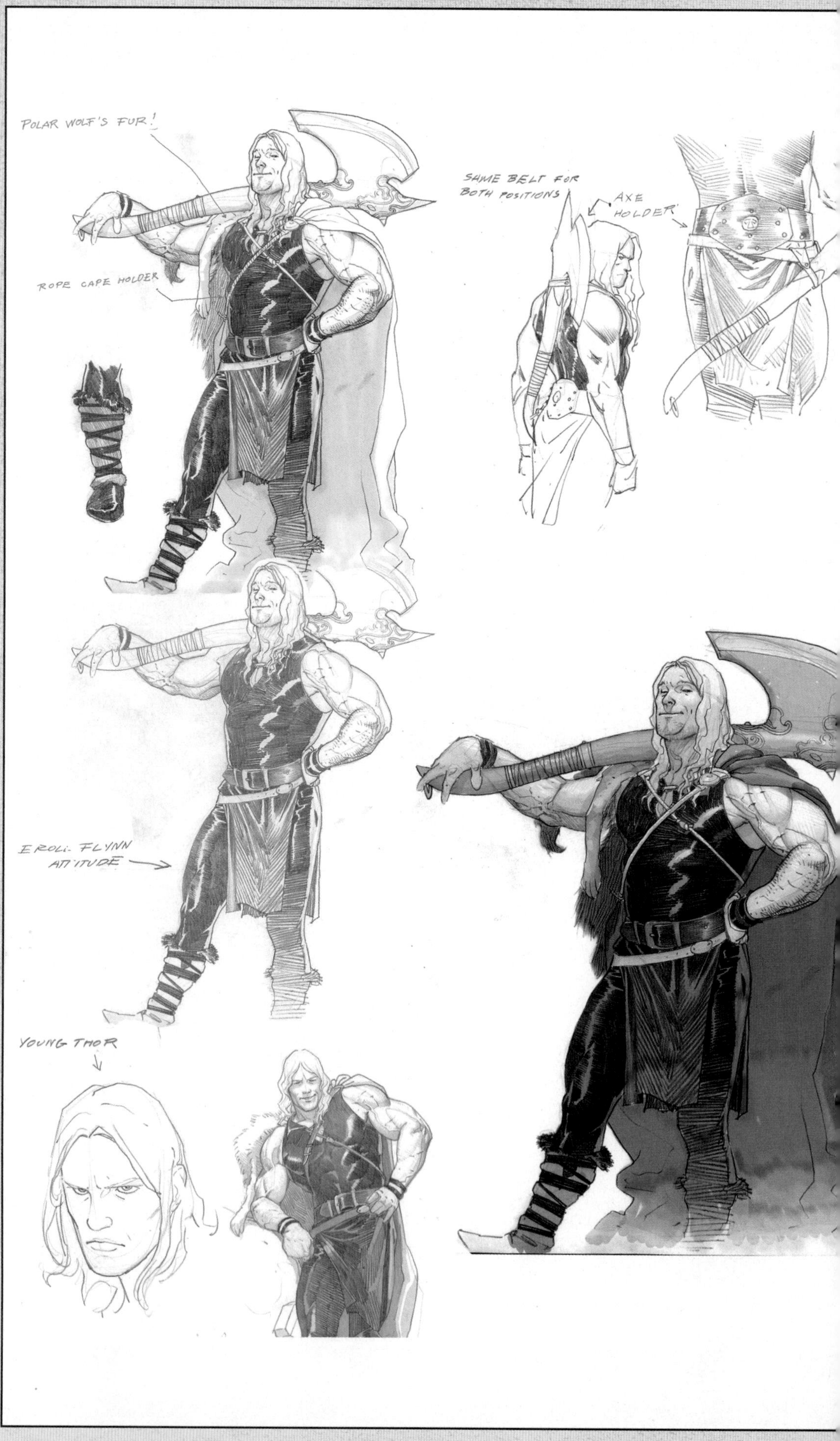
POLAR WOLF'S FUR!
ROPE CAPE HOLDER
SAME BELT FOR BOTH POSITIONS
AXE HOLDER
ERROL FLYNN ATTITUDE
YOUNG THOR

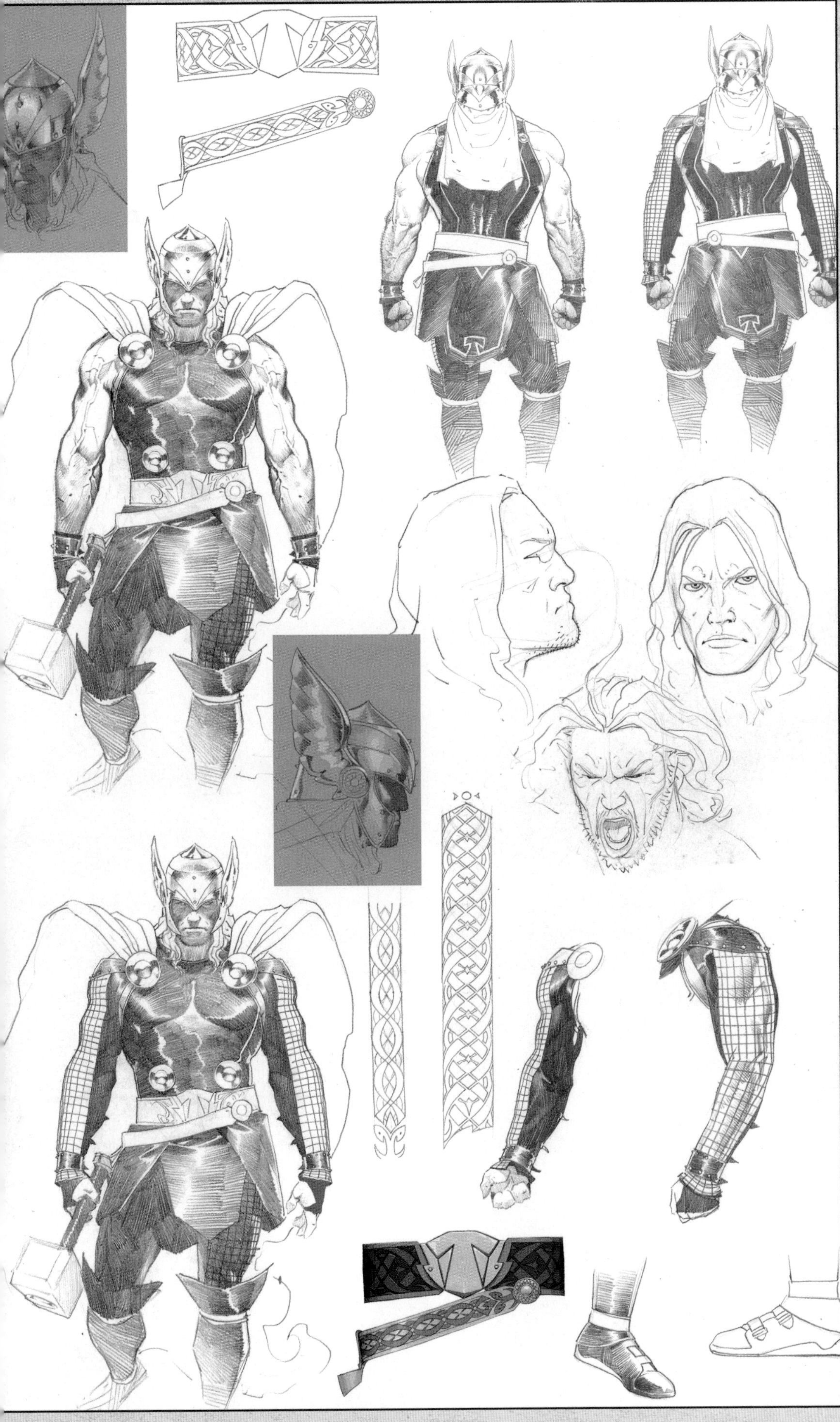

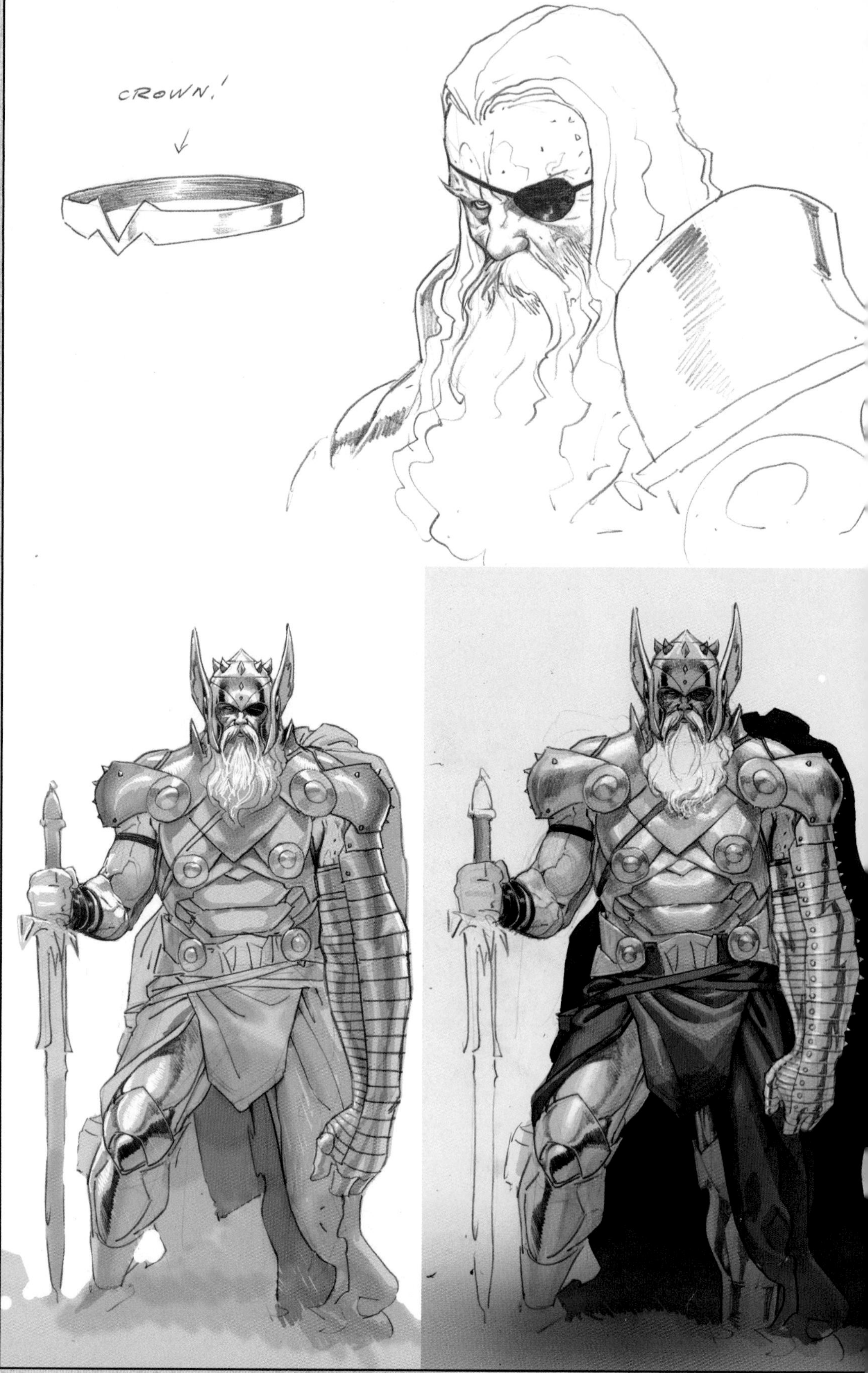
CROWN!

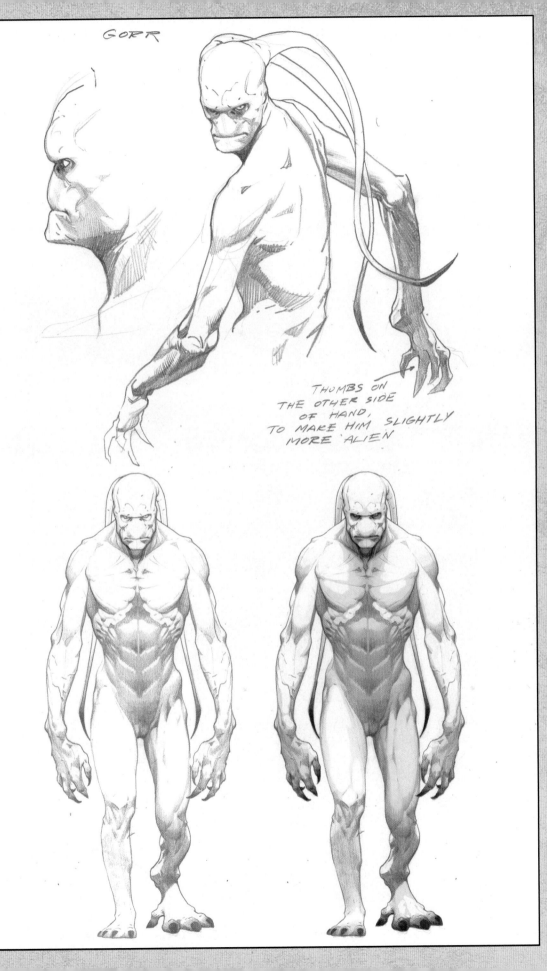

GORR

THUMBS ON
THE OTHER SIDE
OF HAND,
TO MAKE HIM SLIGHTLY
MORE 'ALIEN'

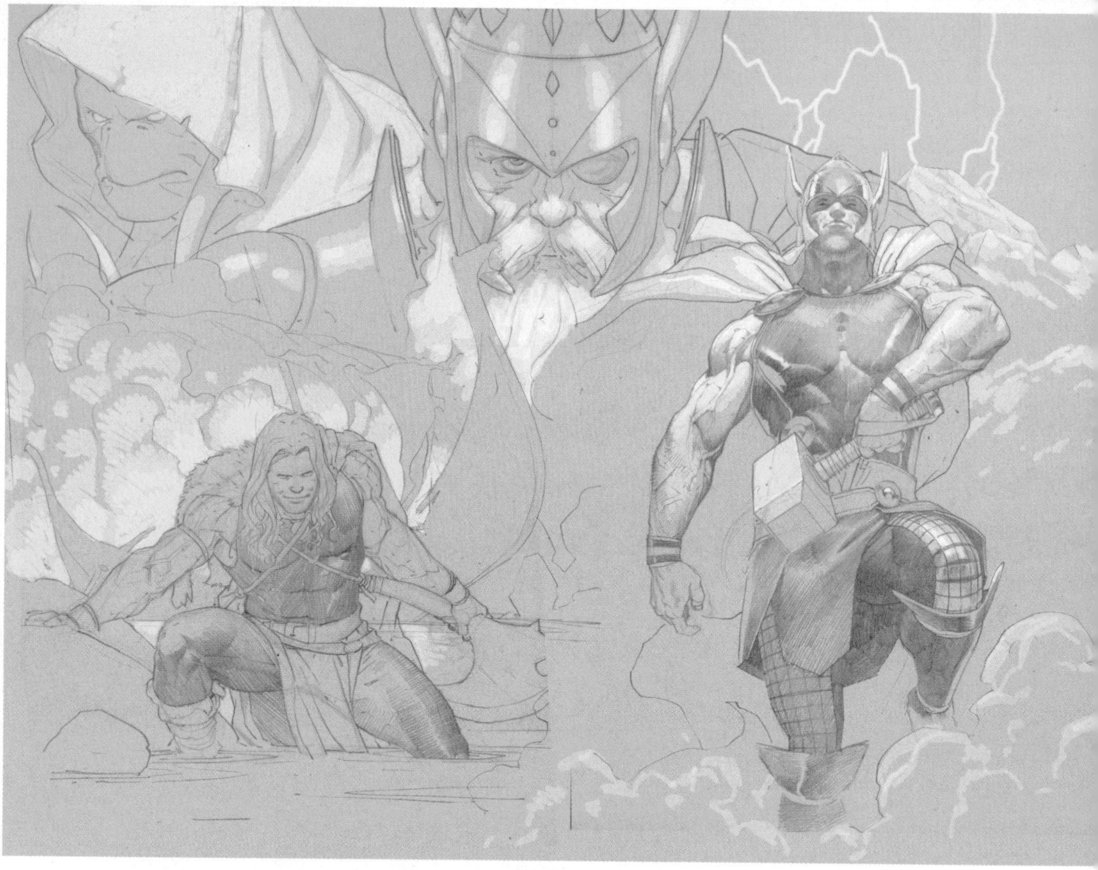

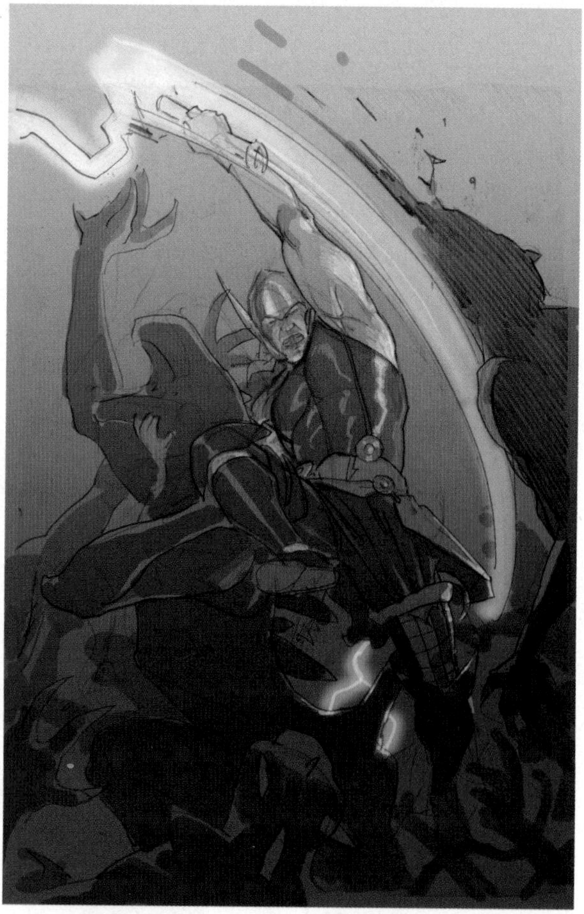

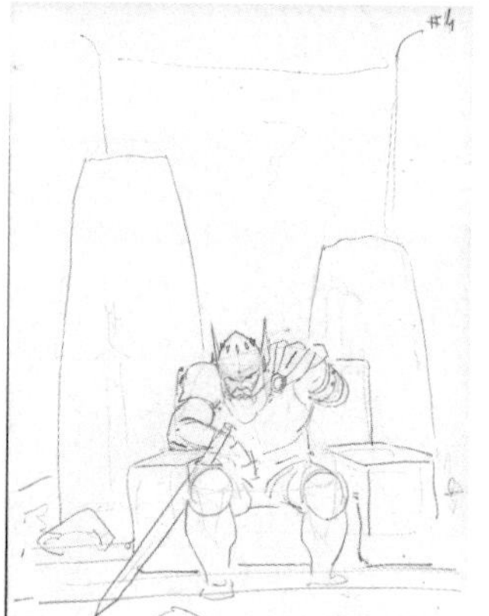
#4

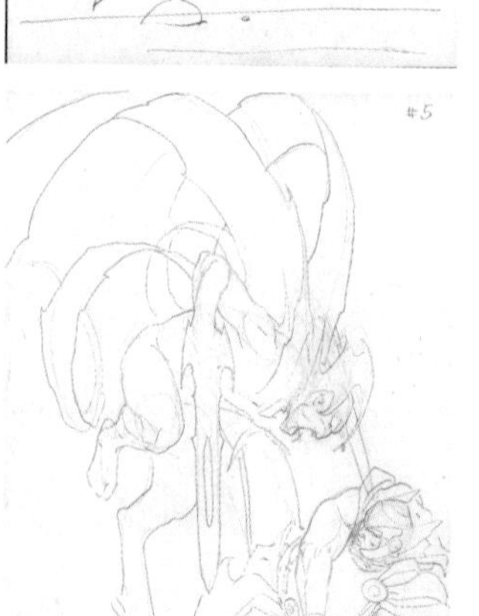
#5

COVER SKETCHES

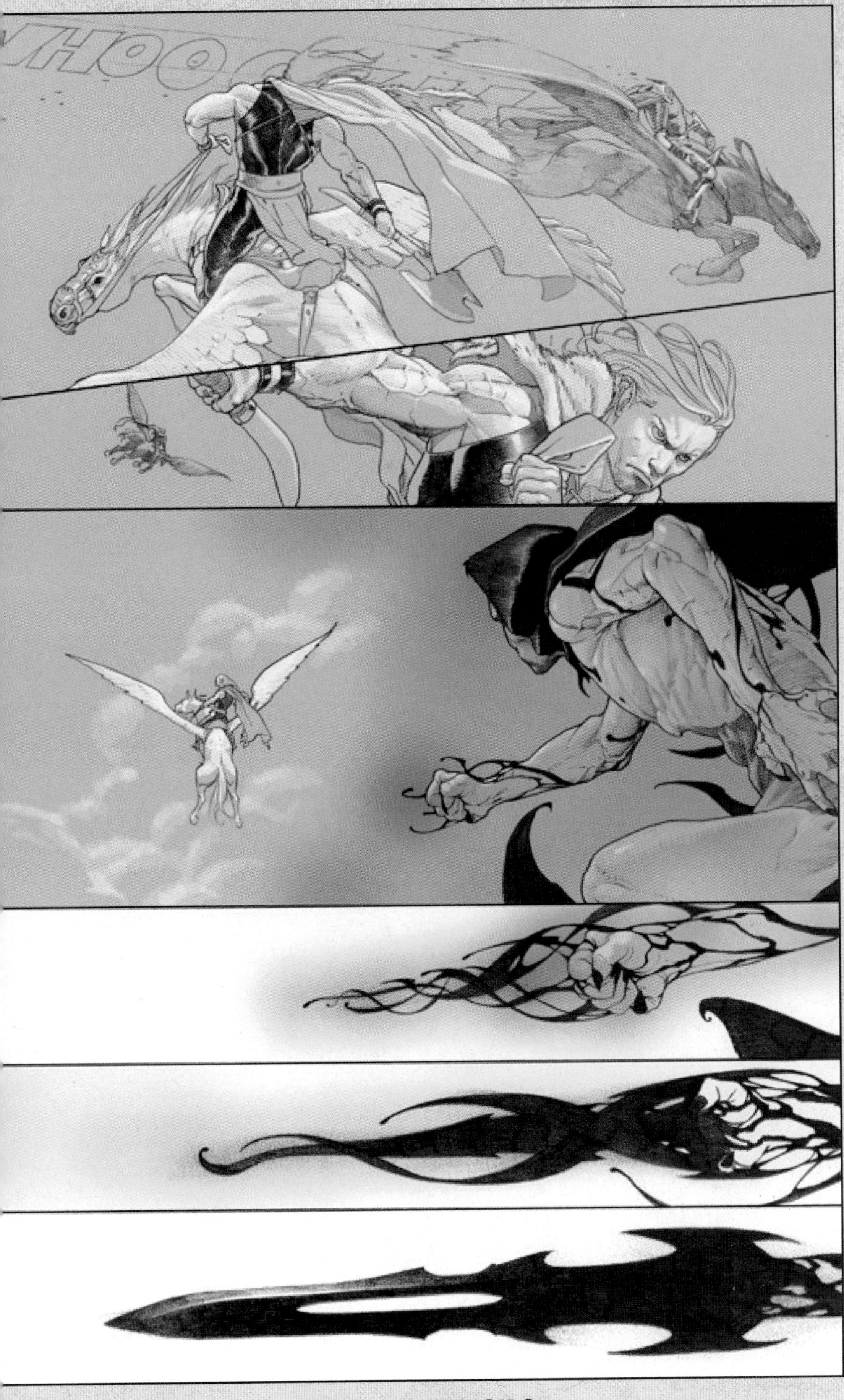

#2, PAGE 9 PENCILS

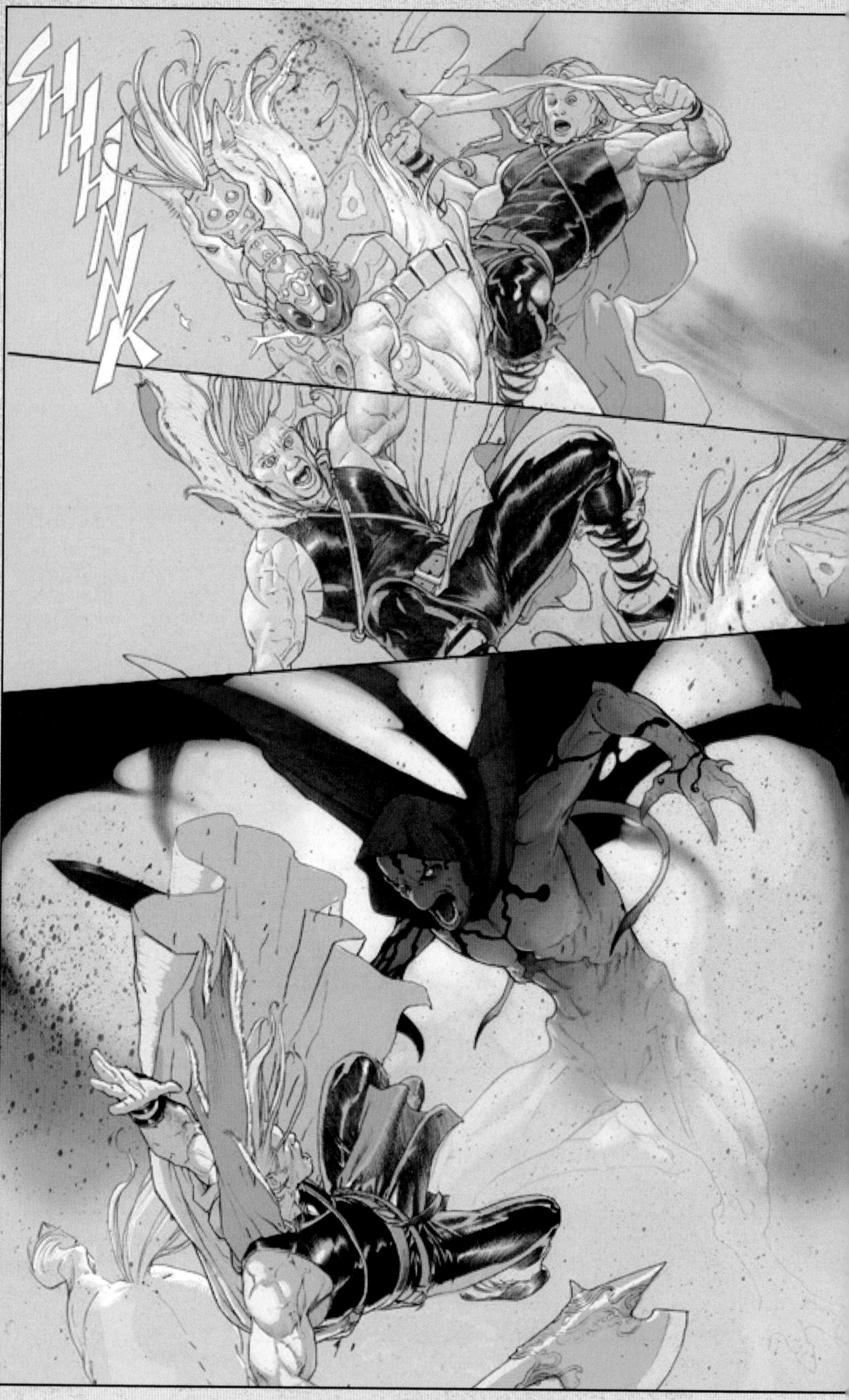
SHHINNK

#2, PAGE 10 PENCILS

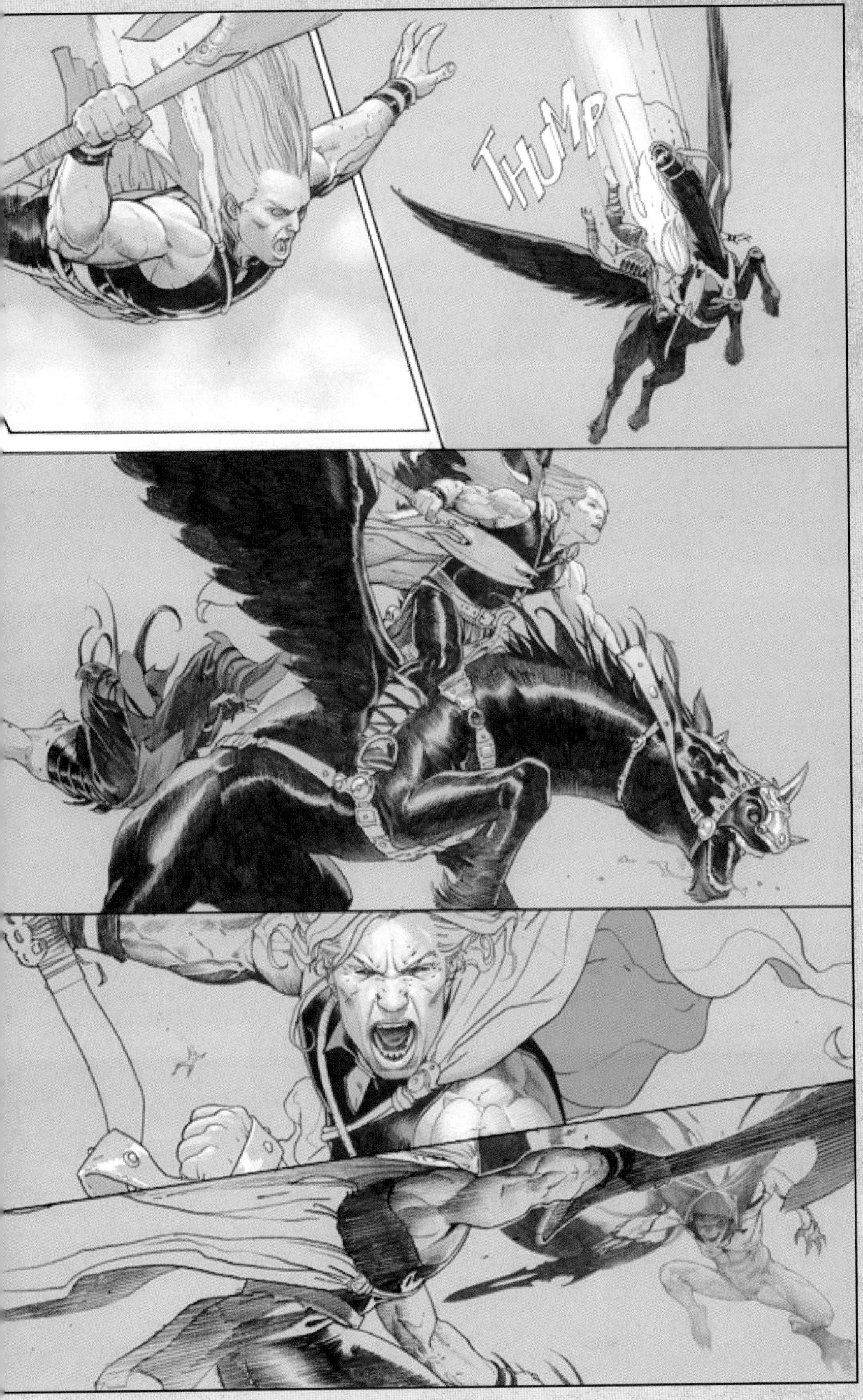
THUMP

#2, PAGE 11 PENCILS

#2, PAGE 12 PENCILS

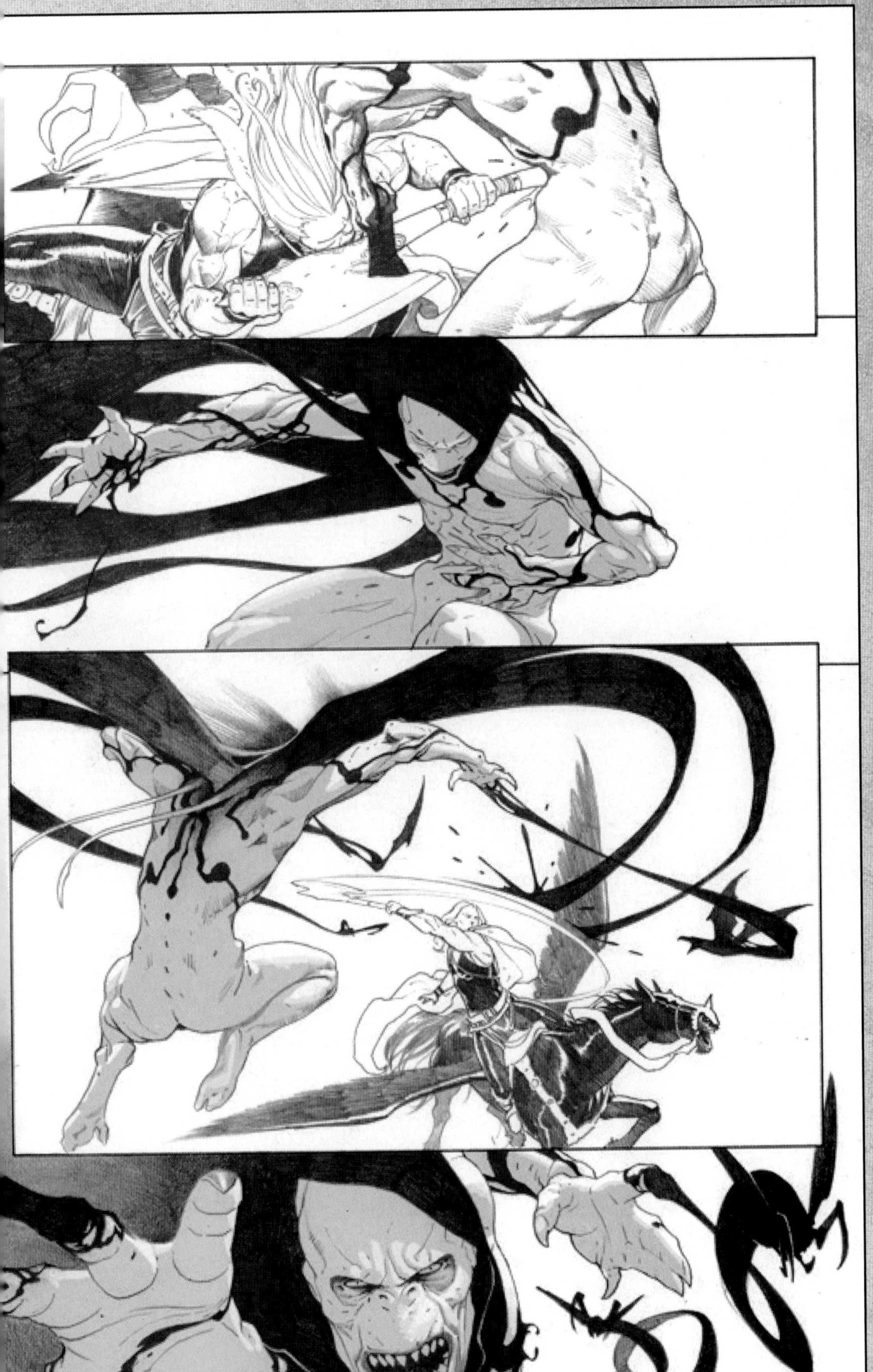

#2, PAGE 13 PENCILS

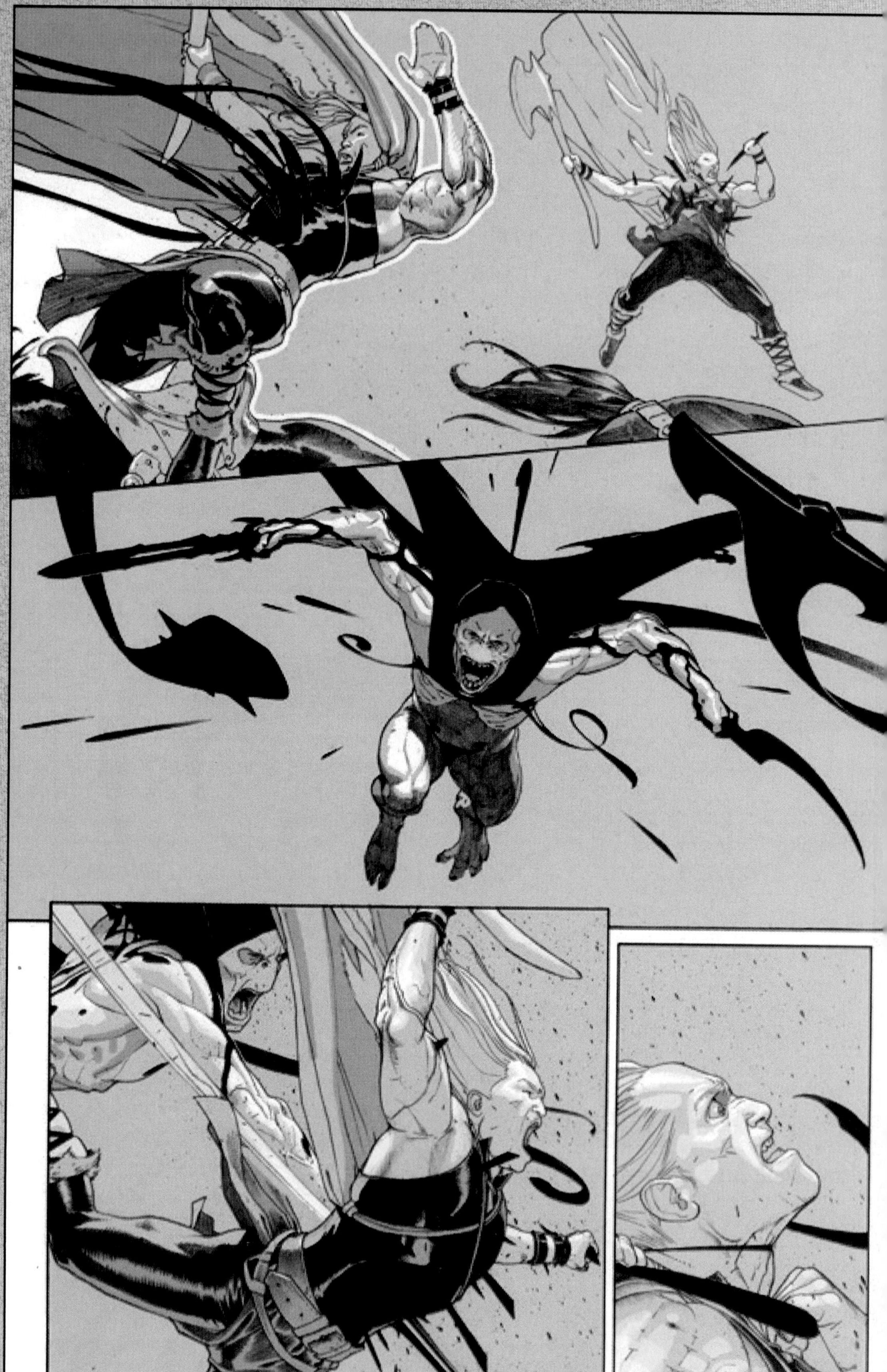

#2, PAGE 14 PENCILS

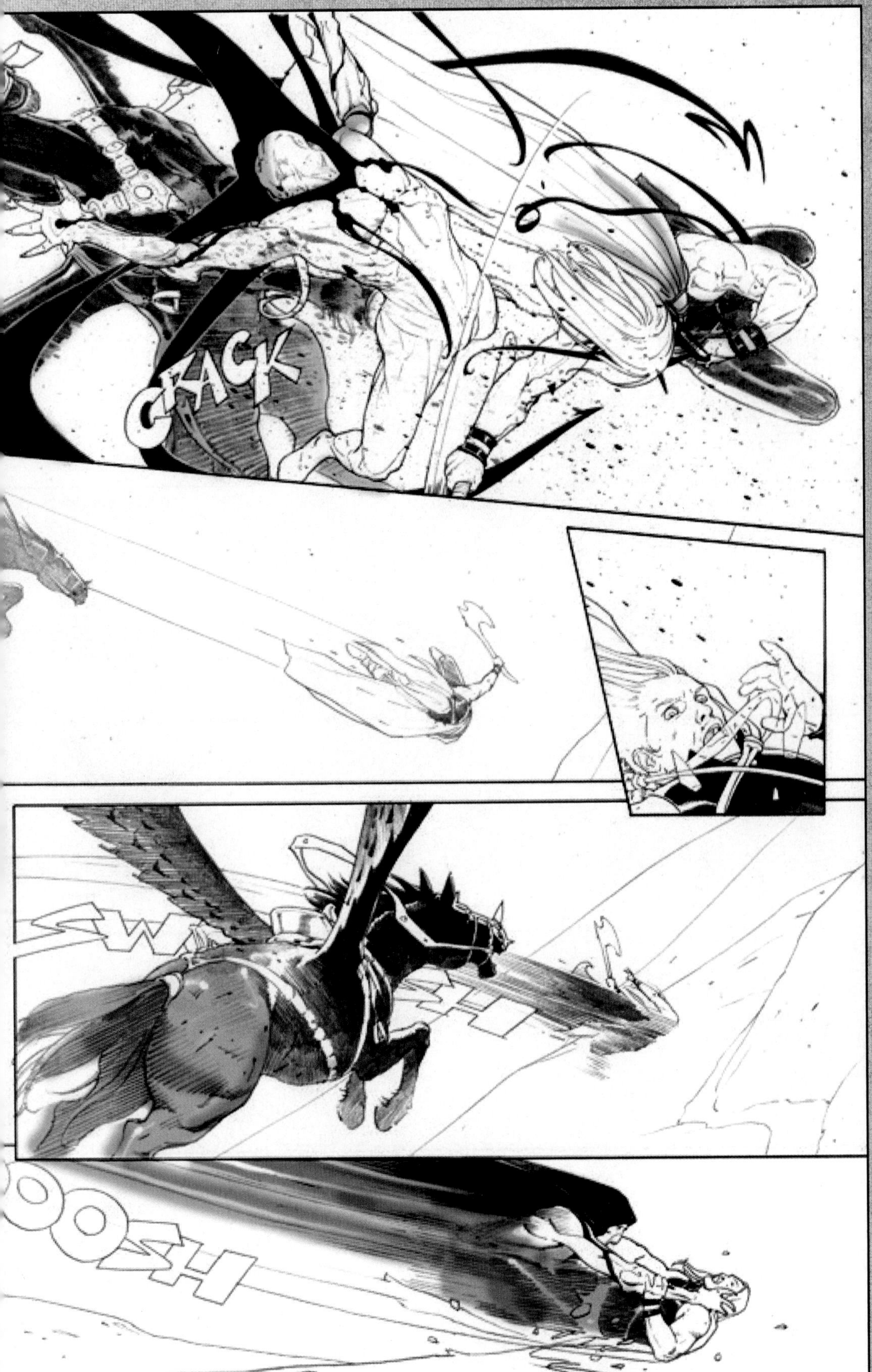
CRACK

#2, PAGE 15 PENCILS

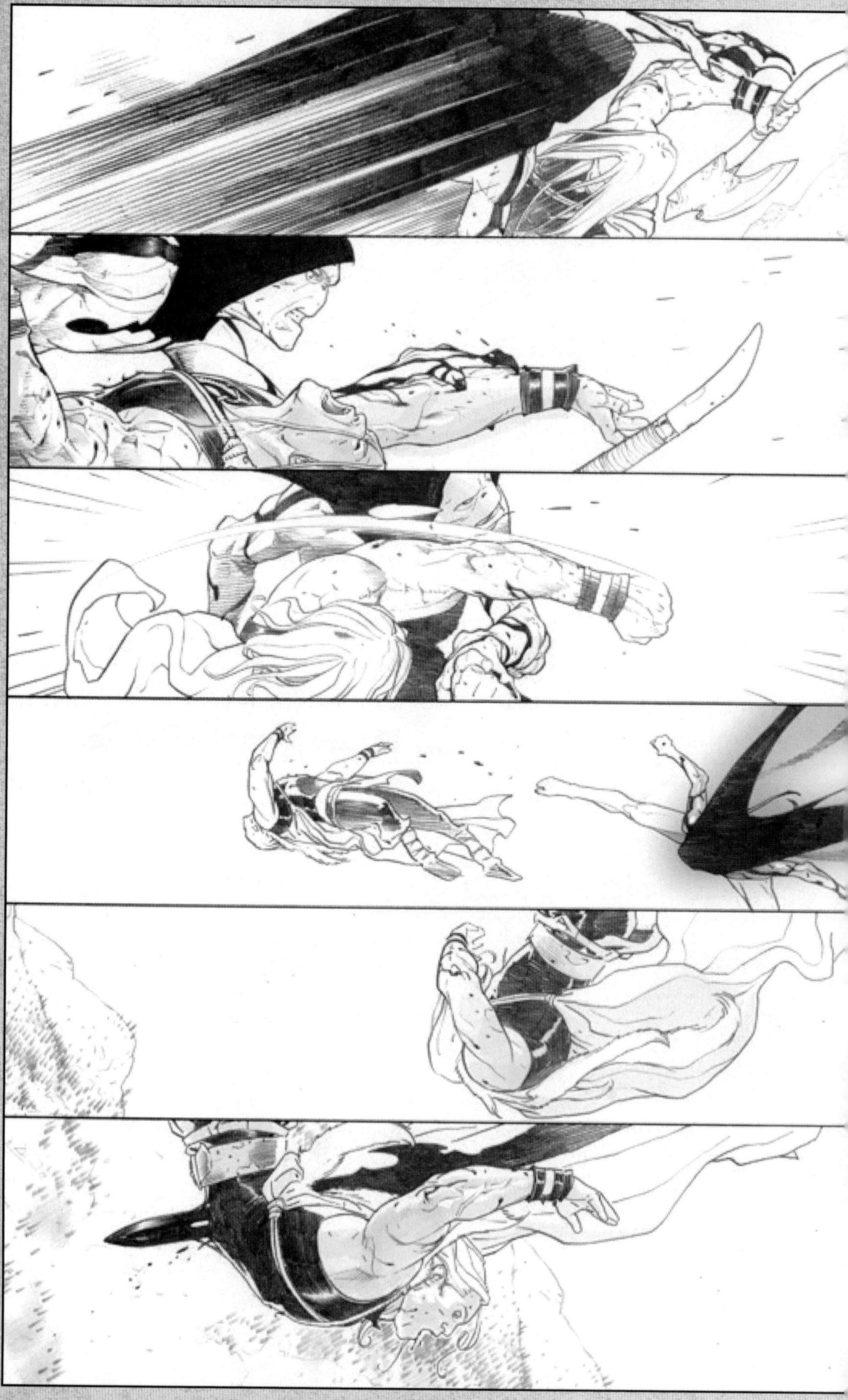

#2, PAGE 16 PENCILS

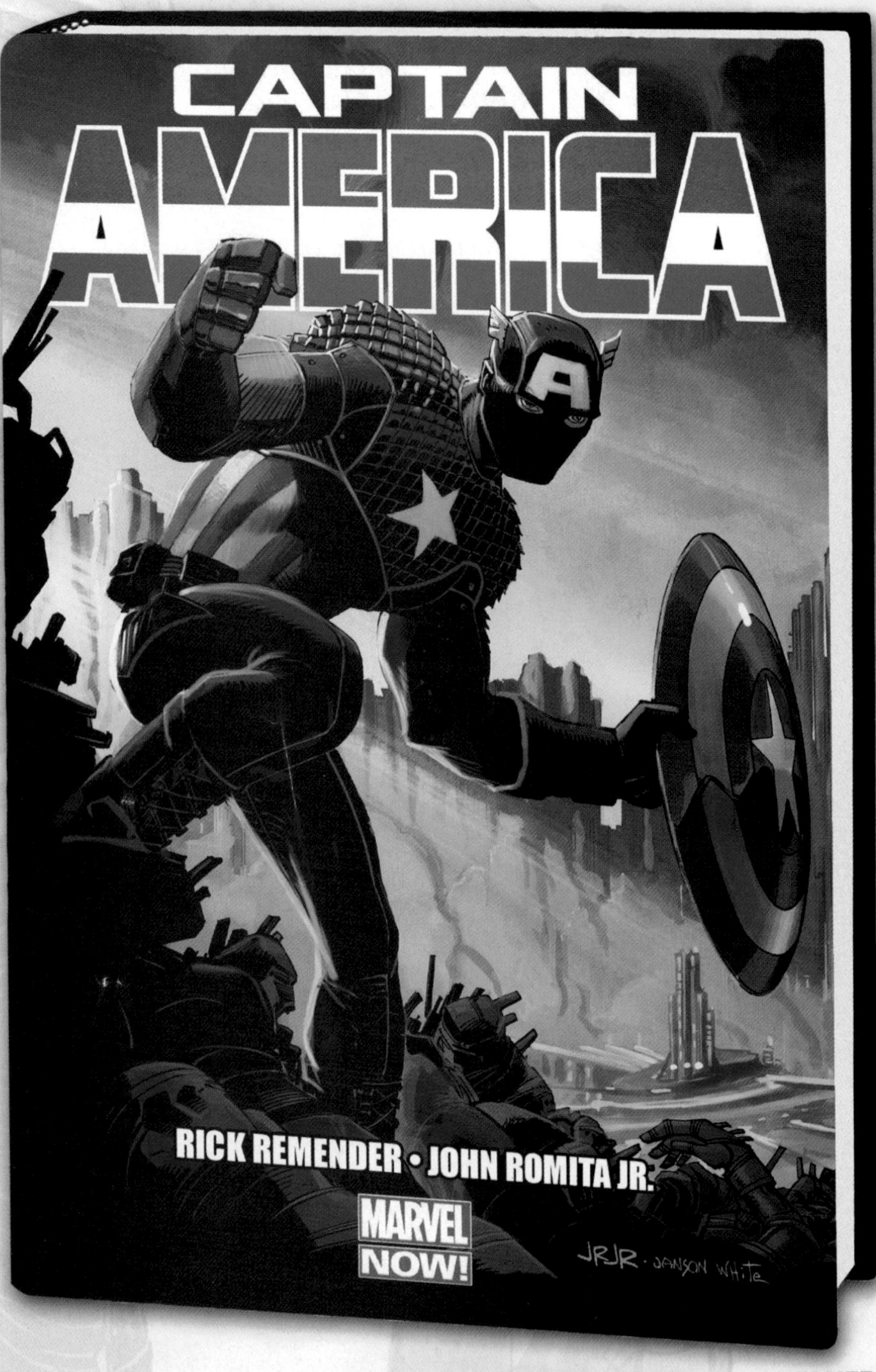
CAPTAIN
AMERICA
RICK REMENDER • JOHN ROMITA JR.
MARVEL NOW!
JRJR · JANSON WHITE

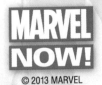

THOR GOD OF THUNDER AR INDEX

Issue #1

Issue #2

Issue #3

Issue #4

Issue #5

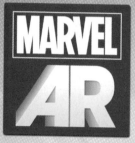

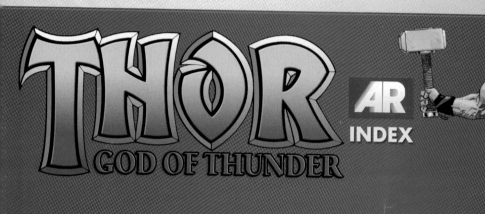

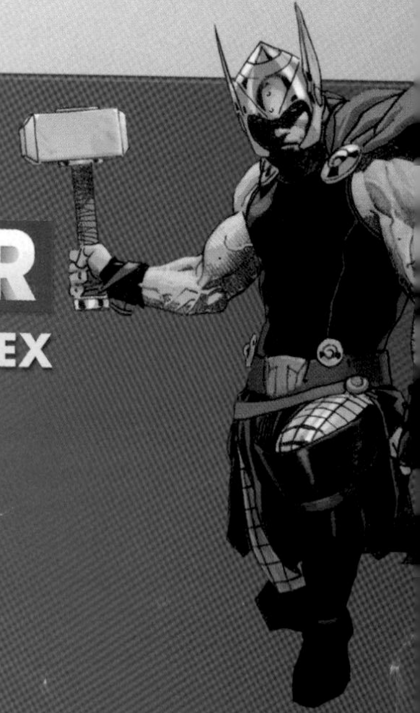